The Junior RE Handbook

Edited by
Robert Jackson and Dennis Starkings

STANLEY
THORNES

First published in 1990 by:
Stanley Thornes (Publishers) Ltd
Ellenborough House
Wellington Street
CHELTENHAM GL50 1YW
England

Reprinted 1996

British Library Cataloguing in Publication Data
The Junior RE handbook.
  1. Schools. Religious education.
  I. Jackson, Robert   II. Starkings, Dennis
  200.71

ISBN 0–7487–2646–2

Typeset by Northern Phototypesetting Co. Ltd., Bolton
Printed and bound in Great Britain at
T.J.Press (Padstow) Ltd., Padstow, Cornwall

Contents

Foreword *vi*
Preface *viii*

PART ONE
Principles and Planning

CHAPTER 1	Religious education after the Reform Act 3
	Robert Jackson
CHAPTER 2	Planning religious education 14
	Mary Hayward

PART TWO
Guides to Religions

Introduction 29

CHAPTER 3	Getting to grips with Buddhism 31
	Peggy Morgan
CHAPTER 4	Looking at Christianity 37
	John Hallows
CHAPTER 5	Being a Christian 44
	John Rankin
CHAPTER 6	An overview of Hinduism 51
	Robert Jackson and Eleanor Nesbitt
CHAPTER 7	Islam in outline 57
	M. Abdel Haleem
CHAPTER 8	A taste of Judaism 64
	Clive Lawton
CHAPTER 9	Introducing Sikhism 72
	W. Owen Cole

PART THREE
Teaching about Religions

Introduction   81
CHAPTER 10   Buddhism in junior schools   83
Peggy Morgan
CHAPTER 11   Teaching Christianity in junior schools   91
Jean Holm
CHAPTER 12   Approaching Christianity in the classroom   96
Peter Doble
CHAPTER 13   Teaching Hinduism in the junior school   103
Ken Oldfield
CHAPTER 14   Islam in the classroom   109
Vida Barnett
CHAPTER 15   Judaism in the junior school   116
Douglas Charing
CHAPTER 16   Sikhism: books and stories   124
Eleanor Nesbitt

PART FOUR
Religious Education and the Arts

Introduction   133
CHAPTER 17   'It isn't true is it Miss? It's only a story. . .'   137
Jack Priestley
CHAPTER 18   Children exploring religious stories   142
Merlin Price
CHAPTER 19   Stories from the Christian tradition   149
Jack Priestley
CHAPTER 20   Hide and seek: an approach to myth and mystery
in the middle years   155
Angela Wood
CHAPTER 21   Living the story: drama in religious education   162
David Self
CHAPTER 22   The role of art in junior religious education   169
Jo Price
CHAPTER 23   Music's contribution to junior religious education   175
Robert Green

PART FIVE
Methods and Issues

Introduction   185
CHAPTER 24   Topic work and junior religious education   187
Rachel Gregory
CHAPTER 25   Visiting places of worship   192
Dennis Starkings
CHAPTER 26   Children as ethnographers   200
Robert Jackson
CHAPTER 27   Learning from the religious experience of children   208
Eleanor Nesbitt and Robert Jackson
CHAPTER 28   One step at a time: RE and children with special needs   214
Jill Davies
CHAPTER 29   Worship in the junior school   219
Geoffrey Marshall-Taylor

Contributors   226
Keyword Index   230

Foreword

This Handbook is designed as a practical resource for teachers in planning and implementing a coherent programme of religious education. It is intended to help teachers in two ways: by illuminating the key elements and ideas of the major religious traditions represented in Britain, and by looking at the theory and practice of religious education in relation to the aims and content of the curriculum as a whole. The Handbook is for use by individual teachers planning work in their own classrooms, and by in-service and initial training courses in religious education.

The 1988 Education Reform Act has given a new significance to religious education in schools. There is in the first place a renewed formal requirement for religious education. The basic curriculum for all pupils consists of the ten core and foundation subjects of the National Curriculum and religious education. The nature and content of formal religious education is the subject of intense debate and, inevitably, of controversy. This Handbook provides a valuable background to the major issues.

The Education Act has also established a more pervasive need for religious education in the curriculum as a whole. A fundamental principle of the Act is that the school curriculum should be 'balanced and broadly based' and that it should:

1   promote the spiritual, moral, cultural, mental and physical development of pupils at the school and of society;
2   prepare pupils for the opportunities, responsibilities and experiences of adult life.

Both of these concerns are at the centre of contemporary developments in religious education. Religious education in schools is essentially concerned with engaging young people in the spiritual and moral issues that impel different religious beliefs and practices. It is also concerned with understanding the roles and dynamics of faith and tradition in different cultural settings. To this extent, religious education is a central element in multicultural education. Consequently, this book is also concerned with the role of religious education in fulfilling the purposes and principles of the curriculum as a whole.

Some of the chapters here, and many of the writers, have appeared previously in *Resource*, the journal of religious education which has been published three times a year since 1978 by the University of Warwick Institute of Education. The policy of *Resource* has been to support religious and moral education at all levels of schooling with articles that closely relate theory to practice. *The Junior RE Handbook* has its origins in the success of *Resource*, but much of the book is entirely new. Previously published material has been revised and updated to take full account of the impact of the 1988 Education Act. The book strikes several balances: it recognises the importance of the Christian tradition and of other major faiths; there is a range of specialist writers from inside and outside particular faiths; and there is a range of theoretical perspectives and of practical experiences.

The Handbook is edited by Robert Jackson and Dennis Starkings – also joint editors of *Resource* – both of whom are leading members of the Department of Arts Education at the University of Warwick, and key figures in the general field of religious education. In addition to religious education, the Department of Arts Education includes specialist work in music, drama, visual arts, literature, history and modern languages. It is therefore particularly well placed to explore the many ways in which religious education interacts with the creative arts and humanities in the development of a coherent and broadly based cultural education. These relationships will be of growing concern in the future development of the department's work, and it is significant that a full section of this book is devoted to exploring the benefits of interdisciplinary work.

Given the avalanche of statutory publications that schools now have to deal with on the curriculum, this Handbook has been planned for easy use and quick reference. It is part of an ambitious and continuing programme of work in religious education at the University of Warwick. Enquiries are welcome about other activities and publications, including subscriptions to *Resource*. For further information, please contact:

The Secretary
Department of Arts Education
University of Warwick
COVENTRY CV4 7AL.

Ken Robinson
Professor of Arts Education,
University of Warwick.
Director, National Foundation for Arts Education

Preface

The 1988 Education Reform Act has brought to schools many changes in curriculum, organisation and finance. This Handbook is designed to help junior school teachers – whether working with colleagues in school or on INSET courses – and students in training, to prepare to plan and teach RE effectively in the post-Act situation. It also deals with issues concerned with collective worship, and gives practical advice on interpreting the Act on this subject. We hope the book will also be read by governors of junior schools and members of SACREs.

The book is designed to provide ideas and information for teachers and students working anywhere in England and Wales and readers are encouraged to use it flexibly in order to meet their particular needs. It is arranged in five parts, with Parts 2–5 each having an editorial introduction which should be read in conjunction with the chapters that follow it.

Part One, Principles and Planning, includes an introductory chapter which explains the 1988 Act's clauses on RE and collective worship, and suggests six key elements which need to be present in a balanced RE programme. Chapter 2 gives detailed practical advice on planning RE in junior schools, including some ideas for INSET activities.

Part Two, Guides to Religions, gives short, authoritative introductions to six major world religions currently practised in Britain – Buddhism, Christianity, Hinduism, Islam, Judaism and Sikhism. Given the historical and cultural importance of Christianity in Britain, and the diverse forms of its denominations, two chapters are devoted to this tradition, one giving an overview and the other presenting an insider's view of the faith. It is hoped that various introductions will help newcomers to grasp key concepts, practices and beliefs and convey something of their spiritual character, as well as pointing to further literature.

Part Three, Teaching about Religions, explores classroom programmes for teaching the world religions introduced in Part Two. The chapters demonstrate a close relationship between the structure of each teaching programme and the structure of beliefs and values in the religions with which they deal.

Part Four, Religious Education and the Arts, shows (with particular attention to the character and potential of religious story) how practical classroom activities arise for religious education in association with music, art, drama and language development.

Part Five, Methods and Issues, appraises issues and suggests possible points of growth and development arising from them. Topic work and school worship are considered, along with techniques of field work and imaginative investigation, and the sharp focus on aims and objectives in the context of special needs education.

Most of the chapters in this book are revised versions of articles which first appeared in recent editions of *Resource*, published for teachers of RE by the University of Warwick Institute of Education. As editors since the emergence of *Resource* in 1978, we would like to take the opportunity of thanking our many contributors and subscribers. Thanks are also due to the Professional Council for Religious Education, to successive chairmen of the Arts Education Department at Warwick – Bill Hammond, Tom Arkell, Professor David Jenkins and Tom Swallow – to colleagues in Warwick's Institute of Education (especially Elsie Robinson and the Director, Professor John Tomlinson) for their continued support and to secretaries Jean Baillie, Heather Meldrum, Jill Perry and Catherine Taylor. Enquiries about *Resource* should be addressed to the Editors, Department of Arts Education, University of Warwick, Coventry CV4 7AL.

Robert Jackson and Dennis Starkings,
University of Warwick,
September 1989

PART ONE

Principles and Planning

CHAPTER I

Religious education after the Reform Act

ROBERT JACKSON

The Education Reform Act has brought challenges and opportunities for teachers in junior schools in delivering an appropriate religious education curriculum. The debate about religious education which accompanied the passage of the Bill through Parliament, however, was often heated, mis-informed and badly reported. The rhetoric of combatants and tabloids alike needs to be separated from what the Act says.

The 1944 Act established what is called 'religious instruction' as part of the educational provision for all pupils in English and Welsh maintained schools, but giving parents a right to withdraw their children if they so wished. Similarly, teachers not wishing to participate in RI could also withdraw. In county schools, RI had to be 'non-denominational' and taught in accordance with a locally determined agreed syllabus produced by a conference consisting of four committees – local authority representatives; (in England) the Church of England; teachers' representatives; and other denominations.

The 1988 Act has retained many of these features (provision, withdrawal and agreed syllabuses), but has introduced changes which strengthen RE's place in the curriculum and acknowledge some recent developments in the subject. A most significant development is the use of 'religious education' to replace the term 'religious instruction' with its overtones of deliberate trans-mission of religious beliefs. The subject must be fully educational with its aims and processes justifiable on educational grounds. Recognising the need for different interest groups to have a say in the production of syllabuses, and for local circumstances to be reflected by them, the arrangements for producing agreed syllabuses have been retained but with some important changes. For the first time in law, representatives of faiths other than Christianity are given a place on agreed syllabus conferences, on what used to be the 'other denomi-nations' committee. Also Standing Advisory Councils on Religious Education (SACREs) now *have* to be set up (post 1944 they were optional) with functions that include monitoring the use of agreed syllabuses and the power to *require* an LEA to set up a conference to review the locally agreed syllabus. SACREs have a composition which parallels that of agreed syllabus conferences, and they can co-opt extra members. Their monitoring function should ensure that agreed syllabuses are up to date and that the RE curriculum is being delivered.

The importance of religious education is emphasised by its being part of the 'basic curriculum'. Religious education and the National Curriculum together form the basic curriculum which is the entitlement of all pupils. RE stays out of nationally agreed assessment arrangements and does not become a foundation subject simply in order to preserve the character of locally determined agreed syllabuses which are able to reflect local circumstances and the contributions of the different interest groups which constitute local agreed syllabus conferences. DES Circular 3/89 states that agreed syllabus conferences may decide to include assessment arrangements in syllabuses that parallel those established in National Curriculum subjects. Chapter Two discusses some of the issues concerned with the assessment of RE and introduces ideas for assessment at key stage 2.

To read some of the rhetoric surrounding the Act's publication one might be forgiven for assuming that its clauses on religious education were a charter for Christian evangelism in the classroom. This simply is not the case. Like most modern agreed syllabuses, the Act is concerned with achieving a balance of content, and identifying the subject as being concerned with *religions* (it may overlap with areas such as social or moral education but it is not identical with them). The Act requires that any new agreed syllabus 'must reflect the fact that religious traditions in Great Britain are in the main Christian, whilst taking account of the teaching and practices of the other principal religions represented in Great Britain'. This says nothing about instruction *in* Christianity. *New* agreed syllabuses need to give proper attention to the study of Christianity and, regardless of their location in the country, should also give attention to the other major religions represented in Britain. In these respects new syllabuses should closely resemble most recent agreed syllabuses which are already in use.

It is earnestly to be hoped that agreed syllabus conferences do not adopt a narrow interpretation of the clause quoted above, on the grounds that children living in certain parts of the country are unlikely to have direct contact with adherents of faiths other than Christianity. Quite apart from the fact the demography of religions is constantly changing, most children are unlikely to spend the rest of their lives in one place. Many will move to work or to study. Many will also travel abroad. Through television, all will be confronted with issues concerned with religions, whether in other parts of Britain or in other parts of the world. It would be a lamentably parochial RE that confined its subject matter to the immediate locality.

This is not to say that RE should not draw on the local environment. It is vital that children and young people get some first hand experience of religion, through meeting religious people and through visiting places of worship and other sites of religious interest. Most of these encounters are likely to take place locally.

There is also the implication in the clause quoted above that there should be an emphasis on religion as it is lived and practised, and a recognition that Christianity itself is pluralistic. This last point is reinforced by the Act's making it clear that although teaching characteristic of any Christian denomination is not permissible in county schools, the *study* of different Christian denominations is a legitimate part of religious education.

It is also important to see religious education in the context of the whole curriculum of maintained schools which 'must be balanced and broadly based' and must promote 'the spiritual, moral, cultural, mental and physical development of pupils at the school and of society . . .' (*Education Reform Act 1988*, Part 1, Ch 1, section 2, para 2(a)). Religious education then, as well as being broad, balanced and open should not simply be a study of religions, but should relate to the experience of pupils in such a way that it contributes to their personal development. Some agreed syllabuses published before the Act have recognised this composite function of the subject. The aims of the 1985 Warwickshire syllabus, for example, are:

> To promote in children and young people an understanding of religion *and* to encourage children and young people to develop well-reasoned views and opinions about religion and about the basic questions of meaning and value with which religions and philosophies are concerned.

Aims are discussed in more detail in the next chapter.

Tolerance, withdrawal and commitment

DES Circular 3/89 is explicit on the spirit of the Act's clauses on Religious Education:

> The Government believes that all those concerned with religious education should seek to ensure that it promotes respect, understanding and tolerance for those who adhere to different faiths.
>
> *(p. 5)*

Such understanding can only be achieved if children of one faith study the faiths of others. Provided that schools teach RE according to educational aims and handle religious traditions accurately and sensitively and have good communications with parents, there should be no grounds for the withdrawal of pupils from RE, unless the parents themselves reject the spirit of tolerance underlying the Act and/or the principle of critical inquiry that characterises education in an open society.[1]

The same comments apply to teachers in schools. Religious education can be taught by teachers of different religious commitments or none, provided that they are professionally committed to the subject, and prepare themselves adequately for the task. The issue of the relationship between the teacher's personal commitments and the process of teaching religious education has been discussed at length elsewhere, for example in *Approaching World Religions, Commitment and Neutrality in Religious Education* and Peter Doble's chapter in *Teaching Christianity: A World Religions Approach*. In the present writer's experience, teachers and students with a wide variety of religious and non-religious commitments have been able to teach RE effectively and with enjoyment by:

- being committed professionally to teaching the subject, through recognising the educational importance of developing an understanding of different religious traditions based on accurate information.
- revealing their own commitments at appropriate times (for example, in answer to questions), but by placing personal views in the context of the views of others (for example, colleagues, pupils, religious figures being studied). This is very different from setting out to convert others to one's own views and allows the religious experience of pupils, parents, teachers, members of the local community and others to be a resource for religious education.
- (if from a religious background) recognising the theological importance of studying other religious traditions. There is now a huge literature, from inside and outside Christianity, on the theological relationship between the religions which recognises the importance of the study of other traditions (see introduction to Part Two).

Those who find serious personal difficulties in teaching an open religious education tend to come either from exclusivist theological traditions which emphasise the absolute truth of particular revelations or from dogmatically anti-religious backgrounds where religion is removed from any agenda of serious discussion. This is not, of course, to say that all 'conservative' religious believers or all atheists fit into these polarised categories. There are many excellent RE teachers who are one or the other of these and who are deeply committed professionally to an open religious education. The main practical and emotional problems teachers and students face are to do with confidence about being adequately prepared to teach RE.

Collective worship

Although this book is primarily about religious *education* in junior schools it would be inappropriate not to comment on the 1988 Act's clauses on collective worship in county schools, legislation which has attracted criticism from educators inside and outside religious traditions and from teachers' unions.

The 1944 Act required county schools to provide a non-denominational act of collective worship for all pupils at the beginning or the end of the day. Parents had the right of withdrawal for their children and staff too could opt out on conscientious grounds. Ironically, withdrawals tended to be from overtly religious families – for example, Roman Catholic, Jewish, Jehovah's Witness – rather than from secular families. By the 1970s many schools were not obeying the letter of the law. Many large comprehensives found it impossible to accommodate the whole school in one place; often heads and teachers found it impossible to provide a stimulating experience for children every day; and many educators questioned the appropriateness of worship as a central if not compulsory activity in a society that was increasingly secular and pluralistic. By 1975 a book had appeared with the title *School Worship: an Obituary*, and many predicted the eventual demise of collective worship. At the same time many schools – especially junior schools – were doing some very creative things with what was commonly called 'assembly'. Instead of being 'worship' in the strong sense – devotional activity from people with a shared religious way of life directed towards a transcendent object – 'assembly' in junior schools typically included ideas such as 'community', 'sharing' and 'reciprocity', promoting values such as respect for others, friendship, honesty and interdependence and including celebrations of festivals of children from different communities in Britain represented inside and outside the school. Good and bad times for the community, school or individuals would be shared and there was often a high degree of pupil involvement. There was likely to be corporate singing and perhaps a short prayer or a period of reflective silence. For some this activity was still 'worship', but in a weaker sense of sharing the worth of the persons comprising the school community, with the prayer at the end being the only element sometimes linking it directly with the Christian tradition. For others 'assembly' provided the *opportunity* for individuals to worship, but was essentially a broad educational activity which included moral and spiritual elements and was of value to all pupils and teachers regardless of their religious or non-religious affiliations. Note that assemblies of this nature were not developed as a result of anti-Christian or anti-religious motivation. They emerged as an educational way of avoiding the illogicality and immorality of mixing children from different secular and religious backgrounds and expecting them to participate meaningfully in an act which in its strong sense assumed both a commonality of belief and a desire on the part of children to participate.

Many had hoped that for county schools the 1988 Act would clearly endorse the kind of activity described above in language that would be non-divisive and acceptable to educators and to religious and secular bodies. In effect the Act *does* allow this kind of activity, but in clauses which some have found potentially divisive and which is easy to misrepresent or to interpret in uneducational ways. So what does the Act say, and how might it be interpreted? The 1988 Act retains the non-denominational daily act of collective worship for all pupils, though allowing it at any time during the school day and allowing separate acts of worship for sub-groups such as year groups (though not in normal circumstances separate religious groups).[2] In county schools collective worship organised by the school is to be 'wholly or mainly of a broadly Christian character' and heads in consultation with governors are responsible for deciding the balance appropriate to their schools. 'Mainly' refers to each act of worship, and to the number of acts of worship in any term. Thus only the majority of acts of worship in any one term needs be of a broadly Christian character. Any of these need only be *mainly* of a broadly Christian character, and can include other material. According to the Act 'collective worship is of a broadly Christian character if it reflects the broad traditions of Christian belief without being distinctive of any particular denomination' (Part 1, 7(2)). Note the use of the word 'reflect' and absence of any specification of what are the 'broad traditions of Christian belief'. When the clause is taken together with Circular 3/89's statement that 'In the Secretary of State's view, an act of worship which is "broadly Christian" need not contain only Christian material provided that, taken as a whole, it reflects the traditions of Christian belief' considerable latitude is offered for a broadly based interpretation of the Act.

Further flexibility is given by clauses which state that those making school policy on acts of worship should take into account:

> any circumstances relating to the family backgrounds of the pupils concerned which are relevant for determining the character of the collective worship which is appropriate in their case; and their ages and aptitudes.
>
> *(Part 1, 7 (5) (a) and (b))*

Chapter 29 attempts an interpretation of the Act which offers ideas to enable heads and governors to keep at least most of the junior school community together while offering an educational activity for all, an opportunity to worship for those who wish to do so and an experience which has both spiritual and moral qualities. The Act can be interpreted in other ways, however. As the Church of England's own document *School Worship* says:

> The worship clauses in the Act could be used in ways which are far from educational, and school governors need to be alert to what is actually happening in their school . . . but given the professionalism of teachers involved and the full support of the governors in the pursuit of professionally acceptable answers, then the problems can be resolved and the potential of the new legislation fully realised.

Elements of religious education

Because there are no national guidelines for religious education, teachers need to plan schemes of work for their schools based on Local Authority Agreed Syllabuses and consistent with their aims. The following check list of elements of RE is consistent with many Agreed Syllabuses. It does not prescribe content, but emphasises the processes of learning and teaching RE. It is intended to help teachers to make religious education exciting and engaging for pupils and to ensure that its methods are open and reflective. The check list can be used both in planning and evaluating RE schemes.

A sensitising element

In religious education we are introducing children to traditions and ways of life that are of deep importance to those who belong to them. It is very important that these ways of life are introduced impartially and accurately and that children are well prepared for their work. This is not to suggest that all religions are the same, that all religions are equally true or that any religion is true or false, but to assert the importance of accuracy, impartiality and sensitivity in presenting material and selecting methods of study.

On their own, accuracy and impartiality are not enough. Unless children have been prepared for encountering unfamiliar dress, practices and symbols, some of them may feel alienated from them, and may give a flippant or a hostile response. This can even happen when children from one religion are introduced to an unfamiliar denomination or movement within the same faith. One idea for sensitising children to new material is discussed below in 'Children as ethnographers'. Another way is to begin with children's experiences of belonging to a group, beginning with the family and moving on to clubs and organisations such as Brownies and Cubs, and then to a religious group.

A knowledge element

The field of religion encompasses an overwhelming amount of information that no individual could possibly assimilate. So how does the teacher select from the staggering range of possibilities? One rule of thumb is to select information and concepts that are central to topics from religions being considered and to introduce them at appropriate stages. For example, a class of lower juniors doing a topic on names, who took part in a simulation of a baptism ceremony with the vicar during a visit to the local parish church, learned terms such as font, godparent, vicar and church and were able to define them simply (including the idea that the principal meaning of 'church' is the people who form the Christian community rather than the building). Appropriate methods for checking that children know and understand information need to be employed by the teacher. In this case the children displayed their paintings of the visit and wrote their own captions (printed out by the computer) to enhance the display. The children then explained their work to parents and children from other classes.

Another rule of thumb is to draw on material from no more than two or three religions during any one topic and to ensure that children do not confuse names and terms from different religions. This is easily done if children are not overwhelmed with information and if teachers take care to check that everyone knows and understands vocabulary before moving on to a new topic. Chapters 3–9 provide basic introductions to six major world religions, while Chapters 10–16 show how these faiths might be approached in junior classrooms. Readers will be able to select material to meet the particular needs of their own pupils.

An experiential element

Religious education is more than gaining knowledge of religions. It should also give some experience of religion, not by requiring children to take part in religious activity, but by observing and reflecting on devotional acts and by gaining insight into the religious experience of believers. Such experience can be gained at second-hand through the sensitive use of audio-visual materials and at first-hand through visits and through welcoming guests from religious communities into the school. Within the classroom pupils' and teachers' personal experiences of religion can make a very important contribution to the process of religious education. Many children with no experience of formal religion may nevertheless have personal experiences of a religious character.

Pupils from religious backgrounds bring with them personal experience and knowledge which may provide material for sharing with others. I am reminded of a lesson with fourth-year juniors in which a class was guessing what was happening in a transparency showing a Greek Orthodox baptism ceremony. Part of the lesson was taken over by a boy who volunteered information about the rites of adult baptism in his own Baptist tradition. He was even able to tell us what the word 'baptism' meant and to outline the symbolism of being 'dipped' into death and rising to new life. On being shown a slide of the Golden Temple at Amritsar the one Sikh child in the class, a rather shy girl, whispered 'I've been there'. She didn't volunteer any more information during the lesson, but afterwards offered to bring in photographs and souvenirs from her visit. Both she and other members of the class (to say nothing of the teacher) were motivated by the experience and informed by her contribution. Sometimes children's contributions may be mediated through curriculum materials. Chapter 27, for example, sketches some information about the varied religious lives of one group of Hindu pupils of junior age, illustrating the potentially rich contribution of children to RE. Children's direct contributions do need to be managed with great sensitivity, however. Children rightly may feel resentful if they feel forced or manoeuvred into contributing their own personal experiences.

An analytical element

Some critics of RE which draws on several religions have accused the subject of 'relativism'. The charge is that an impartial approach results in children getting the impression that all religions are equally true. These critics fail to grasp the distinction between learning about religion impartially and thinking about and questioning the claims of religious traditions; both of these processes are legitimate aspects of religious education. To return to an earlier example, the boy who made a contribution from his own experience as a Baptist believed that adult baptism was right and that baptising infants was a mistake. Further, he was able to give reasons for his beliefs. This did not prevent him from considering with interest and sensitivity the example of infant baptism we were examining and it did him no harm to explain his own point of view. Note too the example quoted in Chapter 26, in which the activity of studying the contents of a shrine in a Hindu temple prompted children to raise questions such as 'Who is God?' and 'Why do different people think there are different gods?'

When studying religions in the classroom there will be children who question all religious claims, who strongly agree with one or another religious or secular position, and who tend to adopt agnostic positions. What religious education should offer is an approach which encourages children to support their commitments with reasons and to be prepared to consider reasonably the views of others.

An imaginative element

The use of the imagination is vital in attempting to understand religions, especially in trying to grasp something of the experience of people who practise religions other than one's own. Imagination can also help children to appreciate different types and levels of meaning in religious language, whether the language of spoken, sung or written story, the body language of ritual or the visual language of religious art and iconography (see the chapters in this book on religion and the arts). Children can also be stimulated to use their imagination in designing methods of study and varieties of classroom activity (see for example 'Children as ethnographers' and 'Visiting places of worship').

An expressive element

Religious education entails more than learning about religions and empathising with practitioners of religion. Children should have the opportunity not only to express their understanding of a topic or issue, but also their reflections on it and responses to it. The creative arts have much to offer in helping children to integrate their knowledge, thinking and imagination as the chapters in this book on story, drama, art and music show. The poem reproduced in Chapter 26 is a good example of the way in which an artistic medium can draw together strands of knowledge, thought and feeling as a child reflects on a class visit to a parish church.

Training in Religious Education

The 1988 Act essentially supports a liberal and open approach to religious education. The opportunities it affords will, however, come to little unless the issues of provision and training are addressed effectively. The Religious Education Council of England and Wales' paper *Religious Education: Supply of Teachers for the 1990s* exposes the chronic shortage of teachers with RE qualifications in junior and secondary schools together with insufficient training opportunities at initial and in-service levels.

The paper's analysis of DES statistics shows a thin provision of INSET at the junior level and an inadequate number of RE curriculum leaders in junior schools. Nationally DES funding needs to be specifically earmarked for RE. Locally, SACREs and LEAs have a responsibility to ensure that adequate training and resource levels are provided, while governing bodies share with SACREs a major responsibility for ensuring that the intentions of the Act are carried out. Individual schools can, however, take the initiative in developing effective RE by designating curriculum leaders, sending teachers on INSET courses, organising school-based INSET, keeping governors and parents well-informed, and lobbying for more resources. We hope that this book will be one resource for helping groups of teachers to develop RE in their own schools and for providing information and ideas for students in initial training.

Notes

[1] On the question of withdrawal, only county *secondary* schools are *required* to arrange for 'denominational teaching' on the school premises if parents request it. DES Circular 3/89 suggests that these arrangements could be extended by mutual agreement to all schools as long as 'alternative provision is consistent with the overall purposes of the school curriculum set out in Section 1 of the Act'.

[2] Heads can apply for exemption from the normal requirements of the Act on collective worship. Circular 3/89 states:

> where it is difficult to reconcile these requirements either in the case of a whole school or of a particular category of pupils, the headteacher may apply to the SACRE for a determination that the requirement for Christian collective worship should not apply in the case of the school or of any class or description of pupils within it.

The head has first to consult the governors, who in turn may seek the views of parents. The purpose of this procedure:

> is to allow for acts of collective worship according to a faith or religion other than Christianity where for some or all of the pupils in a school the requirement that worship should be of a broadly Christian character is inappropriate. (IV, 36)

The SACRE must take account of 'relevant circumstances relating to the backgrounds of the pupils concerned' in arriving at its decision, which must be a straight acceptance or rejection of the request, given in writing to the head, and stating the date from which any change is to take place. The head informs the governing body and the parents of the SACRE's decision. Any such determination ends after five years unless renewed by the SACRE, though the head can request an earlier review, after consulting the governors who, in turn, may seek the views of parents.

The rights of parents to withdraw children, and staff to withdraw themselves, is retained from the 1944 legislation. Circular 3/89 says:

> if the parent asks that a pupil should be wholly or partly excused from attending any religious worship or RE given in the school, then the school must comply. This includes alternative worship given in a county school as a result of a determination by a SACRE. (V, 41, ii)

Bibliography

Important sources are the Act itself and DES Circular 3/89 *The Education Reform Act 1988: Religious Education and Collective worship*

Alan Brown, 'Religious Education and Worship in Schools: Flexibility, Frustration, Foibles and Fallacies', *Resource* (Vol. 12, No. 1, Autumn 1989). This discusses misrepresentations of the 1988 Act on RE and collective worship in the press and educational journals.

Edwin Cox and Josephine Cairns, *Reforming Religious Education* (Kogan Page, 1989)

C. Erricker (ed.), *Teaching Christianity: A World Religions Approach* (Lutterworth, 1987)

John Hull, *The Act Unpacked* (CEM, 1989)

John Hull, *School Worship: an Obituary* (SCM Press, 1975)

E. Hulmes, *Commitment and Neutrality in Religious Education* (Geoffrey Chapman, 1979)

R. Jackson (ed.), *Approaching World Religions* (John Murray, 1982)

Religious Education (National Society, 1989. Available from Church House, Great Smith Street, London SW1P 3NZ)

School Worship (National Society, 1989)

'Teaching Religious Education', an *Education* Digest (Longman, The Pinnacles, Fourth Avenue, Harlow, Essex)

Religious Education: Supply of Teachers for the 1990s (Religious Education Council of England and Wales, available from the Religious Education Department, St Martin's College, Lancaster LA1 3JB)

CHAPTER 2

Planning religious education

MARY HAYWARD

Religious education is at a critical moment in its history. The present moment is one when its place in the curriculum may be once and for all secured on sound educational principles, or when a kind of legalistic tokenism – 'we must obey the Act' – takes over and the subject is marginalised to an extent which, in the end, makes a fool of the 1988 legislation. This chapter, however, starts from the premise that religious education's continuing place in the curriculum will be assured not by law, but by those schools where careful thought and planning make it an indispensable part of children's coming to self-understanding, and to an understanding of the complex world in which they are growing up.

Working towards a school policy for RE

Although an overview of Agreed Syllabuses of the last decade points to an emergent consensus about the nature and purpose of RE, in the preparation of each syllabus there will have been discussion, disagreement, and debate in arriving at agreement. Open and honest debate needs to take place in staff rooms too when a school's RE policy is being shaped; some schools also find it useful to involve representatives of their governing body in the policy making process. A number of issues need clarification and agreement for a sound RE programme to emerge.

Aims

Statements of aims are now commonplace in most Agreed Syllabuses; often an overarching aim sets the tone of a syllabus' provision (5 to 16/18). The opportunity for all the teachers in a junior school – and perhaps their feeder infant school(s) – to *go through the process* of reaching an *agreed* and overarching aim for RE can be illuminating.

Here is one approach. Make a card pack of 15–20 aims derived from syllabuses, 'vox pop', politicians, the media and faith communities – Figure 1 gives some suggestions. Working groups of three or four people each receive a pack and must *agree* on two aims from the pack which they find acceptable and two which must be discarded at all costs. Each group must then present its decisions, and *argue the case* for its choices and rejections.

To make sure children have a knowledge of the Bible.	To help children make moral choices.	To familiarise children with the Christian heritage of their country.	To teach children about Christianity.
To help children understand what it means to hold a religious view of life.	To foster a reflective approach to life in the context of understanding the experience, and beliefs and religious practices of mankind.	To explore those aspects of human experience which raise questions about the meaning of life.	To discover the part religion has played in the history of mankind.
To promote tolerance of and sensitivity towards those with religious beliefs different from one's own.	To provide children with a faith by which to live.	To develop the ability to think about questions of belief and value.	To help children make decisions about which faith they will adopt – to give them a choice.
To give children values by which to live.	To teach children how to behave.	To help children learn more about their own religious tradition and heritage.	To foster spiritual awareness.

Figure 1   Health Warning: only read these aims after you have read the task on p. 14.

The process quickly brings to the fore perennial issues in the RE debate.
- the teacher's commitment, indoctrination, nurture or education?
- moral or religious education?
- which religions?
- what style of teaching?
- and the expectations of parents and faith communities.

The 'game' clarifies staff positions, clears the air, but importantly pinpoints determinants of aims and helps staff to work towards their school's philosophy of RE. 'What is *the* aim?' becomes 'What is *our* aim?'

Which religions?

Part Two of this book attempts to offer a first foothold in each of six traditions, but each school will need to decide which of these children should encounter. A number of factors are likely to influence such a decision: local circumstances – the faiths represented in the school and/or the neighbourhood; the knowledge and expertise of staff; available resources – including the human; opportunities offered by other curriculum areas; and, the most important, the children's experience and stage of development. The arguments that children will be confused if they meet more than *one* religion and that 'explicit' religion, such as is explored in this book, is outside the child's experience are often raised at this point and need laying to rest. They ignore the fact – well exemplified in Chapter 27 – that some children come from family backgrounds where religious faith matters; whilst the latter argument is particularly specious in the context of the range of topics tackled by most junior schools. When for example did your class last meet a Viking or encounter a dinosaur?

What is religion?

Clearly this question won't be answered here! But it is also the wrong question to ask if the required answer is a definition. Consider a different kind of answer constructed from this book: religion is story, myth, symbol, image, picture, music, worship, buildings, sacred books, and people; it is also remembering, questioning, identity and belonging, searching, believing, experiencing, living, dying, celebrating and valuing. And of course much more. But a shift has been made from definition to 'map-making'; it's useful for a school on an INSET Day to begin to make their own map. For example, view some school programmes such as Central Television's *Believe it or Not* series. Select two or three programmes about different religions, and from this concrete experience begin to list and then group the 'ingredients' of 'religion' which emerge: be careful to cultivate a 'listening eye' whilst you do this, and try to leave your personal spectacles in their case! Work towards a map which staff can 'own' and check against others' readings.

Ninian Smart's book *The World's Religions* offers a map which can be helpful in planning RE. Smart outlines seven dimensions which this chapter will pick up later in attainment targets. The dimensions are the

- practical and ritual dimension (regular practices of a religion: worship, prayer, preaching, and meditation for example)
- experiential and emotional dimension (the inner side of a religious faith; also a sense of mystery, awe)
- narrative or mythic dimension (the story side of religion)
- doctrinal and philosophical dimension (intellectual statements and formulations concerning the fundamentals of a particular faith)
- ethical and legal dimension (patterns of behaviour, life styles, laws which mark out paths to salvation/liberation)
- social and institutional dimension (religions are embodied in people, for example, Church (Christian), Umma (Muslim) – in communities which organise and structure themselves in distinctive ways)
- material dimension (community expression in, for example, sacred buildings, art; sacred places associated with a community, for example, the Ganges; Mount Sinai).

What is offered is a tool which reminds us of the richness and variety of religions. The dimensions are of course not found in equal balance in each religion, nor within all groups who claim to be, for example, Christian or Hindu. Variety is endemic in religions! So is complexity – and so the dimensions are also interrelated: a church building may be cruciform in shape, pointing to the worship which takes place there, to the Christian story of Jesus who died on the cross, and to an ideal of sacrificial love. A celebration of *Diwali* uses the symbol of light, and often focuses on a story which tells how God operates in the world, sets ideals of goodness and loyalty and points to a vision of a harmonious and ordered world.

The nature of RE

What was said of religions above pointed to 'inner' and 'outer' aspects of traditions; subsequent chapters of this book show that the inner and outer belong together. If children simply learn to describe the *rak'ah* or postures in Muslim prayer, what have they learnt? But if considering *salah* (the prescribed prayers) has led them on the way to understanding the discipline of mind and body in prayer, of being part of a community which has a particular understanding of the relationship of man and God, and if they have grasped something of a Muslim's sense of God, then we have moved from the outer to the inner.

The use of 'inner' here is a reminder of the importance of the *experiential* dimension which is fundamental to all the others. But it usefully points as well to the kind of *existential* issues noted above (belonging, living, dying, etc.). This is another strand of RE, which needs to be an integral part of the subject. Sometimes it is in danger of becoming divorced from the 'outer' elements.

As long ago as 1977 *Discovering an Approach*, the work of the Schools Council Project on RE in primary schools, neatly summarised such an approach to RE:

> religious education should have two sides to it. It is to help children understand the religious traditions of life and thought that they meet in their environment. It is also to help children to be sensitive to the ultimate questions posed by life and to the dimension of mystery and wonder that underlies all human experience. These two aspects are vital; to neglect one or the other is to undermine the effectiveness of religious education.
>
> *(p. 11)*

Planning the RE programme

Unless RE is planned it doesn't take place! Until this point we have been laying foundations, identifying issues which any school needs to face before engaging in the practicalities of a programme of RE. In many ways the practicalities here are no different from those confronted when planning other areas of the curriculum. The children are rightly at the heart of the school's concern. Providing a stimulating environment, relevant and interesting resources, and a variety of learning experiences; ensuring the development of skills relevant to the area of study and within the capacity of the child; ascertaining 'where the children are' at seven years will all be important. Taking RE seriously means planning ahead.

A school audit

Where RE is seen as important attention will need to be given to a fair allocation of time, to capitation, to staffing, to the physical environment in which RE occurs, to the range of resources which are available (books, AVA, artefacts; staff – and not only teachers – and children who may be living resources, and the community in which the school is set). To review all these matters can begin to point towards the possibility of a living RE programme.

Organisation

As part of the basic curriculum it would be unfortunate if RE did not take its place within the regular organisational pattern of the school. For seven- to eleven-year-olds this will often be through integrated topic work, though it is useful for a school to identify other areas where RE may occur – collective worship, through the development of relevant or related skills and concepts in other areas of the curriculum, or through storytime, for example. Rachel Gregory's chapter (Chapter 24) usefully points out how RE may relate to the organisation of topics in different ways. Some topics will have no religious dimension; courage to recognise this is important! What is clear is that attention needs to be paid to the balance of topics throughout a year, or throughout an age phase and to keeping a record of what is done.

Development and progression

As well as due care being given to 'balance', progression and development are important; some features of religion will occur and re-occur in the junior curriculum: festivals come to mind particularly. Jean Holm's reflections on teaching Christianity (Chapter 11) make it clear that development is more than extending content, it is also acquiring an increasingly complex repertoire of skills. Local work on attainment targets and statements of attainment for RE may help schools to ensure development and progression in their RE programmes.

Attainment targets for RE?

As part of the basic curriculum one of the questions and challenges which faces RE in the present is that of attainment targets. The desirability of targets in a subject which lays claims on operating particularly in the affective and personal domains is an issue which will continue to be debated. But if RE is at a time of crisis, that thought should be given to attainment targets seems vital. At the time of writing a number of discussion documents are currently available (see bibliography): that prepared by the Association of Religious Education Advisors and Inspectors (AREAI) is instructive in its *approach*, which could provide a model for local development. This approach

- derives attainment targets from an agreed map of religion
- suggests that there should be no more than 12 attainment targets, accessible to all children between 5 to 16/18
- shapes attainment targets according to an agreed aim for the understanding of RE
- uses the key stages (7, 11, 14, 16) but not the ten levels of core curriculum documents.

Whilst schools will wish to discover significant LEA initiatives, in the inevitable hiatus between convening an Agreed Syllabus Conference and the production of locally determined guidelines, schools may find this a helpful model to use themselves. Notice that its first and third points endorse the importance we attached earlier to laying foundations for RE.

Recalling the dimensional 'map' of religion what kind of attainment targets might emerge? The grid (Figure 2, on p. 20) is offered for reflection and discussion.

Comments on the grid
In setting out targets in this way a number of observations need to be made:

- Just as the elements in a map of religion are interrelated, so are attainment targets.
- A topic, for example, a festival, might (pedagogically) be drawn from *one* target. But in a study, for example, of Easter prompted by AT 7 teachers of seven- to eleven-year-olds might also be working in relation to ATs 3, 4, 5, and 8. The existence of targets should help to prioritise what is happening *this* term and what might happen *next* time this topic is studied.
- In the listing of these attainment targets no hierarchy is implied in terms of religious traditions, nor suggested in terms of a sequence of learning or levels of difficulty. The sequential learning of maths and science gives way to a more fluid situation in RE, though this does not diminish the need for an organised approach to learning.
- Attainment targets expressed in this way call for a sensitive approach to

AT	Aim: Children should develop knowledge, understanding and skills appropriate to thinking about and interpreting the following aspects of religious traditions:	Key 'map' references
1	Significant beliefs of major religious traditions, especially the ways in which they have spoken of God/Ultimate Reality.	Doctrinal/Philosophical Narrative/Mythical
2	Religious insights into fundamental questions of human existence: Who am I? How do I relate to others? Humankind's use of the created world: suffering; death etc.	Cuts across dimensions
3	The place of story and narrative in communicating religious ideas and interpreting and exploring existential issues.	Narrative/Mythic Experiential/Emotional
4	The ways in which religions convey meaning through the special use of language; through symbols – verbal, aural, visual etc.	Practical/Ritual Narrative/Mythic Material
5	The material expressions of religion and their significance – symbolic and pragmatic – in the life of a tradition: sacred places, buildings, art, music, drama, artefacts etc.	Practical/Ritual Material Narrative/Mythic
6	The place of community in the transmission of belief and in the continuity of religious traditions.	Social/Institutional Doctrinal/Philosophical
7	Celebration, festival and the marking of time in the life of the individual and the community.	Practical/Ritual Narrative/Mythic Social/Institutional
8	The 'spiritual' life of the community and the individual as expressed communally and individually: worship, prayer, meditation, fasting, pilgrimage etc.	Experiential/Emotional Practical/Ritual Material
9	The continuing vitality influence and authority of sacred writings, founders and teachers in religions in the present.	Narrative/Mythic Ethical/Legal
10	Commitments, responses, values and lifestyles shaped by religious insight.	Narrative/Mythic Ethical/Legal Social/Institutional

Figure 2   Attainment Targets for RE: a provisional statement.

religious traditions. The need for comprehensiveness and 'neutrality' in stating attainment targets must not obscure the distinctiveness of religions: not all give the same place or weighting to a calendar of festivals; thus Judaism would 'score' highly, Islam not so high. On the other hand 'pilgrimage' would inevitably draw on Islam, but not on Sikhism.

- The attainment targets stated here have a present, a 'here and now' thrust. They may be 'matched' both to children's experiences and to the opportunities which the local environment offers. Indeed once attainment targets are clear there is a wealth of material available to service them – as this book indicates.

Statements of attainment

Where Agreed Syllabuses have been objective led, and have had an eye to progression and coherence, LEAs and schools are already well-placed to move from attainment targets to statements of attainment. Both Durham (1983) and Cambridge (1982) are noteworthy in this respect. Statements of attainment as they emerge in a school or LEA in relation to a particular attainment target need to be enabling rather than restrictive, but the need for the accuracy which will lend itself to assessment makes this a difficult and delicate balance to maintain. Statements of attainment are also likely to reflect a school's understanding of religious *education*, with regard especially to its aims and methods. The AREAI report referred to in the bibliography contains useful comments on the structuring and phrasing of statements of attainment. See Section 13, pp. 16–17.

A worked example

The popularity of festivals in the junior curriculum means that each of the documents to which I have referred chooses this as a theme for further development – this chapter is no exception! So let us take AT 7 from the grid. Figure 3 suggests how statements of attainment for key stages 1 and 2 might look. This example is obviously a provisional exploration of statements of attainment and would acquire a specific context in a programme of study. In attempting it I experienced a number of frustrations! Firstly the attainment target – even if I had continued with my statements of attainment to 16+ – points to much more potential learning than I will ever assess at the given stages. This I suspect should be encouraging, but it is also a warning against the restrictive nature of statements of attainment. Put in another way, statements of attainment are likely to represent a small amount of the learning which takes place. Secondly – I suspect like many teachers – I wanted to move from the attainment targets to identify specific *topics*. For example, Festivals of Light, Time, the Calendar, Change, Seasons and so on would have allowed me to do cross curricular work with integrity, but my statements of attainment for key stages could again be restrictive: *particular* topics may suggest a different range of statements of attainment but perhaps equally valid and insightful. For the moment I leave this problem open to debate. The strength, however, of statements of attainment for RE is that

- they help to clarify the educational intent of RE
- they identify a range of skills

21

- they point to the importance of progression and development
- together with attainment targets, they help to clarify boundaries and thus RE's potential relationship with other curriculum areas.

Relation of ATs and programmes of study

So far I have been largely concerned with preparing a ground plan for a sound religious *education*. But schools also have to decide 'what to teach' term by term. In National Curriculum terminology this brings us to programmes of study – the organisation of content, skills and processes to achieve attainment targets at set stages. Arguably the construction of these does give a school freedom to remain true to its own philosophy and organisation, and in RE at least attainment targets should not become a restrictive force.

AREAI's Interim Consultative Report suggests that a programme of study is most easily constructed for the key stage age groups in relation to one attainment target but the NCC documents for science and maths offer other models. Relating groups of attainment targets in RE, given their inter-connectedness, seems more helpful. Relating particular attainment targets to age phases might also make sense, since it recognises the complexity of

By key stage 1 (7 years)
Children should be able: • to identify and recall two special days in their own experience and say why they are/were special • to suggest up to three ways in which people remember or recall past events. • to name three key days marked in a Christian calendar and to match them with associated events (and to discover the names of those important to other faith communities represented in school) • to express the story/or another aspect of *one* festival through an appropriate creative activity e.g. movement, mime, collage, music, etc.
By key stage 2 (11 years)
Children should be able: • to give a simple account of the ways in which a major festival in each of two religions is celebrated • to identify the key symbols which are associated with the festivals studied and suggest why they are important • to discover by questioning or research why each festival is important for a follower of the religions studied • to recognise and explore for themselves some of the human experiences which underlie these and other festivals familiar to them.

Figure 3 Statements of attainment for key stages 1 and 2 in relation to AT 7 (Figure 2).

material and offers selection according to children's capacities; this is not to diminish the importance of any one attainment target, but to recognise that at different stages some will have a higher profile than others. Whichever way we approach the clustering of attainment targets, they will offer the possibility of a variety of programmes of study, cross curricular or discretely RE. Cross curricular work needs to be approached with thought and with concern for the integrity of what is done. A review I read recently commented:

> Many teachers will be at a loss to incorporate religious education into for instance, Attainment Target 15: Using light and electromagnetic radiation . . . There is a demand for publications using science, maths, history or geography based topics which can point to 'explicit' religious education material. For example, a topic based on visits to HMS *Victory* and the *Mary Rose* (History) can be linked with water (Science) and the symbolism of water (RE).

Not only do other curriculum areas call the tune here, but the random juxtaposition of content also indicates the pitfalls for RE, and highlights the need for cross curricular planning to occur at the level of statements of attainment. Schools need to face the question, how far can what we (or the LEA) wish to achieve in RE be met by cross curricular work? As part of the basic curriculum, RE requires at least a degree of 'self determination' in the planning of programmes of study. This is not a plea for an isolationist policy, but the danger is that the core curriculum becomes all consuming.

The future shape of Agreed Syllabuses can only be a matter of speculation at present. If LEAs move towards locally determined attainment targets, statements of attainment and programmes of study, many will be more prescriptive than hitherto. In the meantime the school which can agree a set of attainment targets (and not lose sight of specific attainment at key stages in children's learning) is in a position to exercise a responsible flexibility in its choice of content. The point in all this will be to ensure progression, variety, and balance – balance among traditions as prescribed by the local Agreed Syllabus and ERA, balance within a map of religion (expressed through ATs) and balance within the chosen model of RE.

Assessment

In speaking of assessment in RE it needs to be clear that just as the aim of RE is educational, not confessional, so also with assessment. As the Religious Education Council's *Handbook for Agreed Syllabus Conferences SACREs and Schools* (1989) puts it:

> Schools must make it quite clear that, if records are kept in this subject, they represent not the attainment of religious faith and its practice, but the extent to which pupils are sufficiently informed and can understand and respond to religious issues.

(p. 21)

23

Recognition of this is important from two perspectives: from that of parents who would rightly suspect any attempts made in a county school to nurture children in a particular faith and also from that of parents whose faith commitment may see the school as having a nurturing role, and may be uncertain about the educational stance taken in school. Clearly the school will need to be sensitive to the commitments of parents and children and careful to communicate and discuss its RE policy – including assessment.

If an LEA or a school judges attainment targets and associated statements of attainment as appropriate, and if we are concerned for progression and sequence then some form of assessment might be seen as a logical consequence; attainment targets suggest that there is a basic 'religious literacy' which children may acquire in school. We need to be clear however both about its boundaries and its limitations, especially with regard to RE's affective and personal dimensions noted.

Recent writing on assessment in RE relates it to three general approaches: diagnostic (identifying 'where a pupil is' in order to plan for further learning), summative (identifying what children know and have achieved at fixed stages) and formative (to which we must add profiling). Sections 18 and 19 of AREAIs report explores issues relating to assessment. *How do I Teach RE?* also looks at assessment in RE in some detail. The formative approach seems to offer most to RE, but is the most taxing on already overburdened teachers. Formative assessment is integral to the learning process – an ongoing dialogue among pupil, teacher and what is being studied. It is likely to involve the child in self-evaluation, and will draw on a range of techniques. This seems to be a necessary adjunct to the summative (for example, at 7, 11, 14 and 16) if the latter is not to dominate the educational scene, but to be an integral part of its 'flow'. Just as it is hoped that RE will offer a wide range of learning experiences, the means of assessment need to be varied to 'capture' the range of competencies children may develop. At the time of writing this is fertile ground for research.

Bibliography

Association of Religious Education Advisers and Inspectors (AREAI), *Religious Education for ages 5 to 16/18: Attainment and Assessment Interim Consultative Report* (July 1989), available from RE–ME Enquiry Service, St Martin's College, Lancaster LA1 3JD

Believe it or Not, commercially available on video from PEP, Hennock Road, Exeter Devon EX2 8RP

London Diocesan Board for Schools, *Attainment Targets for Religious Education Key Stages 1 and 2* (Draft document), available from The Education Committee, London Diocesan Board for Schools, 30 Causton Street, London SW1P 4AU

G. Read, J. Rudge and R. B. Howarth, *How do I teach RE?* (Stanley Thornes (Publishers) Ltd, 1986)

Religious Education Council of England and Wales, *Handbook for Agreed Syllabus Conferences SACRES and Schools* (1989), Chapter 5: Statements of Achievement and Programmes of Study, available from RE–ME Enquiry Service (see above for address)
Ninian Smart, *The World's Religions* (Cambridge, 1989)

PART TWO

Guides to Religions

Introduction

The aim of this section is to provide readers with brief introductions to the main religious traditions represented in this country. It is not intended as a syllabus, but to provide brief overviews for teachers wishing to orientate themselves to particular traditions prior to designing and producing teaching materials.

There are advantages and disadvantages in overviews. They do, of course, need to be written by people who have a good knowledge of the subject. They can then provide reference points, both for the beginner and for the person very familiar with specific aspects of a tradition, but lacking an overall perspective. Overviews can thus indicate key concepts, practices and events. They can also introduce the reader to some of the best and most reliable literature on a religious tradition.

Some of our overviews are written by outsiders, writers with a strong academic and professional interest in the religions they write about. Others are written by insiders who are in one way or another professionally engaged in teaching about their religion as well as being involved as participants.

So far so good. But what dangers ought the reader to be aware of when using the overviews? One is a tendency to perceive the religions as wholly independent entities, having a minimal relationship with one another. This tendency is implicit in the idea of presenting separate introductions to the various faiths. Despite the attention authors give to the pluralism of the traditions with which they deal, there can also be a tendency to regard religions as monolithic, or at least as abstractions which correspond to an ideal rather than the complex range of examples that occur in ordinary life. We need to remind ourselves of the shared concepts of the Semitic religions (Judaism, Christianity and Islam) and of the Indian religions as well as of the various mutual influences that have occurred in history.

Then there is the fact that all authors are writing from one perspective or other. An outsider attempting to grasp a tradition in all its diversity will describe it differently from an insider whose way of perceiving it will be influenced to a greater or lesser degree by personal or community experience of a particular kind. The chapter on Hinduism, written by outsiders, attempts to indicate something of the range of possibilities covered by the term and would have been written differently by an insider, who would have been influenced perhaps by ethnic background or sectarian allegiance. The chapter on Judaism, written by an insider, splendidly covers the range of the tradition, but reveals some of the author's personal commitments which would not necessarily be shared by all Jews.

The points made above are highlighted in the work of the Canadian scholar Wilfred Cantwell Smith. In his book *The Meaning and End of Religion* (SPCK, 1978) Smith points out the inadequacy of the term 'religion' to denote the complex, historically fluid and internally diverse phenomena that are known by names such as Christianity, Hinduism and Islam. In preference to 'religion', Smith uses the terms 'faith' and 'tradition'. 'Faith' represents the commitments and beliefs of the individual set in a particular place and time and facing a cluster of questions and dilemmas that are of personal concern. 'Tradition' is the cumulative tradition which provides the historical and cultural setting for faith and the family of concepts and structures that give expression to the individual's faith. It is the study of the interplay between faith and tradition that provides the basis for an understanding of living religion. At junior level a study of the religious lives of individuals and families set in the context of the wider tradition can both facilitate understanding and provide links with the children's own experience. Incidentally, one of the accounts of Christianity in this section describes the tradition in general (by a Roman Catholic who 'stands back' from his faith) and is complemented by another (by an Anglican) which refers to the author's personal faith position.

Smith's points raise general questions about the relationship between religions. Some of the cruder attacks on relativism that were characteristic of the debate surrounding the RE clauses in the Education Reform Bill gave the erroneous impression that children are being taught widely that all religions are equally true. What we should be doing as RE teachers is to ensure that pupils grasp that people inside and outside religious traditions have a variety of views and commitments about the relationship between the different religions and that this variety can be found within individual traditions. Within Christianity, for example, that range of views has been classified by some theologians into three types: exclusivism, pluralism and inclusivism.

Exclusivism is associated with conservative and fundamentalist theologies, and takes the line that only those who have committed themselves to Christ can be saved. At the other extreme, pluralism regards religions as different and equally legitimate paths leading to the same goal. Inclusivism, however, maintains a commitment to the uniqueness of Christianity, while acknowledging the reality of divine revelation in the other faiths. This, for example, is the official position of the Roman Catholic Church, based on the documents of the Second Vatican Council.

CHAPTER 3

Getting to grips with Buddhism

PEGGY MORGAN

One of the first points to make is that in many ways Buddhism is one of the easiest of the world religions to encounter in Britain. Most of its teachers and adherents are British, and they can be found in all kinds of environments; in the rural areas of Dumfries, Northumbria, Sussex and Wales as well as the more obvious multicultural centres of Birmingham and London. The distribution of groups and communities can be seen from a glance at the addresses, map and description of activities in *The Buddhist Directory* which is regularly updated. Another way of overviewing the Buddhist presence in Britain is to look at copies of *The Middle Way*. This also comes from the Buddhist Society and contains material on all the schools such as Theravada, Zen and Tibetan that are thriving here. There are also some Pure Land Buddhists and New Buddhist Movements such as the two Nichiren groups, Nipponzan Myohoji and Soka Gakkai. Most forms of Buddhism are being transplanted into the west and it is thought to be entirely in keeping with the methods and teaching of the Buddha that British forms of Buddhism should grow. One such form is the eclectic Friends of the Western Buddhist Order.

A Path to Happiness

Buddhism claims to be a 'Path to Happiness', to quote the title of the first in a trilogy of Buddhist children's books in French. The Buddhist greeting reflects the words of the *Metta Sutta*, a text learned by all Buddhist children in traditional Theravada societies such as Sri Lanka. It says:

> May all beings be happy and secure;
> may their minds be contented.

It is, of course, a happiness based on the inward quality of life, not on externals. If this makes Buddhism sound more like a philosophy, an ethical system or way of life, than a religion, then it is only fair to say that it has been called all of those things; but then so have Hindusim, Judaism, Islam, etc. If the term religion is suspect then it is usually because it can have the overtones of 'empty ritual', a 'Sundays only' activity, of intellectual belief being enough, or of relying on a being 'out there' to solve your problems. Buddhists want to emphasise practice, everyday mindfulness, the transformation of the heart and that 'you yourselves must make the effort; the Buddhas are only teachers'.

To return to the image of a path, it is more accurate to say that Buddhism is not one but many paths which seek to take 'whatsoever living beings there may be, short, small or large, seen or unseen, those dwelling far and near, those who are born and those who are yet to be born' to peace and happiness. The heart of Buddhism is compassion, and 'he who, seeking his own happiness, torments with the rod creatures that are desirous of happiness, shall not attain happiness thereafter'. Since beings are all very different they need different paths to take them on their journey. Some paths follow the natural lines of the countryside and meander carefully and painstakingly along. They take people slowly but reliably to the goal. Often in single file. Other paths are cut out broadly, making a quicker, more sociable climb which is dependent on a way that has been prepared before. There are also direct dangerous routes up rock faces where it is wise to be roped to a skilled rock climber whom you trust. All these ways can take people to their destination. Their inclinations and aptitudes vary.

Buddhists also use the image of a path when they talk of a 'middle way', a way that avoids the extremes of self-denial and self-indulgence. It is illustrated in the life of the Buddha who lived through and rejected both luxury and severe asceticism. One of the most basic summaries of Buddhist teaching is called 'The Noble Eightfold Path', and the path image naturally links with the idea of life as a journey, as a pilgrimage with a purpose, rather than the 'wandering without a purpose' which I once saw as a definition of *samsara*. *Samsara* is the endless cycle of birth and death and describes the wheel of rebirth on which all unenlightened beings are bound. It is a word which Buddhists share with Hindus, and they have a common purpose of release from *samsara*. One Buddhist interviewed by John Bowker in *Worlds of Faith* says that the big difference between people is between pilgrims and non-pilgrims:

> It isn't a division between different world religious systems or different faiths that matters; it's between . . . those who talk about following the path and those who follow it.

(p. 60)

Gautama Buddha is said to have discovered 'an ancient noble path', not to have invented something completely new. It is *dharma*, a word that can be translated as teaching or truth. The truth is the truth about the way things are and is not exclusive to Buddhism:

> But if there are teachings, no matter whose, you are sure will conduce to serenity, not passion; freedom, not bondage . . . thrift, not greed; calm, not restlessness; . . . energy, not sloth; performance of good, not delight in evil – that is the *Dharma*; that is the discipline, that is the master's way.

The goal of the *dharma* is for *samsara* to be transformed into *Nirvana*. The best way to understand what is meant by *Nirvana* is to look at some other imagery used by Buddhists.

The vehicles

In addition to the idea of the path or the way, Buddhists also talk about vehicles such as boats or rafts which carry people safely across a river or a stretch of sea in which are hidden currents and treacherous rocks. *Samsara* in this case is the tumultuous river or tempestuous sea. To be without a boat or raft is to be 'at sea', tossed in the waters of *samsara* without direction or goal. To be on a raft, to have a vehicle, is to know the *dharma* and to be able to steer or be steered towards the 'further shore' or the 'island refuge', both images used for *Nirvana*. The raft is for crossing over and not for retaining. It is to be discarded once it has served its purpose. *Nirvana* can be described only in relation to *samsara*. It is peace after the storm, happiness after unsatisfactoriness, the deathlessness after the agonies of constant rebirth, the extinguished flames after the uncontrollable fires of greed, hatred and ignorance. To attain *Nirvana* people do not necessarily have to be Buddhists, but they do need some kind of path.

Buddhist history and teaching makes reference to three kinds of boat or raft. These are not identifiable with the divisions of the existing schools or sects. The *Hinayana* (little boat) is a way of steady self-discipline and refinement with a careful balance between strict moral norms and renunciation of the world. This balance is maintained in the interdependence of the way of life of householders and members of the monastic *sangha*, the *bhikshus* and *bhikshunis* – monks and nuns – whom the householders feed, clothe and house and who are thought by them to be close to *Nirvana*. In the *Mahayana* (great vehicle) approach, the variety of methods for attaining *Nirvana* increases. There is an emphasis on the ideal of the *bodhisattvas* (enlightenment beings) who vow to stay in *samsara* as long as there are sentient beings who need their help. They have an infinite number of skilful means (*upaya kausalya*) which can help others on the way. One of the most important realisations in the *Mahayana* approach is the emptiness (*sunyata*) of mundane reality and conventional thinking. The wise understanding of this is the nature of *Nirvana*, to be realised in and not apart from *samsara*. The third vehicle or boat is the *Vajrayana*, the way of the thunderbolt or diamond. The thunderbolt goes straight to its mark, and a diamond not only has an indestructible quality, but a sharp cutting edge The *Vajrayana* as a vehicle is said to combine wisdom and compassion. It is as direct and fast as a speedboat, but dangerous in the wrong hands, so a good driver (teacher, guru or lama) is essential; and it is not wise to leave the keys lying around to be misused.

All these three vehicles trace the foundation for their methods back to the Buddha himself. Elements of them can be found in all the major schools, though the means are sometimes more dominant in one school than another: for example Tibetan Buddhism is sometimes identified with the *Vajrayana*, although it should be pointed out that many Tibetan lay Buddhists are almost completely *Hinayana* in their attitudes. Because at one time in Buddhist history the group of schools to which the Theravada belong were criticised for being *Hinayana* in a narrow way, Theravadins do not like this term. They prefer to emphasise the title Theravada which means 'way of the elders' and claims their unbroken continuity with the earliest teachings of Buddhism.

Impermanence

To be in *samsara* is not only like being 'at sea', it is also like being trapped in a burning house, without even realising it. The message of Buddhism is first of all like a fire alarm, to alert you to the fact that 'all is burning'. It is necessary to realise the precariousness of life, as Gautama Buddha did in his encounter with old age, sickness and death. The young and handsome prince realised that instead of turning like a perfectly balanced wheel, smoothly and satisfactorily (*sukha* – a state of happiness), life was *dukkha*, unsatisfactory, especially in its impermanence. This *anicca*, impermanence, can be seen most forcibly in the person who has no fixed core or *atman*, self or soul. Both physically and psychologically one is in a constant process of change, linked with the past and the future in a chain of cause and effect. This state of change is the case equally for states of mind as the cells of the body, and in describing it the Buddhist says *anatman*, there is no eternal, unchanging ego, self or soul. *Dukkha*, *anicca* and *anatman* are the three marks of existence. Unsatisfactoriness and rebirth are kept in motion by the burning fires of human desire, which is like a thirst, a constant wanting, and are expressed especially in greed, hatred and ignorance (delusion or confusion). These are the three root evils at the centre of the wheel of life.

The human predicament is also seen as a sickness for which the Buddha provides a diagnosis in the 'Four Noble Truths' and then a cure in the Noble Eightfold Path. This imagery can be presented visually. The Buddha is the doctor. From his experience and skill emerges the medicine of the *Dharma*, painted in the form of a lotus. From and within the lotus emerges the *Sangha*, which acts as a nurse. It is in 'taking refuge' in these three precious things that a person becomes a Buddhist.

The teachers and the teaching

Teachers are very important in Buddhism. The most famous of all is Gautama

Buddha who lived in north east India in the sixth or fifth century BCE. He taught in the context of the group of religions later called Hinduism. This is why some of the vocabulary and ideas of Buddhism, like *samsara*, the round of rebirth; *dharma*, truth or teaching; *karma*, the deeds that affect one's future birth; *ahimsa*, non-harming and equanimity or non-attachment are the same. The reasons the teaching of the Buddha eventually formed a distinctive religion are complex and controversial. Firstly he seems to have questioned the authority of the Vedas, which are basic to Hinduism, even where they are not fully understood. The Buddha's attitude was:

> Be not led by the authority of religious texts, nor by mere logic or inference . . . nor by the idea that this is our teacher . . . know for yourselves.

Secondly, within the *sangha*, the rules of caste separation did not apply and the Buddha challenged his listeners with questions about whether one was a 'true Brahmin' by birth or by inner moral worth. The third reason probably lies in the radically different understanding of the *atman* in Buddhism. The Buddha taught that everything is in a state of flux and change, and that there is no unchanging entity or self in human or other living beings. It is only by letting go our desire for a separate, eternal soul and the attachments that come from a false idea of 'ego', by becoming 'selfless persons', that there is hope of happiness. The whole of Buddhism is then oriented to the means, the practice for becoming selfless. A common way for Buddhists to refer to the different schools is to ask 'what is your practice?'. The most basic practice is then summarised as:

> Not to do any evil, to cultivate one's mind. This is the teaching of the Buddhas.

The purification of the mind, or the freeing of the heart (*citta* means both mind and heart in Buddhism), is, of course, the goal of the practice of meditation. Meditation, however, especially the most basic practice of mindfulness, is based on ethics and social concern and does not set Buddhists above *sila*, morality. Even the purification of one's own mind and heart is not a selfish act and it is common at the end of a meditation session to hear the giving away of any merit that has accrued for the benefit of others. Giving (*dana*) or generosity is the most fundamental Buddhist virtue and one that will quickly be experienced by anyone trying to get to grips with Buddhism by meeting Buddhists for themselves.

Bibliography

The quotations in the text, unless otherwise acknowledged, are taken from:
W. Rahula, *What the Buddha Taught* (Gordon Fraser, 1959). This is an excellent introduction to basic Buddhist ideas. Other useful books are:
H. Bechert and R. Gombrich (eds), *The World of Buddhism* (Thames & Hudson, 1984)

J. Bowker, *Worlds of Faith* (BBC, 1983)
M. Carrithers, *The Buddha* (OUP, 1983)
E. Conze, *Buddhist Scriptures* (Penguin, 1959)
R. Gombrich, *Theravada Buddhism* (RKP, 1988)
Nyanaponika Thera, *The Heart of Buddhist Meditation* (Rider, 1962)
P. Morgan, *Buddhism* (Batsford, 1987)
P. Morgan, *Being a Buddhist* (Batsford, 1989)
M. Pye, *The Buddha* (Duckworth, 1979)
R. H. Robinson and W. H. Johnson, *The Buddhist Religion*, 3rd edition (Wadsworth, 1982)
H. Saddhatissa, *Buddhist Ethics* (George, Allen & Unwin, 1979)
J. Snelling, *The Buddhist Handbook* (Century Hutchinson, 1987)
A. Watts, *The Way of Zen* (Penguin, 1957)
P. Williams, *Mahayana Buddhism* (RKP, 1989)

The Buddhist Directory and *The Middle Way* are obtainable from The Buddhist Society, 58 Ecclestone Square, London SW1V 1PH

Another useful source of literature (some free) is Buddhist Publishing Group, PO Box 136, Leicester LE2 4TZ

A large mail order catalogue is supplied by Wisdom Publications, 23 Dering Street, London W1

CHAPTER 4

Looking at Christianity

JOHN HALLOWS

The Education Reform Act (1988) states that any new agreed syllabus:

> shall reflect the fact that the religious traditions in Great Britain are in the main Christian, whilst taking account of the teaching and practices of the other principal religions represented in Great Britain.

(Section 8.3)

In many ways this represents a continuity of recent practice. But it is interesting that the Act underlines a view of Christianity which was absent in previous legislation: while Christianity is acknowledged as the dominant faith in Britain, it is seen as 'religious traditions', diverse rather than monolithic.

This underlines the difficulty facing teachers of religious education. Any approach to Christianity in the classroom must reflect the variety of forms and expression within the religion. Standing close to the phenomenon means that we may have absorbed much of Christianity whether or not we profess a Christian faith. But how do you make sense of the diversity between Christian traditions especially if you have been initiated into one of those traditions? Where do you find the ground to stand back and view the whole landscape?

What I intend to do in this chapter is to provide a 'standing back' guide to Christianity. The result will not be an exhaustive résumé of all its traditions but will give an account of its major landmarks in belief and worship.

Jesus of Nazareth

A useful way into Christianity is to take as a starting point its major stories. The key story is that of Jesus of Nazareth. The major sources for this story, the four Gospels, are the result of interpretation and faith responses. The Gospels contain elements which are familiar from other religious traditions; miraculous birth, prodigious happenings, etc. But although the Gospels present challenges in interpretation, recent studies have enabled the religious and political climate of Jesus' times to stand out. Jesus of Nazareth was a Jew living in Roman occupied Judaea in the first century CE. He had beliefs, hopes and fears which belonged to his time and became the inspiration of Christianity. He believed in a God with whom one should enjoy an intimate relationship; he hoped in the commitment of this God to justice which would hasten the overthrow of evil; he felt strongly about the way some types of religious

observance could enslave people; and he feared that in some way his relationship with God, expressed in the familiar term *abba* (father), would shape
his own destiny and lead to his death.

As such the story of Jesus is an accessible account of the career of a prophet
and bears points of comparison with other great religious teachers. But at this
point the story becomes unique; some would say laden with the language of
myth. Some time after his death (the Biblical expression is 'on the third day')
Jesus is encountered alive by his friends. This experience transformed them in
terms of commitment and their understanding of Jesus. Although his death
had all the appearance of failure, his followers soon proclaimed that God
raised Jesus back to life – in short a victory. Resurrection was for early
Christians a powerful symbol of God's readiness to intervene to vindicate the
suffering of the just person. Although 'resurrection from the dead' was
expected to occur at the end of the world, they interpreted their experience as
God acting decisively in the life of Jesus, and expressed their belief by giving
him the title Christ. (This title, meaning 'the anointed one', was used in some
Jewish circles at the time of Jesus to refer to the person who, it was anticipated,
would be God's agent in overthrowing the forces of evil.)

A relationship with God

All Christian teaching revolves around this story. At the centre is the belief in a
God who oversees events in the universe; from its beginnings, as is witnessed
by the two Creation stories in the opening pages of the Bible; through the
history of the human race, represented specifically by the Jews as the people
chosen by God, and latterly by the Christian church. What Christianity
teaches about this God is complex and often in tension with itself. Imagery in
the Bible ranges from the stern judge who is prepared to punish to make a
point, to the intimate lover or parent in the writings of Hosea in the eighth
century BCE, and a forgiving father/parent in the teaching of Jesus. The
imagery is capable of the crudest anthropomorphisms and the loftiest
transcendence. Most Christians have no difficulty with representational
images of God, and their ideas about God can be explored through the rich
tradition of religious art up to the present day.

Humanity's relationship with God is characterised by a call, or election, to a
special status, particularly through membership of the Church. How exclusive
this relationship is varies according to the Christian tradition, from a red-
blooded 'outside the Church there is no salvation' to seeking common cause
with all 'people of good faith'. Election requires a response, keeping to the
Law and participation in worship. The Law refers generally to the rules found
in the Bible, which number more than the Ten Commandments, as well as the
teachings of Jesus. Some Christian traditions also include rules made by the

Church in response to contemporary issues. Keeping the Law is subject to interpretation among Christians. Some insist on as near a literal adherence to the rules as possible; some argue that morality means responding to specific situations according to the requirement of Christian love of God and neighbour.

Salvation in Jesus Christ

The purpose of God's involvement in the universe and election is salvation. Salvation is basically conceived as life with God, and consists in removing anything that estranges the human race from God. (Most Christians consider salvation as applying to human beings, but there are grounds in the Bible for thinking that salvation extends to the whole of creation.) Estrangement is expressed in the term sin, and is illustrated by another series of stories in the first part of the Bible which tells of the increasing sinfulness of the human race. Christianity teaches that God is good and that creation reflects God's goodness, but it also has to give an account of evil and suffering. The answer, in the story of Adam and Eve, is that left to its own devices the human race will disobey God thus causing suffering.

The 'sin' of Adam and Eve, sometimes called Original Sin, highlights the imperfections of the human condition. Christians differ in interpreting this story, some seeing it as a description of an historical event with appalling consequences for humans, some a myth containing insights into human nature. But all traditions agree in stressing human responsibility for sin and the universal need for salvation. Traditionally this is spoken of as being saved from one's own sinfulness. But recently, largely through the influence of Christians living under political oppression in Latin America and Southern Africa, sin is seen as the dehumanising effect of poverty and the lack of civil rights. This means that for some salvation may also take the form of political, economic and social emancipation.

The symbols of salvation and sin are powerful in the consciousness of Christians reinforced by centuries of colourful imagery. The idea of heaven as a place of reward, and hell as a place of fearsome torment, and the notion of a devil as a being only marginally inferior to God, have passed into the folk religion of our times. Again Christians vary in their interpretations of these symbols, some giving them the weight of almost concrete reality, others preferring to use them as illustrations of the struggle towards goodness.

Where there is consensus on salvation in Christianity is the source of salvation. This can only be God. On its own the human race fails. At this point Christianity is trying to address a paradox in human existence, the tension between good and evil. If people are wholly good, then how can they do so much evil? If they are evil, how can any good come about? Within the polarity

39

of good and evil lies the Christian teaching on free will and grace. The discussion owes much to ideas on human nature from Greek philosophy, although nowadays more account is being taken of psychology and psychiatry. But the key elements are clear: people are expected to make a responsible choice for good within a relationship with God which makes a free choice possible. Again one can detect diversity among Christian traditions. At one extreme some Christians believe that salvation depends on making the right choices in following God's commands; some believe that while the obligation to choose the good exists, it is not enough, and that salvation depends on love and forgiveness which are a gift from God.

Christians see Jesus as having played a decisive role in saving the human race. This is a unique claim by Christians. They are saying that Jesus Christ is more than a religious teacher with a programme for salvation. They are saying that in some way the destiny of the whole human race converges in his life, death and resurrection. Modern theologians have come up with a variety of attempts to make sense of this claim but for most Christians it is still understood in the categories of thought used by early Christians. The general expectation at the time of Jesus among many Jews was that God would intervene to end this chapter of history, overthrow the forces of evil and establish a kingdom of justice. This is the view of history known as 'apocalyptic' which features strongly in some Christian traditions today. The events of Jesus's career didn't match the expectation completely, but there was enough correspondence for Christians to interpret the life and death of Jesus in apocalyptic terms. So Jesus, through whom God was believed to be acting, was encountered in some mysterious way as alive after his death. This encounter, described as the resurrection from the dead, was believed to be an event of the end of the world. According to the Adam and Eve story death came into the world as a result of sin. Jesus by scoring a victory over death, had defeated sin.

Sacraments

From their roots in Judaism, early Christians began to interpret the death of Jesus as a sacrifice to take away sin. They developed the ritual traditions of the Jews into their own rituals or sacraments, so called because they expressed the plans of God for the salvation of the human race. Baptism represented the joining of Christians with the death of Jesus. This was expressed through a ritual burial in water. Christians hoped that by participating sacramentally in Jesus' death, they would have a share in Jesus' resurrection. The Eucharist, continuing Jesus' practice of eating with friends and followers, acquired sacrificial overtones through linking the Jewish custom of blessing bread and wine in the Passover meal with the death of Jesus and the establishment of a new relationship, or covenant, with God.

These two sacraments with the Jewish practice of praying, reading from the Bible and singing spiritual songs, form the basis of the whole of Christian worship. Some Christian traditions preserve elaborate rituals which members are expected to engage in and which open spiritual benefits to participants. For example the Roman Catholic tradition extended the concept of sacrament to other rituals to do with key moments in life such as marriage. Those traditions emphasise the sacredness of places, objects and certain members of the Church. Other traditions limit the extent of ritual and emphasise the centrality of the Bible which they celebrate through reading and preaching, and reflecting on its contents. The diversity can be seen in a simple exercise of comparing the interiors and furnishings of different church buildings.

The Trinity

Seeing God as acting decisively through Jesus was a short step from attributing a divine role to Jesus and then divine status. This is expressed by the idea of Jesus as the Incarnation of God. What this means is that to describe Jesus as an outstanding human being is inadequate. He is, in Bishop Robinson's words, 'the human face of God'. How this is explained varies. Traditionally, but oversimplified, it is in terms of God becoming a human individual. One mustn't be surprised if this is a difficult idea. Christians have argued for centuries about how precisely it happened.

What this tension has created is the peculiar understanding that Christians have of God (although some have seen here an insight shared with Hinduism). Christianity, developing out of Judaism, shares its belief in monotheism. 'We believe in one God.' At the same time Christianity teaches that there is differentiation within God. This is expressed in the idea of the Trinity, from a Latin word meaning 'three-ness'. Three-ness does not imply polytheism, that is three gods, but three distinct ways of acting as God; God as the source of divine activity such as creating the world (Father); God as a means or channel of divine activity in so far as we can know it (Son); and God as the energy within the divine which fills the universe and enables a human response to God (Spirit).

The Church, churches and denominations

Although there is considerable unity in the beliefs expressed by Christians, there is at the same time considerable diversity in the ways Christians practice their beliefs. Even a passing acquaintance will reveal a variety of different Christian groups sometimes described as churches, sometimes denominations. This may lead to confusion as 'church' can refer to all Christians taken as a whole, or to a Christian group as in 'the Church of England', or to a specific community and its building.

The diversity within Christianity can be summarised in three main divisions. The Orthodox tradition, mainly encountered in eastern Europe and the Middle East, although there are several Orthodox churches in Britain, puts much stress on the mystery of God, and reflects this in its sumptuous liturgy and its veneration of icons, pictures which communicate the divine to believers.

The Catholic tradition arising in western Europe separated from the Orthodox in the ninth century. Although it is European in terms of its roots, the numerically strongest Catholic regions are in Latin America. The term Catholic is a generic term describing a Christian tradition, although sometimes it refers specifically to the Roman Catholic Church, that is Christians who are united in allegiance to the Pope in Rome. The Catholic approach to worship emphasises the mystery with elaborate rituals. Roman Catholicism fosters the veneration of saints, great Christians of the past who inspire by their example or teaching, and in particular of the Virgin Mary. Much emphasis is placed on the authority of bishops in both the Catholic and Orthodox traditions.

Western Christianity underwent a period of turbulence in the sixteenth century, known as the Reformation, giving rise to what is sometimes called the Reformed or Protestant tradition. Reformed churches on the whole avoid elaborate liturgies and emphasise the place of the Bible in Christian life. Thus preaching and Bible study feature strongly, and while one should not underestimate the authority of preachers, stress is placed on the individual conscience. Often the focus on the Bible's authority has given rise to Biblical Fundamentalism, a view which admits no errors in the Bible. This can sometimes mean interpreting accounts such as Creation stories or the story of Adam and Eve in a literal sense, thus bringing some Christians into conflict with modern science.

The Reformation accounts for most of the diversity within British Christianity where the Catholic tradition of Roman Catholicism is found alongside the Reformed tradition of Presbyterians, Baptists and others. The Church of England contains elements of both Catholic and Reformed traditions.

A developing faith

Christianity as a faith is constantly developing. Three significant trends in the twentieth century illustrate its capacity to address itself to new challenges. First, the ecumenical movement has sought to establish greater communication and sharing between different Christian churches, after centuries of suspicion and even hostility. Among its achievements has been the union of Christian groups into the Church of South India.

Second, the growth of Pentecostalism both in the form of small independent churches, and charismatic movements within existing churches, is giving rise to different types of experience in prayer and worship. This trend emphasises the charisms, or gifts, described in the Bible in the early days of the Church. These are mainly 'speaking in tongues', healing illness, and prophesying.

Finally there is the increasing involvement of Christians in the politics of liberation. The concern in the Bible for social justice and salvation as deliverance from slavery has manifested itself in a number of forms: independent African churches; liberation theology which equates Christian discipleship with challenging injustice in society; the proliferation of development aid agencies associated with Christian churches; and the debate on the rights of women to full participation within the Church, including ordination as priests and bishops.

Further reading

Perhaps the most accessible introductions to Christianity are *The World's Religions* (Lion Publishing, 1982, Part 6) and the *Handbook of Christian Belief* (Lion Publishing, 1982). Another approach might be to consult 'catechisms'. A word of warning: catechisms are handbooks for the initiate and are tied to a particular tradition. However, an example of such catechisms is *The New Catechism* (Search Press, 1967; a product of the *perestroika* in the Roman Catholic Church in the 1960s, and though wordy, it is still fresh and readable). See also Clive Erricker (ed.), *Teaching Christianity: A World Religions Approach* (Lutterworth, 1987), and chapters 5, 11, 12 and 19.

CHAPTER 5

Being a Christian

JOHN RANKIN

Christian variety

Christianity is not a neat package which can be easily described in a way that would satisfy all who claim the title.

But we must begin somewhere, and so a bold decision has to be made to focus on the majority consensus. In terms of simple counting of adherents, the largest single grouping is Roman Catholic. Then comes the Eastern Orthodox Churches if one puts them all together. A third grouping is the Protestant or Reformed Churches. Anglicans and Lutherans have characteristics, especially in liturgy, which distinguish them somewhat from these and indeed some Anglicans are at pains to insist that their Church is Catholic. Since there will be considerable focus on what people *do*, the teacher should take care to attend to the variety of practice in Christianity.

Christianity is what Christians do

Unfortunately, previous Education Acts and their subsequent explanations and intentions tended to suggest that there was a kind of 'neutral' Christianity which was obtainable from reading of the Bible. This led to heavily scripture laden syllabuses. Now the Bible is certainly important, perhaps even essential, in Christianity of any sort, but using it as the exclusive source fails to convey what Christian practice means to a large number. Christianity also means, for example, going to Mass, hearing a sermon, taking part in a procession, serving other people, saying prayers, and so on. The Bible, for many Christians has the words which accompany these activities and the words are almost always heard in some context – a wedding, a funeral, a baptism.

Nevertheless the question of belief often arises and you will find at the end of this chapter a very condensed statement of the general consensus of Christian Belief, which might prove useful for reference.

Christian experience

Every Christian has a personal set of experiences and that makes it very difficult to generalise. I try to describe the experience of *one* Christian while indicating that although I think it will find echoes in the experience of many others, it must not be treated as the sole standard!

Belief

I have been asked sometimes, questions like 'Do you believe all that stuff in the Creed?' or even more specifically, 'Do you believe in the Virgin Birth?' Of course I am intellectually challenged by these questions and may often engage in argument or discussion about them, but it is certainly not what being a Christian is about.

It is about 'making sense' of my life. And about 'making sense' in relation to a particular tradition – which was in some way 'given'. By that I mean that I did not begin 'cold'. The Christian rationale was the assumption of the society in which I grew up. Not that my parents were particularly devout or that Christianity was unchallenged in the wider context. But the internal debate was between Christianity and non-Christianity. My life did not have spread before it the options of 'other' religions. Realistically this is the case for most people. All religions have a culture context. While a noticeable minority feel constrained to break down the culture barriers and adopt 'another' religion, one usually finds that this entails acquiring an understanding of the culture element as well.

'Making sense', for me has only been possible by understanding the tradition in terms of *symbols*. First in order of importance to me is the symbol of 'transcendence'. The Christian message comes from 'out there'. I cannot easily speculate on what that 'out there' is, but I mean simply that I find it impossible to make sense of life if the sense has to be confined to the limits of this life. This sense is given in realising something 'beyond'. In the Christian tradition that transcendence is understood in terms of a personal God who is the maker and sustainer of all things.

But this is not to say that life is illusory or unreal in any way. The symbol of the incarnation of God in Jesus is to say quite emphatically that this life has significance beyond the apparent frustration of the grave. If God himself identifies with human life then it must have eternal significance.

The symbol of the 'Kingdom of God' which Jesus used so frequently extends that feeling of meaning in this life. Not only as a hope beyond this world but as something already present in this life which makes it important. Yet the person who proclaimed this Kingdom was crucified. His resurrection states for me that the horrors and injustices of life are overcome, 'in spite of all'. I do not find it a clear solution to what often faces people in pain and suffering, but it does contain an ultimate assurance while preventing the adoption of facile answers in relation to any concept of the Kingdom.

The symbol of 'sin' recognises the paradox within each of us, where we have a heavenly vision and heavenly potential and yet we seem to be part of its rejection.

Some Christians want to make a much heavier image of evil with the concept of the devil as the power of evil. I do not wish to underestimate the power of evil but the rest of the mythology has no meaning for me. Indeed I am very uneasy about the Church's past record as setting itself up as judge on earth which has all too often led to persecution. I also reject the triumphalist style which is sometimes adopted. I mean the style which claims for Christianity exclusive rights to the truth.

Action

Christians have always claimed that Jesus introduced a radical new way of thinking about ethics. It is not strictly correct to describe Jesus as someone who came to tell us to be good! There have been plenty of such persons in the world! He did not, however, advise the rejection of the *rules* of society. He commended the tradition of Moses.

There seem to be two levels of morality – the one in which one can simply consult the rules and another in which a Christian is called to a creative role, to consider what a genuinely loving response might be in any particular circumstance. In the 1960s this latter response acquired the name of 'situation ethics'.

The important point to understand is that there is no simple code of conduct which you can call 'Christian'. Christian behaviour derives from a personal dialogue with the event in which Jesus lived and died and rose from the dead. Sometimes this is simplified to a 'dialogue with Jesus'. However many people find that expression baffling; even off-putting and sentimental. I have problems with it myself and never express myself in this way. It is misleading because people fail to acknowledge the metaphorical element in expressions in which the name Jesus is used. It is clearly not like the relationship with any other human being, and the personalised style of prayer is in itself a metaphor. This is not to suggest that the relationship is less than personal, but it goes beyond that. For my part it is a matter of a relationship with God in which the Jesus event is incorporated. This is occasionally abbreviated to some sense of dialogue with Jesus; yet it is never self-contained.

Christians have always had big disagreements about ethics – about war, armaments, sexual behaviour, business dealing, politics, family allegiance and so on. Sometimes it is judged ineffective for this reason. Maybe it is because we have been discouraged from thinking of ethics like a blueprint. Accepted standards change over the centuries according to changed circumstances.

Christian action goes beyond the idea of responding to particular circumstances. That would be to assume that your life was fixed and your only problem was to decide how to react. Christians are called upon to *take the initiative*, to undertake tasks, to choose their career and lifestyle. From a Christian perspective it would never be commendable to say only 'I never did any harm'.

This active side of Christianity is one of its most typical features and has been perhaps both its glory and its tragedy. The very vigour of the Church's activity in the past has sometimes led to terrible consequences. Christians have been guilty of the most appalling persecutions and some might say that missionary zeal has sometimes been misplaced. Yet the same zeal has given the most extraordinary fortitude in the face of adversity and great things have been achieved.

Christian churches have been pioneers in the establishment of schools and hospitals and in self-sacrificing works of mercy throughout the last two millennia. Individual Christians would all, I think, feel that their lives ought to reflect something of the goodness of God in their compassion and concern for their fellow human beings. Most would, however, insist that we are in no position to judge the lives of others.

All this shows the problem of a religion which believes that action is important. Some try to focus all their energy in the action of self-denial and of prayer and become contemplative religious. This is a minority, although the whole medieval monastic movement was of decisive importance in the cultural and economic development of Europe. There is some controversy among Christians about the monastic life as the Christian ideal. Certainly, unlike Buddhism, it was not one of the foundation forms of Christianity, but evolved as a response to life in the world. It has always seemed to me an attractive way of being a Christian although it has occasionally developed excesses of austerity which are not justified because they betray a lack of faith in the saving grace of Christ.

Community

To present Christianity as a philosophy for the *individual* is to misrepresent it. From the outset Christianity has been *communal*. And the phrase 'religion is a purely personal matter' can also be misleading. It must be true to say that religion is a matter of personal consent, but if the claim is made to be Christian, then it is impossible to view that as purely personal. There has been a constant reiteration of this theme from the very beginning as, for example in Paul's pronouncement 'You are the Body of Christ and individually members of it' (Corinthians 1 12.27). It is because the idea of the community is so strong that we have seen over the centuries such bitter quarrels about the nature of the Church. If it didn't really matter there could be no reason for dispute. There remain today sharp differences of opinion about the nature of the Church but at least there is no longer actual conflict or persecution of one group by another! The same conviction about Christian community underlies the ecumenical movement of the twentieth century in which there has been a sustained effort to overcome differences – or in the language of Christian symbolism 'to heal the wounds in the body of Christ'. For my part, I no longer find myself caught up in debates about the nature of the Church, but I am acutely conscious of Christianity as a religion based on community and find my identity in communal worship.

Worship

The community needs to have some kind of expression, otherwise it remains simply an idea. Community identity is expressed principally in worship.

Christian worship receives its distinctiveness from the belief in the 'person' of God. God is shown in Christ as someone who 'addresses' us, and all Christian prayer and worship is speaking to or praising God. So Christian worship is a time when the community is in deliberate dialogue with God. Of course the community itself in Christ is already bound up with God, and worship is the attempt to articulate and value something already there.

The most typical act of Christian worship is the Eucharist – sometimes called the Mass or Holy Communion. Nowhere is the aspect of community so clearly expressed. It is a shared meal, which is one of the most universal ways in which human beings express their togetherness. The language emphasises the 'oneness of the worshippers ('though we are many, we are one body, because we all share in one bread'). Even the word Communion derives from the Greek *koinonia*, which means 'fellowship'.

For me this act of worship is the most significant element in my allegiance to Christianity and is the one meaningful feature which has always remained even at times of severest doubt or despair. I do not mean this in a facile way as if it were a panacea for all ills, but it has always remained an anchor even when I was unsure what it meant. Indeed I am still unsure of what it all means!

It holds together in such simple form all that Christianity is. It rehearses and makes present the event of Jesus' coming; his death and resurrection. It celebrates his Church and his continued presence with his people in the Spirit. In concrete symbol it brings forgiveness and grace to the participants. It strengthens their awareness of their membership of the Body and fortifies them for their lives as Christians in the world. I and many others also feel that the celebration has in itself an inherent value in some mystical way, as bringing the saving act of Christ into focus in the world. I would nevertheless reject the kind of magical view which would consider that the consequence is 'the more masses the better'!

Not everyone finds the sacrament so significant and some groups do not use it at all. Yet it is the most widespread specifically Christian act of worship, however diverse its form.

My 'Christian' life has more problems than solutions, but I trust that one day I will see all things clearly.

Christian Belief

This overview has been something of a personal statement. In conclusion here is an attempt to make a list of statements to which the majority of Christians would subscribe.

1 There is one God, Creator and sustainer of the Universe.

2 God is personal in the sense that he can both speak to people and can be addressed by them.

3 Jesus, called the Christ, born as man in Bethlehem approximately 6 BCE was also God in human flesh. He died by crucifixion during the Roman occupation of Palestine about 30 CE. He rose from the dead on the third day. By that death and resurrection those who believe in him are on earth made righteous in God's sight and will after judgement, enjoy a blessed rest in heaven.

4 The power of God by which this salvation is accomplished is known as the Holy Spirit. This power was felt especially by the assembled disciples of Jesus, 50 days after his resurrection. The Holy Spirit now guides and strengthens believers.

5 God as Creator, as Redeemer in Christ and as Power in the Spirit, has shown God's nature as dynamic. That is, there is a divine activity within the one God which involves a continuing saving activity in the world. This belief is expressed in the doctrine of the Trinity. This is not understood as making God more than one, but simply as recognising that the mystery of God's oneness is more complex than can be expressed in one 'person'.

6 The activity by which God redeems mankind is known as 'grace', a word which emphasises the sense of the need of God's loving help.

7 Christ caused a continuing life to be fostered among his disciples which is called the Church.

8 The sacred books known as the Old Testament, being the authoritative scriptures of the Jews, together with the collection known as the New Testament are called the Bible, and thus form the authoritative scripture for Christians. For many Christians this is not understood in a direct or uncritical sense. That is, the words are not seen simply as direct messages from God.

9 The Christian salvation lays particular stress on 'community'. That is, religion in the Christian sense is always in relation to a community.

Note: there is an understandable tendency, when teaching about Jesus to young children, to attend only to Jesus as a 'good man', considering that anything else would be too confusing. Certainly there are difficulties in teaching, but it is important to present Jesus as having greater status than simply a man, otherwise it is not faithful to the central tradition. For example, the notion of Jesus' resurrection is quite essential to the main thrust of Christian doctrine, however interpreted, and it should not be, so to speak, 'kept for later'.

Bibliography

Alan Brown, *The Christian World* (Macdonald, 1984). This is a beautiful pictorial survey of the Christian spectrum in the world.

David Edwards, *Your Faith* (Mowbray, 1978). From within the Church of England tradition, this book is an attempt to clarify faith and practice for those recently confirmed.

Gerald Priestland, *Priestland's Progress* (BBC, 1981). This is an exploration by a well-known broadcaster on what it means to be a Christian in Britain. Thirteen broad topics are examined across Church boundaries.

John Rankin, *The Eucharist* (Lutterworth, 1985). This is a 'Chichester Project' book designed for lower secondary pupils, but is quite a useful outline for teachers.

John Rankin, *Christian Worship* (Lutterworth, 1981). This is another 'Chichester Project' book which explores the range of Christian worship.

CHAPTER 6

An overview of Hinduism

ROBERT JACKSON and ELEANOR NESBITT

The word 'Hinduism' is a western term intended to make sense out of the Indian religious tradition. It is derived from the Persian word which originally meant the Indus river.

Hindus often use the term *sanatana dharma*. *Sanatana* means eternal. *Dharma* defies exact translation into English. It can mean, for example, 'sacred duty' and 'function' (the *dharma* of fire is to burn). *Dharma* represents the range of moral and ritual obligations that apply to a member of a particular caste. Within the extended family *dharma* is transmitted especially by example and by myths and stories. For instance a wife's *dharma* is to be as faithful as Sita was to her husband Rama in the Ramayana epic. The Hindu family ethic is strong and the various roles and responsibilities in the moral sphere are generally taken very seriously. Related to *dharma* are the doctrines of *karma* (every action has an inevitable result) and the belief in a cycle of birth and rebirth which the soul goes through (a concept often referred to – usually in text books by outsiders rather than by Hindus – as *samsara*). People who are true to their *dharma*, will generate good *karma* and will be reborn at a higher point on the scale of ritual purity. *Dharma*, in the sense of the acquisition of religious merit through right living, is also one of the traditional aims of life, the others being *artha* (making a living), *kama* (the satisfaction of desire) and *moksha* (liberation from this world). So although *dharma* is often translated by the English word 'religion' we can see how these two concepts have different areas of meaning.

When we look at ideas and practices that have grown up in India over thousands of years the English words which we use to describe them are often misleading in their connotations. For example a range of Indian words such as *bhagvan*, *ishvara* and *deva*, are usually translated into English as 'God' or 'god'. By granting or withholding a capital G the writer has already passed a culturally inappropriate value judgement. This is because 'god' commonly refers to the divinities of pre-Christian Europe and suggests something discredited and obsolete where 'God' is understood primarily in terms of Jewish and Christian monotheistic belief.

The nature of western religious history also inclines westerners to frame particular questions and expect answers that fit. When did Hinduism begin? Who founded it? Do Hindus have a creed? What is their concept of God? To such questions there are no clear cut answers. India's geographical, cultural and linguistic variety, and its complex social hierarchy, both influence and parallel the diversity of beliefs and practices. Any attempt to encompass India's religious firework display – whether made from inside or outside the subcontinent – will inevitably result in distortion. To use an old Hindu (and Buddhist) parable in a different way, those who attempt to describe Hinduism fully are in the same position as blind men trying to perceive an elephant. One blind man, grasping the trunk, believes the elephant to be a snake. Another, who encounters the elephant's leg, believes the animal to be a tree!

Since, in Hinduism's case, we are all in the position of blind or, at best, partially sighted people, let us risk comparing Hinduism with a very old tree. Some roots of the tree are over 5000 years old: they represent the contribution of the Indus valley civilization to Indian religion – perhaps the origins of the goddess cult, perhaps a male divinity resembling Shiva, perhaps the use of water in religious rituals. Another old cluster of roots represents Vedic religion, which was probably brought to India in the second millenium BCE as a result of conquest and settlement by the Aryans, a semi-nomadic people whose name is etymologically linked with the word Iran. One of these roots gives us Hinduism's oldest text, the Rig Veda, with its details of sacrificial offerings to the gods or *deva*s. Another reveals the search for a single cosmic force underlying the *deva*s, sometimes pictured in anthropomorphic terms as Purusha or Prajapati and sometimes as the impersonal Absolute, *Brahman*. Yet another is the body of texts known as the Upanishads which examine the relationship between the individual self (*atman*) and the One (*Brahman*) – an exploration which spawned some of India's great philosophical systems. They also introduce the idea of *moksha* meaning the eventual liberation of the individual from death and rebirth in another body.

Many Hindus do not consider themselves particularly religious but their attitudes are imbued with such concepts. Many, for instance, accept that when their children are grown up it is appropriate to shift from material to spiritual concerns. This view is influenced by the classic Hindu model of life as a sequence of four stages (*ashramas*). According to this the individual progresses from *brahmachari ashrama*, the period of being a celibate student, to *grihastha ashrama*, the period of married life with family responsibilities. *Vanaprastha ashrama* (which means literally living as a forest hermit) follows. Lastly a person enters *sannyasi ashrama*, when all family ties have been severed. Few follow all these stages in practice, but they are influential as an ideal.

From birth a Hindu is part of a family, not in the narrow sense of two parents and their children but in the wider sense of grandparents, uncles, aunts, cousins and other relatives. Cousins are called 'brother' and 'sister' and kinship bonds are strong. Each family is part of a *jati* (usually translated by 'caste', a less specific word of Portuguese origin).

The *jati* is a distinct hereditary group. Marriages are expected to take place within it though not between those who are already related. Nowadays a person's caste and occupation are not necessarily connected. For example a *darzi* (member of tailor caste) may not actually work as a tailor. But although the caste system is changing it is certainly not disappearing, as a glance at the matrimonial advertisements in Indian newspapers reveals. Indeed if Hinduism is like a tree, then the caste system is part of its trunk. Marriages will normally be arranged between members of the same caste and love marriages between members of the same caste seldom face the opposition which intercaste marriages often arouse. Urban life means that people of different castes come into contact in ways unthinkable to their forebears. Nonetheless some concept of a hierarchy of castes persists. If asked to put local castes in rank order people from various castes may produce slightly different lists but all would rank castes hierarchically with Brahmins at the top. At the bottom would be those whose traditional tasks – skinning animals for example – were ritually polluting.

In relating their own caste to other castes Hindus also refer to the four *varna*s or classes mentioned in an ancient Sanskrit text, the Rig Veda. These were the priests (Brahmins) warrior (Kshatriyas), merchants (Vaishyas) and menials (Shudras). Members of a particular caste (*jati*) may regard themselves as belonging to a high *varna* whereas members of other castes allocate them to a lower *varna*. Although the idea of a hierarchy of *varna*s is widespread the local preponderance of, say, Brahmins or Vaishyas and the degree to which they are respected by members of other *varna*s vary considerably. Many castes are specific to particular regions. Hindus sometimes use the English term 'caste' loosely to refer to *varna* or to regional and religious communities different from their own.

The trunk of our tree of Hinduism also incorporates the principal religious practices. These include devotional rituals which are particularly elaborate for devout Brahmins, the *samskara*s or life cycle rites (marking the main transitions of a Hindu's life such as initiation, marriage and death) and worship. Worship (*puja*) may take place in the home or in the temple, and in the *bhakti* (devotional) tradition may be performed through the group-singing of devotional hymns. Another meritorious religious act is pilgrimage to local, regional or national sites such as Varanasi (Benares). The most colourful feature of Hindu practice is the annual cycle of festivals which again may be local, regional or all-Indian (for example *Diwali* and *Navaratri*). The festivals are a yearly reminder of religious values and they bring gaiety and life to Hinduism. Special delicacies are enjoyed.

Food is not incidental to Hinduism. The nature of one's diet is inseparable from being a Hindu and many Hindus live up to their ideal of strict vegetarianism, eating dairy produce but no eggs, fish or meat. Devout Hindus observe many fasts, days when they further restrict their diet and perform an associated ritual often in furtherance of a wish. Hindus who eat meat will avoid beef because the cow is respected as a mother, the giver of milk, *ghi* and pure life-giving products.

If Hindus are highly restricted in the realm of conduct, they are relatively free in the domain of belief. Nevertheless there are certain tendencies which are strong enough to make belief part of the tree trunk of the religion. One is the notion of *Brahman*, the impersonal Absolute or World Soul that pervades the universe. The fact that *Brahman* is considered to be immanent as well as transcendent gives rise to a pantheistic tendency in Hinduism – a belief that the divine principle is present in everything. At the same time there is a tendency to personalise the divine, perhaps as *bhagvan* or *ishvara* (the Lord) and in this sense Hindu religion has a strongly monotheistic current. Hinduism is certainly not crudely polytheistic for the *deva*s, the gods, are generally regarded as different facets of the same jewel or (as a priest in Coventry put it) like different photographs of a beloved relation. A Hindu may make offerings to several *deva*s and still affirm *bhagvan ek hai* – 'God is one'. By focusing on one's favourite representation of the divine, one's worship of the one universal God is deepened. The *ishtadevata* is the chosen deity who is worshipped by a person as the supreme God, while that same individual denies neither the reality of other gods nor that other people will have different chosen deities.

The main branches of our tree represent the three main theistic strands of Hinduism, involving devotion to Vishnu (Vaishnavism), to Shiva (Shaivism) or to the Goddess (Shaktism). Vishnu is regarded as a benevolent deva, who in times of moral decline appears in the world in various forms (*avatar*s, literally 'descents') to restore justice. Generally there are thought to be ten such *avatar*s (animal, semi-human or human), the most important being Krishna and Rama. Krishna is worshipped as a divine child, a mischievous flute-playing young man and as a great hero. In the popular text known as the Bhagavad Gita, Krishna appears as a divine charioteer who speaks of *moksha* (salvation) through enlightenment, action and especially through *bhakti*, loving devotion to the Lord. Rama is a god-prince who, by destroying Ravana, a demon who had abducted his wife Sita, restored righteousness to the world.

Shiva's character is complex. He may be loving and full of grace, but he is also the destroyer. He is both a great ascetic and a god of procreation. He is generally depicted as grey in colour (smeared with ashes, like an ascetic), carrying a trident (*trisul*), wearing a necklace of cobras and with the *Ganga* (Ganges) river escaping from his coiled hair. The *linga*, probably originating as an ancient male fertility symbol, also represents Shiva.

The cult of the Mother Goddess may have originated in devotion to Shiva's wife – Durga in her fierce form, Parvati in her benevolent aspect. Her devotees came to be called *Shakta*, since they believed the goddess to be the *Shakti* – the energy, immanent and active in the world – of the remote and transcendent Shiva. In Britain anyone who has witnessed Gujaratis dancing on the evenings of *Navaratri* will have seen the goddess portrayed in a variety of forms – Ambe Ma, Kali Mata and so on. Hindus often refer to the female divine principle simply as *Mata* (mother) or *Devi* (goddess).

There are many sects devoted to an *avatar* of Vishnu (generally Krishna), to Shiva or to the Goddess, typically having a founder whose teachings are followed closely by adherents. Many of these sects have had a profound importance in providing a bridge between some of the basic forms of Hinduism and its more sophisticated aspects as well as being a source for many Hindus of religious and moral renewal. Again the English language can mislead us. 'Sect' suggests mutually exclusive groups whereas generally speaking, devotion to one of the principal *deva*s does not preclude worship of the others. A temple dedicated to Krishna, for example, may have shrines to Shiva and Durga.

Our tree of Hinduism is a tree in full leaf. Personal and local details of worship and the names for deities are innumerable. In its infinite diversity Hindu tradition is thriving, not only in India, but in many countries of the world.

Sometimes distinctions are drawn between village Hinduism and the Hindusim of the cities but this is to oversimplify. *Devata*s (the first 'a' is not pronounced) are 'godlings' who are not only worshipped in rural India but also in East Africa and in western cities.

From increased global communication Hinduism draws new strength. Preachers, revered saints and acclaimed hymn singers draw huge audiences among the Hindu diaspora in Britain. Video films record the details of religious events and give the myths a new credibility with the growing generation.

Of course our image of a tree lacks historical perspective and over-simplifies the relationship between the constituent elements of Hinduism. We have also omitted important elements. Observers may argue over its form, but agree that it is an organism which is very much alive.

Hinduism is not just a tree from which we pluck our selected fruits. As teachers, often with Hindu pupils in our class, and some of us Hindu, we ourselves are affecting the tradition by the way that we include and exclude it. Hindu children are learning about the story of Rama or belief in reincarnation not only from elders and videos but at school, from books and RE teachers.

Bibliography

A guide for teachers to the Hindu tradition is Robert Jackson and Dermot Killingley, *Approaches to Hinduism* (John Murray, 1988). Themes covered include the family, society, life cycle rituals, worship, mythology and the gods, festivals, pilgrimage, sacred literature, sects and movements, and Hindus in Britain. As well as material on the tradition, there is a chapter on teaching methods, an account of a junior school visit to a temple, numerous teaching ideas for juniors and wide ranging reviews of available schoolbooks and AV resources.

Material for teachers on Hindu ethics is available in Robert Jackson and Dermot Killingley, *Moral Issues in the Hindu Tradition* (Trentham Books, 1990). This includes material on family, marriage and environmental issues.

Patricia Bahree, *India, Pakistan and Bangladesh: A Handbook for Teachers* (1982), available from External Services, School of Oriental and African Studies, Malet Street, London WC1E 7HP, includes valuable background material and literature reviews on history, geography and art as well as religion. See Chapter 27 for an account of the religious lives of some Hindu children in Britain of junior school age.

Robert Jackson and Eleanor Nesbitt, *Listening to Hindus* (Unwin Hyman, 1990) is a schoolbook containing some original material about Hindu children in Britain.

CHAPTER 7

Islam in outline

M. ABDEL HALEEM

The noun Islam (from whose root also came the word *salam*, meaning peace and *salama*, meaning safety) denotes submission to God 'Allah rabbil-alameen', the Lord of all men and all creation. Practising Muslims repeat at least 17 times a day 'Praise be to Allah, Lord of all men and all creation', placing themselves in sympathetic relationship with all beings under the Lordship and care of Allah. The essence of submission to Allah is to be righteous and this is the criterion by which Allah judges all people. Allah speaks to mankind in the Qur'an saying:

> Oh mankind, we have created you male and female and made you nations and tribes, that you may get to know one another. The noblest among you in the sight of Allah is the most righteous. Allah is all-knowing, 'all-Aware'.

The Five Pillars of Islam

The first of the 'five pillars' of Islam is to bear witness to the fact that, 'there is no God but Allah, and Muhammad is His messenger', the belief in Allah as Lord of all mankind and creation, the merciful, the just, the all-knowing, to cite but a few of his 99 'most beautiful names'. Then follows the belief in His messengers or prophets, prominent among whom are Abraham, Moses and Jesus, with Muhammad the seal of the prophets. All these prophets have no divine essence but are concerned with receiving, communicating and explaining the message. All Muslims are thus required to acknowledge the messages of earlier prophets since, according to the Qur'an, they have all preached the same basic message, which is submission to God, have all spoken of His angels and taught His laws, and all warned of God's judgement.

Salah (prayer), the second pillar of Islam, consists of five daily prayers to link the believer with Allah, to maintain and increase his awareness of his Lord. The Muslim through the vehicle of prayer sees himself always in relation to God, and this world always in relation to the next to come. On this point the Prophet said:

> work for this world as if you are going to live here forever, and work for the hereafter as if you are going to die in the morning.

Prayers are a duty to be performed at appointed hours (4:103). This ritual link with God should be maintained from childhood to the moment of death. Alongside the principle of obligation to pray, however, is placed that of dispensation for those who for genuine reasons cannot fulfil this particular obligation: namely where Muslims are so incapacitated as to make prayer impossible. Where they are deemed capable of performing prayer then degrees of dispensation apply; for example, they may not have to conform to the ritual of ablution, considered a fundamental prerequisite to Salah, or may be given dispensation to shorten and combine prayers, to pray sitting or lying down. The *Adhan* (call to prayer) summons the faithful at the beginning of the period for each prayer in the words: 'come to prayer, come to prosperity, Allah is greater'. Prayer at the Mosque must be peformed facing the *Qibla*, which is shown by a niche in the wall indicating the direction of the Ka'aba, the House of God in Makka, which represents the beginning of Islam. Built by Abraham (whose submission to the will of God went to the point of being ready to sacrifice his son) the Ka'aba represents the model of obedience to God.

In Islam prayer can be performed at any place, either alone, or in a congregation. Islam, however, favours communal prayer, for 'praying in congregation is 27 times better than praying alone'. Any Muslim can lead others in prayer, excepting women who, for reasons of modesty and moral propriety, may not kneel and prostrate themselves amongst or in front of their menfolk, but may do so anywhere else. Women may lead women in prayer. Muslims all over the world share the same ritual, and by choosing to pray in Arabic, provide a common language of prayer through which they can share the same religious experience.

The third pillar of Islam is *zakah* (wealth tax) where a fixed portion of one's wealth, ranging from 2.5–10 per cent is paid annually, to be spent on the poor, the needy, or those burdened with debts arising from bona fide reasons. This obligation is distinct from the practice of *sadaqah* (charity), a deed which is highly commended, and for which Allah promises great rewards in this world and in the next. The Qur'an indeed reminds the Muslim community that the poor have a right to a share in the wealth of others throughout this community tax. The term *zakah* itself denotes purity/growth: i.e. the practice of *zakah* purifies the soul and frees the donor from the sin of selfishness. Thereby, at the same time, it maintains the prevalence of social justice in the community. Once the Muslim has paid his quota, Allah promises to bless the remainder of his income by increasing it accordingly. No capable Muslim can be exempted on a point of conscience from paying this right demanded by God on behalf of the poor and needy, and although he may technically evade paying it, surely he will not evade the All-knowing, the Master of the Day of Judgement. Thus the individual's financial responsibility to the community constitutes an essential 'pillar' of the Islamic faith.

The fourth pillar, *sawm* (fasting) is prescribed during the month of

Ramadan, calling for a complete abstention from food, drink, and sex from dawn to sunset. It is a discipline that requires an exercise of will power, involving all members of the Muslim community, except the sick, or those engaged in travel who may qualify for certain exemptions. For example the latter two categories may fast a similar number of days at a later date. More extreme cases may be completely exempted from the ritual but must redeem themselves by offering food to a poor person for each day the fast is broken. If one cannot endure hunger for a day one should feed a hungry person for a day. Fasting can be a difficult exercise for Muslims in non-Muslim lands because the local pattern of work and rest continues normally without regard to the Islamic practice of fasting. It remains all the more an important practice. Fasting has a sobering and uplifting effect on the believers since doing without food and water for long periods helps them reflect on the nature of their existence; it is also a reminder of those who in ordinary times fail to receive enough daily rations to sustain themselves. In addition a Muslim on a fast often undergoes unusual spiritual experiences and develops a greater clarity of the mind; this is but one of the many rewards resulting from the practice of this fourth pillar of Islam.

The fifth pillar of Islam, *hajj* (pilgrimage to the 'house of God') requires a Muslim to make the pilgrimage to Makka at least once in his or her lifetime. *Hajj* affords the Muslim the opportunity to go physically to the place that he faces five times a day during his life. There he enacts rituals performed by Abraham, his wife and son in a place:

> first established for men . . . a blessed place, a beacon for the nations. In it there are veritable signs and the spot where Abraham stood, whoever enters it, is safe.
> *(3:96–97)*

Hajj also affords Muslims from all over the world, both rich and poor, the opportunity to meet together sharing a common religious experience in which social status becomes unimportant, since all pilgrims wear humble clothes and eschew the wearing of perfumes, shaving, etc. for a few days of worship. The ceremony begins and ends with Muslims walking round the Ka'aba, the House of Allah, which they face daily in their prayers, often repeating:

> here I am, O Lord, Praise, blessing and sovereignty belong to you and I am at your service!

Ethics

The Qur'an consistently enjoins Muslims to adhere to and obey God's law: it states why something is enjoined or recommended, prohibited or discouraged. All conduct is judged. Nothing is arbitrary. At the same time there is conscience within each person by which he or she can judge him or herself before others can judge. The Prophet says:

> Consult your heart . . . righteousness is that about which the heart feels tranquil and wrongdoing is that which wavers in the soul even though people again and again have given their legal opinion.

The Qu'ran speaks of itself as confirming and complementing the scriptures that preceded it. We thus find that moral teachings present in the Ten Commandments of Moses (apart from the Sabbath) and in the Sermon on the Mount are also there in the Qur'an, not in one section, but in different parts of the text.

Whereas the Bible says, 'an eye for an eye and a tooth for a tooth' and, 'Whosoever shall smite thee on the right cheek, turn to him the other also', the Qur'anic injunction states:

> If you punish, let your punishment be proportionate to the wrong that has been done to you. But it shall be best for you to endure your wrongs with patience.
>
> *(16:126)*

and further urges believers to 'Requite evil with good, and lo! your enemy will become like a close friend' (41.34).

The Qur'an has far more to say about morality than about ritual or law. Islam requires its followers to pledge their absolute loyalty to truth and justice above personal interest or family loyalty (14:135). Nor should enmity (5:8, 2) difference of religion (60:8) or having superior power (16:92) lead them away from achieving this objective. Neither should Muslims apply different standards in their moral conduct towards non-Muslims or consider something unlawful to be lawful when dealing with them (3:75–76). Each Muslim enjoins the other to keep to this path:

> I swear by time that perdition shall be the lot of man, except for those who have faith, and do good works and counsel one another to the truth and to being steadfast'.
>
> *(103)*

An important obligation incumbent on the individual and society in Islam is the duty to enjoin what is good and forbid what is evil, a Qur'anic injunction considered fundamental in its application to the well-being of the Muslim community (3:110). To this end the Prophet tells all Muslims:

> Whosoever of you sees an evil action, let him change it with his hand; and if he is not able to do so then by his tongue; and if he is not able to do so, then with his heart – and that is the weakest point of faith.

Law

The primary source of Islamic law is of course the Qur'an. The *sunna* or *Hadith* (sayings, actions and tacit approvals of the Prophet) derive authority from such Qu'ranic commands as 'obey Allah and obey the Prophet' (5:92). The relationship between the Qur'an and the *sunna* is well-defined: thus the *sunna* either emphasises what is in the Qur'an and explains it, or introduces teachings which are not overtly mentioned there. However, the *sunna* cannot contradict the Qur'an. If there is no ruling in the Qur'an or in the *sunna* then the third source of Islamic law is invoked, namely the exercise of independent judgement, by analogy or other methods which must not contradict the principles or objectives of the religion. The interest of the community constitutes another principle of Islamic law.

Naturally the Qur'an and *Hadith* are limited texts, and since Islam maintains that it is a religion for all times and places it is the **principles** in the Qur'an and *Hadith* and the subsequent sources that ensure the vitality and lasting relevance of Islamic law. Here, Islamic legal scholarship becomes important, and there has been a revival in this field, following a long period of neglect, in order to meet the challenge of modern times. In this way Islam, with all its components outlined above, remains a comprehensive way of life.

The specifically penal element of the code is also based on the Qu'ran and has as its principal objective the protection of what the religion considers inviolable: life, mind, property, and honour. The Qur'an and *sunna* stipulate several specified penalties but leave to Muslim legislators the task of defining and laying down such penalties which do fall not in the category defined by the Qu'ran. These limited penalties are well-defined, and stringent procedural safeguards are built into them. This deters crime which is seen as a flagrant violation of the accepted order. The ultimate penalty for adultery, for example, can be applied only if a married person commits the said act in a manner to be seen by four trustworthy witnesses: what is involved here is not simply the exercise of individual liberty but a flagrant affront to public decency and order. Concern for society is central to Islamic rituals, ethics and law. The Qur'an also states that if a thief repents and rights his wrong the ultimate penalty may be lawfully suspended, as it also is in times of famine, or when it was recognised that the thief was clearly under a compulsion determined by circumstances beyond his control. When the Qur'an deals with such matters as chastity and the conduct of women, particularly with regard to the way they should dress, it addresses its injunctions to men first and then to women, as follows:

> Enjoin the believing men to turn their eyes away from temptation, and to restrain their carnal desires, that will make their life purer. Allah has knowledge of all their actions. Enjoin the believing women to turn their eyes away from temptation and to restrain their carnal desires, to cover their adornment, save such as is outward.
> *(24:30–31)*

61

Clearly similar teachings are also enjoined on Jewish and Christian men and women by the Old and the New Testaments. The difference is that society in the west, for instance has generally overtly chosen to conduct its life on these matters in a way which apparently leaves aside religious teachings.

The concept of *Jihad* constitutes another aspect of Islamic Law that assumes a particular relevance when the relationship of Muslim society to that of a non-Muslim one takes on a nature of conflict. *Jihad* is a concept much talked about, but its meaning, scope and purpose in Islam has been widely mis-understood. The word in Arabic and in the Qur'an means exerting effort or struggling in general. Thus the Prophet is ordered in the Qur'an not to obey the unbelievers, but to struggle against them with the Qur'an: 'argue with them by it' (25:52). The Qur'an also says, 'there is no compulsion in religion' (2:256).

The Prophet Muhammad lived to become leader of a Muslim state, whose relationship with its neighbours was regulated, whether in peace or war, by the Qur'anic teachings. Thus, in the case of aggression against the Muslim state, war is justified in this way:

> Permission to take up arms is hereby given to those who are attacked, because they have been wronged. Allah has power to grant them victory: those who have been unjustly driven from their homes, only because they say: 'Our Lord is Allah'. Had Allah not repelled some men by the might of others, monasteries and churches, synagogues and mosques in which His name is often mentioned would have been utterly destroyed.
>
> *(22:40).*

The Qur'an here talks about defending religion in general – not just Islam – against aggression. Thus defence against aggression is the justification of war in Islam and 'must stop when aggression is ended' (8:61). In this context Muslims are bound to respect any treaty they make with an enemy, however unbalanced against their interests it may be, and however superior in force they may be to the enemy (16:91–92).

Muslims will always read in the Qur'an about themselves and others:

> We have ordained a law and a path for each of you. Had Allah wished it He could have made you into one nation, but in order to test your faith in what He has given you, He has made you as you are. So vie with one another in good works for to Allah you shall all return and He will declare to you what you have disagreed about.
>
> *(5:48)*

The Day of Judgement

Belief in the Day of Judgement is paramount in the Qur'an and Islamic worship. A practising Muslim cites the name of Allah at least 17 times a day, referring to Him as Master of the Day of Judgement, an exercise which leads to the strengthening of one's responsibility and increasing one's sense of accountability. These two aspects of the Muslim's conduct are reflected most vividly in the Qur'an where they are brought alive in graphic descriptions of the Day of Judgement. This affects both the good and sinners alike who will receive rewards or punishments. The consequences of conduct whether good or bad are set before the individual to contemplate, with the good being granted access to Paradise. There they will dwell with their spouses, children and grandchildren (36:55) (52:21) in good dwellings in the gardens of Eden, and what is greater, in God's pleasure (9:72). They will say:

> Praise be to Allah who had made good to us His promises and given us this land to inherit, that we may dwell in Paradise wherever we please. Blessed is the reward of the righteous. You shall see the angels circling round the Throne glorifying their Lord. . . . all shall say, 'Praise be to Allah, Lord of the Creation!'
>
> *(39:75)*

Bibliography

A. Yusuf Ali (trans.), *The Glorious Qur'an* (Allen & Unwin, 1976) with commentary
E. Ibraham and D. Johnson-Davies, *Forty Hadith Qudsi* (Qur'an Publishing House, 1980)
Hammuda Abdal Ati, *Islam in Focus* (American Trust Publication, 1975)
Fazlur Rahman *Islam*, Second Edition, (University of Chicago Press, 1977)
Fazlur Rahman, *Major Themes of the Qur'an* (University of Chicago Press, 1986)
J. Robson (trans.), *Mishkat al Masabih* (M. Ashraf, 1981) a collection of Hadith
S. Hossein Nasr, *Ideals and Realities of Islam* (Allen & Unwin, 1971)
R. Tames, *Approaches to Islam* (John Murray, 1982)

CHAPTER 8

A taste of Judaism

CLIVE LAWTON

It is perhaps useful to realise that Judaism, too, has its trinity. In this instance, it does not involve God, but instead the concepts of People, Land and Torah. Any approach to Judaism and any attempt to understand it properly requires that one deals with these areas.

People

The first concept is Peoplehood. The Jews perceive themselves as a People, a tribe, a clan, a large extended family. It is this sense of common identity which enables a Jew to remain a Jew irrespective of what he or she believes or with whom he or she identifies. A Jew is born a Jew, of a Jewish mother (with the small exception of those converts who join the Jewish community and are, thereby, as it were, 'adopted'). This People traces its origin back to its 'fathers and mothers', namely Abraham, Isaac and Jacob, Sarah, Rebecca, Leah and Rachel. Their stories are to be found in the Book of Genesis in the Bible.

It is worth remembering that Jacob's other name is Israel; therefore, the phrase 'children of Israel' is a distinctively family term. This people is distinctive, a 'chosen' People (not *the* 'chosen' people, as most translations would have you believe), and different Jews will interpret this identity differently.

Certainly, most Jews will believe that throughout history there has been a distinctive quality to Jewish experience. Some will see their role as the responsibility to witness to God in the world; others will see it as the responsibility to hasten the coming of the Messianic Age by their own correct behaviour. (Jews, of course, are still waiting for the coming of the Messiah. Jesus of Nazareth, for example, has no religious significance for Jews and it is important in any teaching about Jews that Jesus is not introduced as an important figure. One would not expect Muhammad to figure at all in a course on Christianity.) Still others will see the role of the Jew as simply a challenge to civilisation to deal with a community that insists on being different from the mainstream.

This People does not have a racial identity since there are clearly Jews of Arab, African, Scandinavian, Central European, Asian, and other appearances.

This sense of distinctiveness and yet responsibility to the world at large is illustrated by consideration of Passover (*Pesakh*) and *Shabbat* (the Jewish day of rest and recreation). On *Pesakh*, which is primarily a celebration and re-enactment of the Exodus from Egypt (the story of which is to be found in the Book of Exodus in the Bible), it is customary in many families to draw particular attention to those Jews who are not yet free (for example, many lay an empty place at the table for a Soviet or Syrian Jew). At the same time, on *Pesakh*, Jews pray for the Messianic Age, which is hoped to be a time when all tyranny will cease and all humanity will be free.

Similarly, on *Shabbat*, there is the tradition that, if all Jews kept two *Shabbatot* consecutively correctly, the Messianic Age would ensue. Therefore, there is a sense of collective identity on the one hand and a sense of responsibility to the world at large on the other.

Land

The second facet of this three-way pursuit of Judaism is the Land. Any programme on Judaism that does not consider the place of Israel in Jewish thought and aspiration would be missing an essential feature. Jews do not see the Land of Israel as merely, or even mainly, a place of pilgrimage. While Jerusalem stands pre-eminent in the Jews' perception of the Land, relationship to Israel is not mainly because of the events which happened there (most of the formative events took place outside Israel anyway) nor even because of any place that can be seen there. The main reason for the Jewish commitment to Israel is because of the Jewish understanding of the promise made to their family that this will be their ancestral home.

This is not necessarily a political statement but it is a statement of belief about the Jews 'hereditary' right to live in the Land. This explains why feeling was so high when Jordan enacted its law forbidding Jews to live within its borders while it was still in control of the west bank of the Jordan river. Jews will differ over the boundaries of the Land and will argue about what sacrifices of land should be made to establish peaceful relationships with neighbours. Nevertheless, just like a family might view the land on which it has lived for many generations to be its inalienable right, irrespective of who rules it, so too do most Jews see it like this.

The existence of Zionism gives an added dimension to this. Zionism (by believing in the right of the Jews to govern their own state) attempts to translate this into political reality so that Jews cannot only live there, but live there independent of the whims and dangers of rulers who do not necessarily have the best interests of Jews at heart. Bearing in mind the historical experiences of Jews over the last couple of thousand years, this nervousness is at least understandable, if not plain common sense!

While Israel is not a state ruled by religion (any more than Britain is anyway), it is certainly influenced by, and reflects, Jewish religious pre-occupations. The Law of Return (which allows any Jew the right of instant citizenship – the first law to be passed by the new government after independence in 1948) is an immediate manifestation of these first two principles, the People and the Land and their interrelationship.

This relationship to the Land is evident when one considers how many of the festivals are necessarily linked to the agricultural cycle. One of the reasons why the Jewish lunar calendar cannot cut loose of the seasons as, for example, the Muslim calendar does, is because the Spring festivals need necessarily to fall in the springtime, because they reflect harvest patterns. Wherever Jews may live, and throughout the centuries, they have always prayed for rain and dew, and celebrated harvest or the time of planting trees in line with the agriculture of Israel and not necessarily in any relationship with the agricultural cycle of the country in which they live.

Many Jews remark amusedly at the need to pray for rain while living here in Britain, and for Australian Jews the celebration of the autumn harvest of fruits, just at their springtime, would be disorientating if they were not so sure that their eyes were firmly fixed on the land of Israel. Now we can see that the word Israel for a Jew simultaneously implies a Person, a People, and a Land.

Torah

The third leg of this tripod is the Torah. While this is loosely translated as Law, it is of course much more. The simplest definition of the Torah is the first five books of the Bible, the Pentateuch, in which is contained not only an extensive number of commandments and rules (613 in all), but also an explanation of the origin of things and the early history of the Jewish people, establishing their fundamental relationship with each other, God and the world.

When Jews use the word Torah, they often include more than simply this text. Running side by side in Jewish tradition is an Oral Torah, a traditional interpretation which has grown over the years due to the need to respond to changes in life, technology and circumstances.

The first great text in which is written down the initial stages of this Oral Torah is the Talmud, an eighteen-volume encyclopaedia of rabbinic discussion. While the two versions of that were completed in the fifth and eighth centuries respectively, more and more commentaries on the Talmud, and responses to individual issues, have been written and compiled through the centuries, and continue to emerge today. Therefore, a Jew's understanding of Torah will not be based on the written text alone, to which most non-Jews will have access, but will be based on this vast body of traditional interpretation as well.

The way in which a Jew interprets, for example, the requirements in the written Torah to 'write these words on the doorposts of thy house' (Deuteronomy 6), is to produce a *mezuza*, the small box with pre-determined texts from the Torah written on a parchment scroll inside it, fixed to the right-hand doorpost of the house and the rooms inside. It is the Oral Torah that requires that this particular commandment should be fulfilled in this way. Obviously, knowledge of only the written Torah would not give one even the faintest inkling of how a Jew might comply with this rule.

It is, therefore, always necessary to try and find out how a Jew will understand the requirements of the written Torah and it is not sufficient to know, for example, that it says 'love your neighbour as yourself' or 'six days you shall work and on the seventh you shall rest'. Those who think they may know Judaism, because of a knowledge of the Jewish bible, are no more acquainted with it than someone who could claim to know present-day Christianity by an acquaintance with the Gospels – with this difference: no Jew argues that the text must only be taken at face value and it is never acceptable to say about the Torah text, 'If that's what it says, then that's what it means'. Rather, the tendency will be to say, 'If that's what it says, then what does it mean?'

The rules in the Torah, and their interpretation, can be broadly divided into those which relate to ritualistic activities in one's worship of God, and those which relate to human interrelationships. In the first category fall the more famous aspects of Jewish practice, since they are those which most distinguish Jews from other religions; the numerous festivals during the year, the weekly *Shabbat*, Jewish dietary laws and, until the Temple in Jerusalem was destroyed nearly two thousand years ago, the sacrificial cult. (All sacrifices were discontinued with the destruction of the Temple in 70 CE.)

In the second category, are a range of inspiring ethical teachings about the organisation of a society including not stealing and not murdering, respect for the family, for the life and property of others, and caring for the socially less fortunate.

Lying between these two groups of rules are those of agricultural significance, establishing a relationship, as it were, with the earth.

Relationship with God

The reason for a Jew observing these requirements correctly is to maintain his or her relationship with God. Most of the rabbis are agreed that, in order to have a successful relationship with God, one must also maintain a successful relationship with one's fellow human beings.

The 'normal' relationship with God for a human being is neutral, or possibly one of favour, particularly if one comes from a family with a history or pedigree of religious and spiritual grandeur. The idea of 'original sin', or that humanity has a damaged relationship with God, is alien to the mainstream of Jewish thought, but this relationship *can* be damaged by failing to observe the rules (*mitzvot*) in any way. Put more positively, observance of the rules helps to cultivate the good relationship that a Jew has with God from birth.

Since it must be impossible for any individual to be scrupulous in every way, and fail to make any mistake, Jews believe that God is not only just but merciful. Thus He does not judge people on His scale but on theirs. The aim for each person to live up to her or his greatest potential explains why a moral giant such as Moses was punished severely for a relatively small misdemeanour, while others seem to get away with much more.

Wrongdoing and repentance

Since God either makes no particular judgement on people at birth or, in some cases, actually thinks well of them (because of the quality of their ancestors), it is not surprising that the Hebrew word for repentance really means 'to return'. By repenting, Judaism believes that one can re-establish the original relationship which is a naturally pure state. There is no Hebrew word for 'sinner' but there is obviously a concept of sin.

Commission of sins can be corrected at any time but, in particular, in the annual review of the high holy days between the Jewish New Year (*Rosh Hashana*) and the Day of Atonement (*Yom Kippur*). At that time, with genuine repentance, Jews hope to correct their relationship with God. But if their misdemeanours have involved other people, they can do nothing with God until they have attempted to correct their relationship with the people they may have wronged.

Festivals for a people of history

The Jews are very definitely a people of history. Many of their festivals celebrate historical events quite directly. The three pilgrim festivals, Passover, Pentecost and Tabernacles (*Pesakh*, *Shavuot* and *Sukkot*) commemorate events and experiences in that formative phase of the Exodus from Egypt and the travelling to Israel. (Although these are still called pilgrim festivals, the requirement to make pilgrimage to Jerusalem and the Temple ceased when the last Temple was destroyed by the Romans.)

The meaning of *Pesakh* has already been indicated above. *Shavuot* is the festival on which Jews celebrate the giving of the Torah at Mount Sinai.

Sukkot, which lasts about a week, is an occasion for Jews to remember the Wandering in the Wilderness for 40 years. The journey and time was significant because it made the Jews aware of their dependence on God and it also gave them the time they needed to cease to be a slave people.

Other historical events have also been commemorated in festivals and fasts. The destruction of the Temple in Jerusalem by the Romans (and the Babylonians before them) is marked by a fast, the re-dedication of the Temple in Greek times is marked by a festival (*Hanukka*), the saving of the Jews of Persia is marked by the festival of *Purim* and the alleviating of the plague in Roman times is marked by the minor festival of *Lag B'Omer.*

Since events in the Jewish calendar reflect the experience of the Jewish People, the development of the Jewish calendar does not cease. Jewish history is still unfolding, and so slowly edging their way on to the calendar now are three twentieth-century events, each with their own day. Each requires the devising of services and ceremonies and the gradual acceptance of the Jewish people worldwide.

The most widely accepted of these, so far, is *Yom Ha'Atzmaut* (Israel Independence Day), which is celebrated to a greater or lesser extent all round the world by Jews, except for those who feel that the establishment of an independent Jewish state should not have happened until the Messianic Age. This small section of the Jewish community, mystical charismatics known as Hasidim, nonetheless see it as a virtue to live in the land of Israel and many of the most vigorous Jewish opponents of the Jewish state choose to live firmly within its jurisdiction. Their opposition to it is a theological one rather than a political one so, obviously, they are unable to recognise and celebrate Israel Independence Day, as do the vast majority of other Jews in the world.

They are less uncertain about Holocaust Day (*Yom Hashoa*). This event, striking more chords with Ashkenazi (Central and Eastern European) Jews than with Sephardi (Mediterranean and Oriental) Jews, has slowly been gaining recognition over the course of the last 15 years, so that many families will make some act of mourning on this day and an increasing number of communities will devise some ceremony or commemoration to mark the loss of six million Jews from the Jewish people. The number of six million is, in itself, already mind-bogglingly large but when one remembers that the total number of Jews was, before the Holocaust, only about eighteen million around the world, it becomes still more forceful how swingeing a blow to the Jewish people it must have been.

The third event which has yet to make a significant impact on the worldwide Jewish community is Jerusalem Day. This event commemorates the reunification of Jerusalem in 1967 and it is characteristic of the Jewish tendency to see God and the Jewish people in relationship through history to interpret this, not merely as an historical, political, or military event, but to read into it religious significance.

By and large, all these celebrations do not stress human achievements but rather more the intervention of God. The original model for this religious view of history is the *Pesakh* (Passover) *Seder*. Jews re-tell the story of the Exodus on *Pesakh* evening in an extensive and varied liturgy, performed around the table in the home. During the whole event no mention of Moses is made, for fear of detracting from the essential message that it was God who saved the Jews from slavery.

(It is perhaps also worth noting that there is no one in the Jewish community, even in any given country, who has the authority or power to direct to the whole Jewish community to observe one or other of these festivals, until a consensus grows up – often over hundreds of years – across the world.)

Celebration of time

This marking of time is a significant aspect of Jewish practice in general. Not only is history marked, commemorated and celebrated, but the regular passing of time is also identified within Jewish practice. The seasons affect the liturgy and the timing of the festivals. The months are calculated by the changes of the moon. The day is punctuated by three daily services (evening, morning, and afternoon), and the week, of course, is marked and crowned by *Shabbat*.

This weekly festival from Friday sunset to Saturday nightfall, gives an opportunity for leisure and reflection, family and community solidarity, and recreation. It has been a means for the Jew to maintain dignity in the face of a deriding world and has been a significant contributing factor to the survival of the Jewish people. Two other features have also contributed to this survival.

The synagogue

The synagogue is not really a little temple. It is a community centre where social and educational activities are easily as important as liturgical performances. Synagogues are built with provision for the educating of children and adults, and most will also have catering facilities to provide for parties and celebrations.

The success of the Pharisees in ensuring the survival of Judaism past the destruction of the Temple, and the dispersion from the Land, rests largely on the success of the synagogue, and the vigour of the Jewish people has largely been a product of its democracy where all Jews are equally able to lead the liturgy or participate in the service. The only hierarchical qualification is based on knowledge, an asset which has been determinedly made available to all.

Celebrating diversity

Another dimension of Judaism which has aided survival is the concept of separation, which is closely related to the Jewish concept of holiness. Jews are asked to make a virtue of distinction and so they distinguish in their dietary laws between acceptable and unacceptable foods and, within those, the acceptable and unacceptable parts of those foods. What is more, milk and meat foods must be separated.

Shabbat must be distinguished from week days sharply and clearly, and so too should Jews distinguish themselves from the wider Gentile community. This perception of difference as something to be celebrated rather than to be played down is obviously a crucial concept for any community that has traditionally and for millennia been a minority group wherever it has found itself. It is also perhaps an important attitude of mind for a multicultural society.

Bibliography

There are several books that might help to give insight into Jewish life and self-perceptions. Herman Wouk's *This Is My God* (Pocket Books USA, 1959) is an excellent personalised introduction to the day-to-day and year-to-year life of a Jew, and Lionel Blue's *To Heaven With Scribes and Pharisees* (Darton, Longman and Todd, 1975) is an attractively written insight into the ways in which the rabbinic system works. For more precise information on rabbinical attitudes on ethical matters one could do worse than read Louis Jacobs's *What Does Judaism Say About . . . ?* (Keter, 1973) and, for those questions that none of these books seem to answer because they are non-Jewish rather than Jewish, I would recommend my own little booklet *The Jewish People – Some Questions Answered* (Board of Deputies of British Jews, 1983).

The Summer 1981 *British Journal of Religious Education* is devoted entirely to the issue of teaching Judaism today and there is now an increasing range of well-written books about Judaism in the classroom suitable at various levels. Jenny Rose's *Jewish Worship* (Holt, 1985) Angela Wood's *Judaism* (Batsford, 1984), and the section on Jewish festivals in the Shap book, *Festivals in World Religions* (Alan Brown ed., Longman, 1986) will all be helpful by way of general introduction.

There are also insensitive and inaccurate books and it is wise to be as careful as possible, otherwise the intended process of developing understanding will produce exactly the opposite effect. This is also true of some books which refer to Judaism incidentally, for example when dealing with the New Testament story.

To gain an insight into the range of Jewish history which, after all, spans about 4000 years and the whole world, one could do no better than to turn to Martin Gilber's *Jewish History Atlas* (Wiedenfeld and Nicolson, 1969). For issues relating to teaching about the Holocaust I would recommend my video lecture on the subject, produced by ILEA, as part of its Auschwitz pack. Teaching about the Holocaust is one of the most provocative and relevant areas of teaching but also one of the most problematic and it is important to be fully aware of the pitfalls and philosophical issues that the subject necessarily raises before embarking on this field.

If the task seems daunting, don't worry. In the words of the rabbis 'We are not able to complete the task, but neither are we free to desist from it'.

CHAPTER 9

Introducing Sikhism

W. OWEN COLE

The Sikh religion has been viewed in a number of different ways by Sikhs and by people outside the faith. In an age which is ecumenical Guru Nanak has sometimes been described as a man dedicated to Hindu-Muslim reconciliation. In a world which venerates the work and ideas of Mahatma Gandhi he has been shown to be his precursor, preaching, 500 years earlier, a gospel of social, sexual and spiritual equality. Both interpretations reflect certain Sikh values and teachings.

Hindus regard Sikhism as a heterodox form of Hinduism, often displaying pictures of Guru Nanak in their mandirs. Their view may be more accurate than other interpretations but even then it can only be accepted with considerable reservation. Guru Nanak, the founder of the Sikh religion, was certainly born and brought up a Hindu. Sikh understanding of *samsara* (the world into which souls are re-born until they achieve liberation from this cycle), *karma* (the cosmic principle of cause and effect) and *moksha* (ultimate liberation from rebirth) has its origins in Hindu thought. It is against certain aspects of Hindu culture (using that term in its fullest sense to cover conduct, practices and beliefs), that Sikhism reacted or protested. It was especially critical of class and caste, the inequality of women, and the whole structure of brahmanical religion. Even the Sikh concept of Guru, perhaps its central and most distinctive teaching, is a refinement of the Hindu idea.

Origins and development

Sikhism began with Guru Nanak, a Khatri Hindu who lived in the Punjab from 1469–1539 CE though he undertook a number of missionary journeys to other parts of India and beyond. He shared a number of ideas common to a group of North Indian teachers known as *Sants*. The use of the vernacular rather than Sanskrit as the medium of religious teaching, egalitarianism, including the acceptance of women disciples, the inefficacy of ritual and the importance of the inner experience of God were some of them. This latter point was of particular importance for Guru Nanak, who did not regard himself and should not be explained simply as the inheriter and refiner of a *Sant* form of Hinduism, for he had an acute sense of being called and commissioned by God. Consequently Sikhism is not to be understood merely as a daughter religion of Hinduism, but, like its parallels Christianity and Islam (in relation to Judaism), as a religion in its own right, divinely revealed.

In one of his hymns Guru Nanak describes his religious experience:

I was a minstrel out of work,
The Lord gave me employment
The Mighty One instructed me,
'Night and Day, sing my praise.'
The Lord summoned the minstrel
To His high court.
On me he bestowed the robe of honouring
Him and singing his praise.
On me he bestowed the nectar in a cup,
The nectar of his true and holy name.
Those who, at the Guru's bidding,
Feast and take their fill of the Lord's
Will attain peace and joy,
Your minstrel spreads your glory
By singing your word.
Nanak says, Through adoring the truth
we attain the supreme reality.
                (Guru Granth Sahib, p. 150)

His mission was not to create a new religion but to reawaken the world to the forgotten primary truth that everyone could experience God and attain *moksha* through God's grace.

Guru Nanak travelled widely preaching this message. The *Janam Sakhis* or 'lives' of Guru Nanak, written some time after his death, contain many episodes which show how he presented this teaching to the people he met – Hindu priests, imams, peasants, businessmen, kings, and robbers. In 1521 Guru Nanak settled in Kartarpur, a village which practised the Sikh way of life. The day began and ended with devotions based on the Guru's teaching and hymns which he had been inspired to compose. The remaining time was given to work in the fields and village for the benefit of the community.

Before Guru Nanak died he designated and installed a successor. In all there were ten Gurus each of whom faithfully passed on the message given to the first and sustained and developed the community which grew up in response to it. During this period, which ended in 1708 with the death of Guru Gobind Singh, three major developments took place, each fundamental in the life of the religion.

In 1604 Guru Arjan, the fifth Guru of the Sikhs, completed the first compilation of a book known as the Adi Granth. This contains his own compositions and those of his four predecessors as well as some works by such Hindus and Muslims as Namdev, Kabir and Sheikh Farid. Authorised and authenticated copies of the teachings of Sikhism could now be made available

73

to local communities separated by considerable distances from personal contact with the Guru for their spiritual nurture and to counter the teachings of rivals such as the Guru's own brother.

In 1699 the tenth Guru, Gobind Singh, created the institution of the *Khalsa*. By now the *Sikh Panth* (or community) was large and scattered. If the compilation of the Adi Granth had ensured some unity of doctrine, the problems of organisation, allegiance and discipline remained. The solution was the *Khalsa* which men and women entered through initiation, not birth, by making promises and accepting a code of conduct. Most noticeable is the wearing of the turban by men and the adoption of the uncut hair as one of the five K's, so called because in Punjabi they begin with the initial 'K'. There are the *Kesh* (uncut hair), *Kirpan* (sword), *Kara* (wristlet), *Kangha* (comb), and *Kachcha* (short trousers). However, equally important are injunctions against smoking, drinking alcohol, and sexual incontinence. As well as receiving the command to observe the teachings of Sikhism, the *Khalsa* came to share his guruship.

In 1708, on the eve of his death, the tenth Guru declared that the succession of human Gurus was ended and conferred guruship on a revision of the Adi Granth to which he had previously added his father's compositions. Thus the scripture is now known as the Guru Granth Sahib though the title of Adi Granth is also used. Had Guru Gobind Singh's sons not predeceased him, the guruship might well be disputed as in earlier times; this must have been an important reason for investing the office in the scripture and the *Khalsa*. In effect it has made the Sikhs a community whose life is focused upon its scriptures, ritually as well as doctrinally.

Ideals and teachings

Sikhism is an intensely democratic religion. One might describe it as theocratic, bearing in mind that there are no priests. Guruship is an essential property and characteristic of a self-revealing, gracious God. It was imparted to men whose birth is regarded as non-karmic who were sent into the world to reveal the message of deliverance to mankind. This is contained in the scriptural Guru or in the community which obeys it and witnesses to it. Ultimately in an ideal sense the *Panth* is one with God who is often described as 'The one without a second' in the scriptures.

God is also beyond the categories of gender, being neither male nor female but the creator of both, though writers in English often use the masculine pronoun in referring to *Akal Purukh*, The Being Beyond Time, God.

In an individual sense, unity with God is realised partly through enlightenment, when one becomes aware of the presence of God, and partly through *nam japna* or *nam simran*, meditation. This is facilitated by using the scriptures, which are really a collection of religious poems running to 1430 printed pages, and by living in the company of similarly enlightened people.

Personal religion takes on a social aspect, not only in corporate worship but also through the principle of *kirt karna*, an ethic of honest hard work. By the practice of *wand chakna*, almsgiving, the Sikhi is encouraged to help all who are in need, whether they are members of the *Panth* or not.

From these ideals all else in Sikhism emanates. Other religions are to be respected for in these also God, as Guru, is revealed. The unity of God and humankind cannot accept sectarianism as having any ultimate reality. Similarly distinctions of sex or rank are illusory and to be rejected in favour of an egalitarian society. In brief it might be said that Sikhism takes the *varnashramadharma* of Hinduism and replaces it with a society in which there is only one *varna*, namely humanity (though the sanctification of armed resistance in the *Khalsa* ideal might argue that the *varna* is *kshatriya*) one *ashrama*, that of householder (*grihastha*), for the ideal of Sikhism is married family life, and one *dharma* of service to God and humanity. One reason for the early appeal of Sikhism must be that it accepted the lot of the villager (of necessity a hard working, family person) and idealised and sanctified it.

The gurdwara

The Sikh place of worship, the gurdwara, is where the principles of Sikhism can most easily be seen, though they also regulate the life of the home. Immediately one notices the importance of the scripture. Raised above the level of the worshippers, it is uniquely enthroned. Everyone else sits on the ground, facing it. Men and women are usually in separate groups, but both sexes will be present and women will be found reading the scripture as well as playing musical instruments backing the singing. The hymns used are passages of scripture; the homilies which are given will be based on them.

Worship may take place at any time. Just as no person is regarded as more important than another so all days are the same. True, *Gurpurbs*, the birth or death anniversaries of the Gurus, are specially celebrated as are the festivals of *Baisakhi* and *Diwali* and *Hola Mohalla* (in distinctively Sikh forms), but not in such a way that the importance of regular, even daily, corporate worship is diminished.

All acts of worship as well as child naming, marriages and the *amrit* or initiation ceremony take place in the presence of the Guru Granth Sahib and all end with the corporate sharing of *karah parshad*, an act of commensality. This emphasis upon eating together is extended and intensified in the institution of *langar*, the communal meal which everyone is invited to share. It has developed from the kitchen begun by Guru Nanak whose insistence that all who would share the Guru's teaching should eat together thus rejected religious or caste prohibitions. To provide food for *langar* or to serve in the kitchen is an act of service (*sewa*) eagerly undertaken by men, women, young and old. Just as the act of worship itself calls to mind unity and equality so *langar* promotes and fosters the principles of service and almsgiving. Though Sikhs are opposed to begging, the free kitchen is a place where the hungry may find food, whether they be Sikh or not. To cause no one offence only vegetarian meals are served there.

Sikhism in Britain

In Britain Sikhism has undergone some practical modifications. The gurdwara has often replaced the extended family of the village as the medium through which children are educated into Sikhism, and into the Punjabi language. It has become a social centre as well as a place of worship. Services may be held daily but Sunday has become the main day of worship, for it is then that most British Sikhs are free from work. Instead of weddings on the flat roofs of houses or under an awning on a piece of open ground, Sikh weddings in Britain usually take place in the gurdwara.

Besides these restrictions there are potential benefits which the Sikh communities of Britain may enjoy. Sikhs say that as a minority in India, they have been unable to rid themselves of the influence of caste and male domination. In Britain their egalitarian, democratic spirit might flourish. As yet, of course, the 300 000 or so Sikhs living in Britain are struggling to establish themselves in the conurbations to which Sikhs came 20 or 30 years ago bringing their great attributes of adaptability and the work ethic. It will take time for them to influence either British society or world-wide Sikhism whose attachment to Punjabi language and culture is likely to be questioned by them, though not in the near future.

Teaching Sikhism and resources for teaching and study

With younger children those aspects of Sikhism which are likely to prove most intelligible are those which are most tangible in terms of their own experiences, for example the birth of a baby, a wedding, everyday life. We are not so much introducing children to Sikhism but to Sikhs. The key to success lies in humanising religion especially as something here and now. *Pavan is a Sikh* does this well portraying him as normal but his normality includes a father who wears a turban, a mother dressed in a sari, Pavan and his sisters growing their hair long, and eating puries as well as fish and chips. In *Amardip and Rema*, a Coventry Sikh family makes a visit to Punjab, a journey which middle juniors could share, especially through the excellent colour photo-graphs. *The Sikh World* is more comprehensive and more middle school than top junior but could be used with them selectively and the photographs have a universal appeal. *Understanding Your Sikh Neighbour* could also be used with this age group and provides the teacher with necessary background information as does *A Sikh Family in Britain*, and *Baisakhi*, and *Visiting a Sikh Temple*.

Artefacts are essential. A ready-made-up turban, a turban length, the *kirpan* (explained with care), *kara*, *kangha* and *kachcha*, costume dolls, saris and *salwar kameez* (which parents may donate when children have out-grown them), pictures of the Gurus (bought, or from old calendars; see your friendly neighbourhood Sikh grocer), and greetings cards, can easily be obtained.

Examples of aspects to be covered in topics are:

Turban and 5 'ks'	clothes
karah parshad and *langar*	food
Golden Temple	journeys/pilgrimage
Sikh family in Punjab	journeys/pilgrimage
wedding	families
naming ceremony	families
Baisakhi	festivals
gurpurb	festivals
gurdwara	buildings, worship

Stories should be used as back-up. By themselves they are likely to be passively received and soon forgotten. Anthologies are covered in detail by Eleanor Nesbitt in Chapter 16. The *Believe it or Not* series produced by Independent Television has shown a number of programmes about Sikhs or including them with other religions. Teachers may wish to use these in clips, tying a turban for example, or the inside of a gurdwara, rather than as a whole for they cover vast areas in a brief space of time. Used as videos these programmes are especially valuable for schools unfortunate enough not to be located near a Sikh community.

For further reading and information see *The Sikhs: Their Religious Beliefs and Practices*, W. O. Cole and P. S. Sambhi, *The Popular Dictionary of Sikhism*, W. O. Cole and P. S. Sambhi, and *Religion in the Multifaith School*, W. O. Cole (ed.).

Bibliography

D. K. Babraa, *Visiting a Sikh Temple* (Lutterworth, 1981)
O. Bennett, *Listening to Sikhs* (Unwin Hyman, 1990)
W. O. Cole, *A Sikh Family in Britain* (Religious and Moral Education Press, 1973)

W. O. Cole (ed.), *Religion in the Multifaith School* (Stanley Thornes & Hulton, 1983)
W. O. Cole and P. S. Sambhi, *Baisakhi* (Religious and Moral Education Press, 1986)
W. O. Cole and P. S. Sambhi, *The Popular Dictionary of Sikhism* (Curzon Press, 1990)
W. O. Cole and P. S. Sambhi, *The Sikhs: Their Religious Beliefs and Practices* (Routledge, 1972, second reprint 1989)
Steve Harrison, *Amardip and Rema* (Macmillan, 1986)
Sean Lyle, *Pavan is a Sikh* (A & C Black, 1977)
P. S. Sambhi, *Understanding Your Sikh Neighbour* (Lutterworth, 1980)
Daljit Singh and Angela Smith, *The Sikh World* (Macdonald, 1985)

PART THREE

Teaching about Religions

Introduction

When we are framing the curriculum various influences and considerations come round and round again – until, at some critical point, we have to emerge with a practical programme. The apparent starting point might be the requirements of an Act of Parliament, a local authority Agreed Syllabus, or just some awareness of what an all-round education requires. Impetus and ideas seem to come from everywhere – from parents, from the SACRE, from the governors and so on. But then the immediate professional challenge lands on the desk of the class teacher. Within a given curriculum area, what do we teach – and how – and in what order, with what sequence of development?

The chapters in this section are all about what we can teach in junior schools, and how it can be done. But so are other sections – say, on Religious Education and the Arts, or on Methods and Issues. So what is the difference? The difference is that here the practical teaching ideas stem directly from reflection about the central values, traditions and practices of religions. To put it another way, they depend upon the sort of material presented in the preceding section, Guides to Religions. Of course this is not the only influence upon the RE curriculum. As a programme is built up, it soon becomes apparent that other sections of this book, and the real-life approaches they represent, are complementary to this section and to each other. Nevertheless, the contents of this section are centrally important; for the religions themselves must be a major source of inspiration.

Inspiration from the religions

In this section, practical topics, themes and activities are at the forefront. The chapters will suggest what to do, how to do it, and where to look for further help or stimulus – for once we are 'hooked' on the exploration of religion with children, there's no end to its possibilities.

All the chapters, however, derive their inspiration from thought about what is important and interesting in the religions themselves. Eleanor Nesbitt's chapter takes us straight away to stories that are close to the heart of Sikhism. Ken Oldfield (on Hinduism) and Vida Barnett (on Islam) take us on a journey through a range of topics. As we read through them, we become aware that their very character instrinsically acknowledges Hindu and Muslim insights, principles and practices. Then again, consider Douglas Charing's chapter alongside Clive Lawton's chapter from the preceding section. We see how directly our junior school topics can represent fundamental principles of Judaism – and not just information but sensitivity to atmosphere and values.

Peter Doble directs our attention to exploring the living practice of Christianity and reasserts the educational values of the enterprise against the background of the Education Reform Act. Jean Holm emphasises considerations of sequence and development in the teaching of Christianity – from incidental encounters to collection and categorisation, for example. For both writers, the sort of reflection upon Christianity exemplified in Part One is basic.

Peggy Morgan makes perhaps the most explicit affirmation of the way in which her topics depend upon and reflect Buddhist insights and values:

> Buddhist teaching claims to be 'the truth about the way things are', but that truth, Buddhists say, does not have to be labelled Buddhism to be true. The heart of Buddhist practice is meditation, and the heart of Buddhist meditation is mindfulness, a total alertness and attention to the reality of things both inner and outer. This is combined with an emphasis on testing truth out in experience, an approach which harmonises very well with western educational attitudes.

That is why Peggy Morgan's suggestions (for helping children to explore 'the way things are') count as intrinsically Buddhist in character. At the same time they are educationally sound and self-justified explorations of the inner and outer worlds of human experience.

Conclusion

It is not a matter (in any of the world faiths) of just cutting up a religion into teachable bits, like an instructor. It is not a matter of taking a stand outside the faiths and giving information about beliefs and practices in suitably brief chunks. Nor is it a matter of standing inside the faiths and converting children to a different world-view. It is a matter of structuring insights – reflecting the essential values of other people and challenging our own in an atmosphere of sympathetic understanding.

CHAPTER 10

Buddhism in junior schools

PEGGY MORGAN

Buddhist friends at Amaravati Buddhist Centre (whose address appears in the bibliography) produce a magazine for children who go to the centre for teaching at their family weekends and summer camps. It is called *Rainbows*, a title which immediately suggests a topic bursting with possibilities for the junior school. Here are some starting points and interlinking ideas.

Beginning from experience

- Who has seen a rainbow? Can you describe it?
- When do they happen?
- Are rainbows cheerful and happy sights? Why?
- Can you describe how you feel when you see a rainbow or someone says 'Look, there's a rainbow!'?
- What colours are there in a rainbow? Can you remember the order?
- What makes the colours?
- Can we make rainbows?
- Has anyone read *Pollyanna*? Can you remember what a prism is?
- Who likes blowing bubbles or washing up milk bottles?
- What have they got to do with rainbows?

Poems and stories about rainbows

Captain Noah and His Floating Zoo has a song which helps you to remember the colours in their right order.

'The Rainbow' in *How Things Began* says of the colour violet that it is:

> The colour of the shimmery mist at the top of the Himalayan mountains at dawn.

'The Rainbow', written for children by the composer Peter Maxwell Davies, has in its conclusion the idea that objective, scientific descriptions are not enough. The imagination declares that the rainbow is a mystery.

Discussion

In addition to some of the questions asked above there are others.

- What is the best thing about a rainbow?
- Why is it so special?
- Is it its natural beauty?
- Is it because we don't see rainbows very often?
- Is it because they seem so fragile?
- Is it because a rainbow makes us feel hopeful when the sun shines in and through the rain?

Since Buddhists think it good to reflect upon the truth about the way things are, and upon our own reactions, this imaginative exploration is obviously worthwhile in Buddhist terms. It can, in fact, be counted as *Dharma*, teaching. There are, however, even more explicit links with Buddhism here. The Amaravati children's magazine is called *Rainbows* because the rainbow is Amaravati's symbol. It is printed on its booklets and notepaper and dramatically spans its beautiful entrance gates. *Amaravati* literally means realm or land (*vati*) without (*a*) *Mara*. *Mara* is the Buddhist personification of death, desire and whatever works against enlightenment. Another way of translating *Amaravati* is 'the deathless realm'. This is synonymous with the state of *Nirvana*, a state to which the centre hopes to provide a rainbow bridge of hope through the rainstorms of *samsara*, the round of suffering birth and death. Amaravati also tries to offer itself as a centre which teachers can use as a resource, both in terms of the people that are there and in its many visual aids and special exhibitions like that on lay Buddhist life set up in 1989. Apart from its rainbow symbols it also has many styles of Buddha images, a hanging temple bell, meditation and shrine rooms, a stupa, a special children's room and the beginnings of a grove of trees which symbolise the meeting of eastern and western culture. All of these have been annotated in a special 'trail'. All this is part of the rainbow bridge of understanding which the centre hopes to provide.

If you look at the children's books telling the story of the Buddha called 'Prince Siddhartha', you will find that the pictures are full of rainbows. They act as halos to the figures and give the illustrations a jewel-like quality. In the pictures of the enlightenment (pp. 102–3), the rainbows begin to flow outwards, like ripples in water, suggesting the outgoing effect of this event upon the world. The illustrations in the book echo the Tibetan use of colour, and the inclusion of the rainbows probably reflects their particular drama and beauty in the high altitudes of the Himalayas. This is illustrated in a quotation from A. Harvey's book *Journey in Ladakh*.

Dark, threatening clouds massed above us and the air chilled, and the grass around us shivered and darkened. Before us through the half-parted curtains of rain and hail, we could see the valleys folding down to the long valley of Ladakh . . . When the hail cleared and the sun came out again, we walked slowly down the long stony gorges. Across nearly every gorge there shone a large rainbow. I counted nine. 'When there is a rainbow in the mountains', Wangchuk said, 'We say the mountains are dancing. The rainbows are the scarves they wind round their wrists.'

(p. 40)

Stories

I have mentioned above one children's version of the story of Gautama Buddha (Siddhartha was his personal name). This is a favourite starting point for younger children and I have elsewhere documented the many different versions and places where it is included in text books in my *Buddhist Stories*. Two of the most colourful texts have been produced by the Buddhist community themselves. These are *Prince Siddhartha* and *The Story of the Buddha*. There are also colouring books which give outline drawings and activities and cartoons based on traditional Buddhist art.

One of the best experiential beginnings for telling the story of the Buddha is the question of happiness. Do riches bring happiness? Would you be happy if you had been born a handsome prince or princess? Can a person be happy without trying to help others who are unhappy? The story of Gautama Buddha is a challenging reversal of the rags to riches, beggar to prince ideal so often presented in children's literature. For teachers who prefer not to start with existential questions but do not want to plunge straight into the 'Life', there is a delightful story of a Chinese artist by E. Coatsworth called *The Cat Who Went to Heaven*. The artist is commissioned to paint the death of the Buddha and prepares himself for the task by thinking about the events in the Buddha's life which lead up to his death. He has taken in a stray cat which keeps him company as he begins to paint, and the cat becomes central to the understanding of the Buddha's compassion, shown towards the animals at his death, at least according to the Chinese legend.

The story of the Buddha's life can also be linked with the theme of festivals. The Japanese *Hana Matsuri* or flower-festival involves making models (for temple courtyards) of the Lumbini gardens where Gautama Buddha was born. This is a delightful activity for any junior school classroom, as is finding out what Japanese children do when they visit the temple. *Wesak* celebrates the birth, enlightenment and death of the Buddha amongst Theravada Buddhists and is now annually advertised in the *Middle Way* in Britain. It is often called Buddha Day to encourage all Buddhists to take part. Good introductions to festivals in general are suggested in the *Exploring Religion* series, although

Buddhism is not given as a specific example. Teachers can find good material on Buddhist festivals for their own use in *Festivals in World Religions* and in the 1987 edition of *World Religions in Education*.

There are, of course, many other kinds of Buddhist stories which can be enjoyed at story time or integrated into a wider topic. The lives of Buddhist children can be explored from various sources. *Our Buddhist Friends* focuses on a Sri Lankan family living in London. *Ananda in Sri Lanka* is colourfully set in a Sri Lankan village. *My Home in a Monastery in Nepal* is about a boy who wants to be a monk. *A Family in Thailand* provides a traditional background and my *Buddhist Stories* begins with three examples of Buddhist families here in Britain, bringing up their children in the Theravada, Zen and Tibetan traditions.

Other very popular sets of stories are the *Jataka Tales*, which are available in many inexpensive illustrated collections. These overlap with Indian folklore generally and recount the stories of the Buddha's former births (*jataka* means birth) as a golden deer, monkey king, hare etc. They illustrate the moral perfections such as generosity, patience and compassion. They also illustrate the interrelatedness of the animal and human world, a theme with which children have a natural sympathy. If it raises the more difficult question of rebirth, this is best tackled at the junior school stage with a discussion of how life flows in a cycle of cause and effect. The poem 'Whatever Miss T eats turns into Miss T' might be helpful here as will ideas in the next section.

Implicit themes

All the above suggestions make some explicit mention of Buddhists or Buddhism at some point. There are, however, many 'themes' that are 'implicitly Buddhist' and which can provide the junior school teacher with a wealth of enjoyable and interesting material. I have linked them once again to stories, but they all flow naturally into mathematics, environmental science, creative writing, etc. with all the integration that makes life in the junior classroom such a rich and wholesome experience. Here religious education and the inclusion of Buddhism is very much a matter of the way we look at the world, the kind of questions we ask and the kind of explanations we find interesting.

How we see the world, explorations and surprises

Illustrations can be drawn from dramatic changes to knowledge, for example, that the earth is round and not flat, that the earth moves round the sun not the other way round, that matter is made up of constantly moving energies and is not static and solid.

What does the world look like to a snail, a bird or a bat? Do they see things as we do? If not, why not? What makes the differences? What different limitations do different people have? (for example, blind, deaf, dumb, lame, not able to speak a language). What differences do they make?

The stories of 'The Blind Men and The Elephant', 'The Chicken and The Egg' help to explore the above theme.

The cycle of nature with its dramatic changes

Things are not always what they seem to be. Illustrations can be drawn from bare twigs which produce leaves and flowers; the brown earth which becomes a lawn; the cold, runny egg which produces a wriggling, fluffy chick; the caterpillar which becomes a butterfly and the tadpole which turns into a frog. These are all topics which lend themselves to a whole range of activities which make up the junior school day. The story of *The Very Hungry Caterpillar* might also provide stimulus with its dramatic pictorial end. What do we need, apart from food, to grow and change, to realise our potential? What might we become? Other possibilities of transformation are shown in the story of Helen Keller, the experience of the Buddha and a Tibetan folk-tale called 'The Frog' which has reverberations with the western story of the princess and the frog. 'The Ugly Duckling' is another old favourite on this theme.

Who or what do we value most? How does it show?

Can we live without trees? How can we respect trees? What have the Buddhists at Chithurst done with the wood they were given? How are they looking after it? There is a lot of interesting material on this topic in *The Forest Sangha Newsletter* (which, like *Rainbows* is available from Amaravati); it links well with the material on trees and Buddhist economics in Schumacher's book *Small is Beautiful*.

Another question of value which relates to Buddhism is why people support Buddhist monks and nuns. How are these monks and nuns 'helpful' to society? Read the story of *Frederick Fieldmouse* for help with this kind of question.

When the inevitable criticism arises at the end of a section like this 'How is this religious education?', let me remind you of the translation of *dharma* given earlier. Buddhist teaching claims to be 'the truth about the way things are' but that truth, Buddhists say, does not have to be labelled Buddhism to be true. The heart of Buddhist practice is meditation, and the heart of Buddhist meditation is mindfulness, a total alertness and attention to the reality of things both inner and outer. This is combined with an emphasis on testing truth out in experience, an approach which harmonises very well with western educational attitudes.

Bibliography

For teachers

This bibliography complements the one given in Chapter 3, pp. 35–6 of this book. I have discussed other ideas for the classroom and the appropriateness of teaching about Buddhism in A. Wood (ed.), *Religions and Education* (1989, available from BFSS RE Centre, West London Institute of Higher Education, Borough Road, Isleworth, Middlesex).

Amaravati Buddhist Centre, *The Forest Sangha Newsletter* (available from the Amaravati Buddhist Centre, Great Gaddesden, Hemel Hempstead, Herts HP1 3BZ)

A. Brown (ed.), *Festivals in World Religions* (Longman, 1986)

A. Brown (ed.), *The Shap Handbook on World Religions in Education* (available from The Commission for Racial Equality, Elliot House, 10–12 Allington Street, London SW1E 5EH)

The Buddhist Society, *The Middle Way* (available from The Buddhist Society, 58 Eccleston Square, London SW1V 1PH)

A. Harvey, *A Journey in Ladakh* (Flamingo, 1984)

M. Palmer, *Faith and Nature* (Rider, 1988)

P. Morgan, *Being a Buddhist* (Batsford, 1989). This contains original Buddhist sources, scriptural and contemporary and explores the world of Buddhist belief and practice.

P. Morgan, *Buddhism – an Illustrated Dictionary* (Batsford, 1987). This book has short survey articles on Buddhist ideas and practices.

P. Morgan, *Buddhist Iconography* (available from the author at Westminster College, North Hinskey, Oxford OX2 9AT at £3.50)

P. Morgan, *Buddhist Stories* (available from the author at £2.50). There is a list of books and sections of books for teachers and pupils on the Buddha listed on pp. 15–16.

P. Morgan, *Buddhism in the Twentieth Century* (Stanley Thornes & Hulton, 1985). This book is based on themes such as pilgrimage, worship and festivals.

Shap journal, *World Religions in Education* (available from Alan Brown, 23 Kensington Square, London W8 5HN). The annual issue of the journal contains articles on Buddhism.

E. Schumacher, *Small is Beautiful* (Abacus, 1974), especially Chapter 4

World Wide Fund for Nature Newsletter often contains articles on Buddhist activities and reviews relevant books.

For pupils

Stories are often meant to be told, not read, so a text that is for the teacher or older children is still usable as a basis for storytelling. I also have a reluctance to state an exact age level for books, as the language of well-told stories transcends the normal limits of language levels.

Books mentioned in the chapter

Amaravati Buddhist Centre, *Rainbows* (see address above)

J. Ascott, *Our Buddhist Friends* (Denholm House Press, 1978)

The Association of Buddhist Women, *The Story of the Buddha* (available from London Buddhist Vihara, 5 Heathfield Gardens, London W4 4JU)

Buddhist Painting Book (available from Throssel Hole Priory, Carrshield, Hexham, Northumbria NE47 8AL)

The Life of the Buddha (available from Sacred Trinity Centre, Chapel Street, Salford, Manchester M3 7AJ

C. Barker, *Ananda in Sri Lanka* (Hamish Hamilton, 1984)

O. Bennett, *Exploring Religion* series (Bell and Hyman, 1984). Although only the book on worship includes material on Buddhism, the six topic books are bursting with useful introductory ideas.

B. Candappa (ed.), 'How things Began' in a set of four booklets called *Tales of South Asia* (Ginn & Co., 1975)

B. Candappa (ed.), 'The Blind Men and the Elephant' in Fools and Wise Men from *Tales of South Asia* (Ginn & Co., 1975)

E. Coatsworth, *The Cat Who Went to Heaven* (Collier Macmillan, 1958)

P. Hawker and B. Campbell, *My Home in a Monastery in Nepal* (Evans Brothers, 1982)

F. and A. Hyde-Chambers, 'The Frog' in *Tibetan Folk Tales* (Random House, 1981)

P. O. Jacobson and P. S. Kristensen, *A Family in Thailand* (Wayland, 1985)

J. Landaw and J. Brooke, *Prince Siddhartha* (Wisdom, 1984)

L. Leoni, *Frederick Fieldmouse*, (Picture Puffin)

P. Morgan, *Buddhist Stories* (available from the author, address above)

P. Morgan, *Jataka Tales*. A full list of the many versions with some examples can be found in *Buddhist Stories* above.

E. H. Porter, *Pollyanna* (Puffin, 1984)

Some additional material

A. Bancroft, *Festivals of the Buddha* (Religious and Moral Education Press, 1984)

P. and H. Connolly, *Religions through Festivals: Buddhism* (Longman, 1988)

J. Rankin, A. Brown and M. Hayward (eds), *RE Topics for the Primary School* (Longman, 1989)

D. and U. Samaraseka, *I am a Buddhist* (Franklin Watts, 1986) and *Our Culture–Buddhist* (Franklin Watts)

J. Snelling, *Buddhist Festivals* (Wayland, 1985), *Buddhist Stories* (Wayland, 1986) and *Buddhism* (Wayland, 1986)

Audio-visual aids

Slides

Ann and Bury Peerless, 22 King's Avenue, Minnis Bay, Birchington, Kent CT7 9QL, have various sets with flexible use, for example:

Sri Lankan Festival-Torchlight Procession
Sri Lankan Pilgrimage to Adam's Peak
Burma: Swe Dagon Pagoda, Rangoon
India: Sanchi Stupa, carved scenes from Jataka stories

Posters and photographs

Pictorial Charts Education Trust, 27 Kirchen Road, London W13 0UD:

E43 My Neighbours' Religion, 1 chart
E44 Acts of Worship, 1 chart
E735 Religious Artefacts, 16 charts
E749 Buddhist Festivals, 4 charts
E732 Religion in Art 1, 8 charts
E733 Religion in Art 2, 8 charts
E752 Holy Writings, 8 charts
E726 Holy Books 1, 4 charts
E730 Founders and Messengers, 4 charts

Some Buddhist publishers and organisations have posters and postcards which can be useful, for example:

The Buddhist Society, 58 Eccleston Square, London SW1V 1PH
Manjushri Institute, Conishead Priory, Ulverston, Cumbria LA12 9QQ
Tharpa Publications, 13 Bendemeer Road, London SW15 1JX
Wisdom Publications, 23 Dering Street, London

CHAPTER 11

Teaching Christianity in junior schools

JEAN HOLM

Christianity, like other religions, is complex. It is much more than beliefs, morals and Bible stories! If the pupils are to gain any understanding of what Christianity means to Christians, they should be introduced during their primary school days to the features which make up the framework of a religious person's life:

- **places and forms of worship:** architecture, furnishings, ornamentation, symbols, a special day for corporate worship, cathedrals, monasteries, etc.
- **festivals:** the way they are celebrated today
- **scriptures:** their use in church, their role in festivals, the story of their translation, the finding of ancient manuscripts, life in Bible times
- **pilgrimage:** places of pilgrimage in the locality (as a foundation for a general topic on pilgrimage in the secondary school)
- **rituals:** saying grace, distributing palm crosses in church, genuflecting, etc.
- **rites of passage:** birth, initiation, marriage and death, dealt with incidentally (more systematic topics on growing up in Christianity – to include birth and initiation – death and burial, and marriage are appropriate in the secondary school).

In addition we shall need to introduce pupils to such things as symbols and the expressive arts, especially music and art, which are significant in all the features listed above.

I offer here some suggestions for dealing with two important questions: first, what is the best stage in children's development to tackle particular topics and secondly, how can children be helped to build up their understanding of Christianity in a reasonably systematic way?

The Church

In the infant school most of what children will learn about Christianity will be incidental, and will be related mainly to what they bring into the classroom from their own background and experience. It may be a contribution to 'news time' about a baby brother or sister who is to be 'done', with the child asked to tell the rest of the class about it after the event. This will include, at the very least, the ceremony taking place in a church, the use of water and the giving of a name. It may include the giving of candles to parents and godparents (an early stage in understanding the symbolism of light), and a child from a Christian family may know about the baby being signed with the sign of the cross.

In the same way, a wedding or a funeral or a present of a book of Bible stories may stimulate a news item in the classroom.

The subject of baptism may also arise in a topic on babies. A topic on colours lends itself to a visit to a church to look at stained glass windows, and the liturgical colours – on the altar cloth, Bible marker and vestments.

At the junior stage children will still do much of their learning about Christianity incidentally, (for example discovering the symbol for a church on maps), but now we can also enable them to learn more systematically. Two of the characteristics of junior age children are their curiosity and their delight in collecting things, so the emphasis should be on 'finding out'. For example, a topic for lower juniors on the local environment will include a church, and children enjoy being able to put names to such things as font, pulpit, lectern and altar, discovering the prominence given to the Bible, and seeing how many crosses they can find.

Upper juniors enjoy not only collecting things, especially facts, but also classifying them. In a multifaith scheme on sacred places, for example, they can penetrate more deeply into the significance of the church as they think about what it has in common with the places of worship of other religions and in what ways it is different. Like the seven- to nine-year-olds they may enjoy seeing how many crosses they can find in a church, but now they can also see how many different types of cross they can find. They can make a pie chart of the seasons of the Christian year, showing the liturgical colours. They can find out about the different kinds of service of worship a church has, and who takes them, and think about why there is always a reading from a Gospel at a Communion service. A foundation is thus laid for a study at secondary school of the church as a community of people, and for a study of different Christian denominations, and eventually for a study of worship.

Learning about monasteries and monastic life is one way to introduce top juniors to particular developments in the history of Christianity, to the disciplined life of groups of Christians, and to the role which the religious orders played – and in different ways still play – in the community.

Children's fiction is another way of making aspects of Christianity a natural part of children's learning. Books such as J. Tomlinson's *The Bus that Went to Church* and Graham Oakley's *The Church Mouse* for the infants, and the other Church Mice books for the juniors, are well written and illustrated, have delightful touches of humour, and are refreshingly free from the moralising that characterises so many religious stories.

Festivals

Festivals are by definition celebrations, so it is essential that children associate the experience of celebration with learning about a festival. In addition to parties, letting the children enjoy and use the Christmas imagery is more important than 'telling' the Christmas story. A joyous collage could include Father Christmas, presents, candles, Christmas trees, etc., as well as the Holy Family, manger, angels, shepherds and kings. The inclusiveness of the celebration is an accurate reflection of the nature of religious festivals: it is impossible to draw a definite line between what is religious and what is not religious.

One possible Christmas topic for lower juniors involves finding out about the origin of Santa Claus and about the customs associated with this figure in different countries (one of the ways in which we help children to realise that Christianity is a world religion). Other possibilities include finding out about some of the Christmas customs – puddings, robins, etc. – using stories such as *Baboushka*, making Christmas cards, and learning to recognise Luke's and Matthew's nativity stories.

The festivals can be dealt with more comprehensively in the upper junior school. Christmas lends itself to a study of nativity scenes in art, or to an exploration of the way in which the story of the wise men has fascinated poets and musicians and artists down the centuries. Other possibilities are finding out about the origins of Christmas customs and the significance they have been given within the Christian festival (including the fourth-century choice of 25 December as the birthday of Jesus), or a study of Christmas cards to discover and explore the different aspects of the festival which are respresented – a useful reminder of the close relationship of religion and culture.

Another way for top juniors to become aware of the relationship of religion and culture is to study past copies of the *Radio Times* and *TV Times* at the end of the autumn term, listing in one column all the programmes which make any reference to Christianity, in a second column those which refer explicitly to Christmas and in a third those which refer to the biblical story. The pupils should then be encouraged to listen to and watch some of the programmes during the holidays (also enlisting parents and friends), in order to discuss next term how the media handled the Christian faith, and especially the festival of Christmas.

Easter is a much more difficult festival to handle, and needs to be approached with great sensitivity. At the five to seven stage it is appropriate to put the emphasis on celebration, through new life in spring, and parties and the enjoyment of things like Easter eggs.

For lower juniors spring is still the appropriate focus of new life. Making a spring collage helps the children to reflect on their experience of wonder as they see the new life emerge in the bulbs they have grown and in the world outside the classroom. Watching chicks hatch can give children an even more profound experience of new life. Other possible activities include painting eggs (and discovering that this is an important custom in the Eastern Orthodox Church), making Easter bonnets, hot cross buns, palm crosses and Easter cards. These last activities, which might have been undertaken in the infant school, bear repetition because they provide significant affective experiences, in contrast to the more cognitive aspects of the curriculum in which children expect to be moving on to more grown up levels.

We can go into more detail with the upper juniors. A study of Easter customs and their Christian significance, for example, the use on Ash Wednesday of the ash from the burning of last year's palm crosses, the Maundy money, the covering of the cross on Good Friday, the lighting of the Easter Fire, can be rewarding. Another possibility for top juniors is discovering which passages from the Bible are read in church from Ash Wednesday through to Easter Day.

The Bible

A reminder should be made here that everything in the Bible was originally addressed to adults. It is *Christian* scripture, with authority only for Christians. And too much emphasis on Bible *stories* creates the impression that the Bible is a book that people grow up out of rather than one which Christians grow up into.

Some Bible stories, such as those about Joseph and David, are appropriate for lower juniors but there are many other ways in which children can become familiar with the Bible. Schemes on life in Bible times, for example, the home life of Jewish children at the time of Jesus, and what boys would learn in the synagogue school at the time of Jesus, provide some of the background information without which the Bible can't be understood, but they also perform the important task of helping children to realise that Jesus was Jewish. Another form of background scheme is the biblical image theme, which helps children to learn about the way of life out of which the great biblical images emerged. Two of these – Shepherd and Bread – can be explored with the seven to nine age group. Biblical background schemes are also appropriate for upper juniors, though they should now include more detail of Jewish religious life such as synagogue and Temple. The biblical image theme of Water is excellent for this age group. A study of the achievements of certain characters (not just the 'stories'), for example David, Elijah, Nehemiah and Judas Maccabaeus, is also suitable for this age group. Schemes about the translation of the Bible, perhaps focusing on William Tyndale, and about the discoveries of biblical manuscripts, perhaps the Dead Sea Scrolls or the famous Sinaiticus manuscript, are other possibilities.

Jesus

Teaching about Jesus is much more interesting – and more complex – than just telling stories from the Gospels. Children will be able to see Jesus in his Jewish setting through some of the background schemes already mentioned. If the emphasis at junior school level is put on his life as a man – a Jewish man – in first-century Palestine, pupils will have a much sounder foundation on which to build at secondary level when they meet such schemes as What is a Gospel? and Who was Jesus? or undertake a study of what the festival of Easter means to Christians.

This does not mean that at junior level children's thinking about Jesus is restricted to his life in Palestine. In many ways, for example through learning about the church and about Christian symbols, and through the imagery of the festivals, children become aware of the greater significance which Jesus has for Christians. A more systematic study of what Jesus means to Christians is appropriate in the secondary school.

Finally, a reminder that children can obtain much of the factual information which they should have by the time they leave junior school through general topics. Some brief examples: Seasons – the Christian year; Books and Writing – scrolls, codices, Hebrew and Greek script, the order of the books in the Jewish Bible; Light and Darkness – the symbolism of light, including the Eastern Orthodox Church's Easter; Signs and Symbols – the Chi Rho, Alpha and Omega, ICHTHUS, the pilgrim shell, different kinds of cross, the symbolism of food, light and water.

Bibliography

Olivia Bennett, *Colin's Baptism* (Hamish Hamilton, 1986). This has simple but informative explanations and colour photos.

Alan Brown, *The Christian World* (Macdonald, 1984). This shows Christianity as a world religion.

Marion and Olivia H. H. Cole, *Things to Make and Do for Easter* (Franklin Watts, 1979). This is full of stories, games, recipes and colour drawings.

J. Tomlinson, *The Bus that Went to Church* (Faber, 1975)

Graham Oakley, *The Church Mouse* and other Church Mice stories (Macmillan, 1972)

Brenda Pettenuzzo, *I am a Roman Catholic* (Franklin Watts, 1985) This is told by a nine-year-old.

W. Ellwood Post, *Saints, Signs and Symbols* (SPCK, 1966). This contains hundreds of Christian symbols, including 60 different crosses.

Maria Roussou, *I am a Greek Orthodox* (Franklin Watts, 1985). This is told by an eleven-year-old.

R. O. Hughes, *Religions through Festivals: Christianity* (Longman, 1989). This is suitable for use with top juniors.

Brian Wildsmith, *The True Cross* (OUP, 1977). This is about the legend of the True Cross and contains superb colour illustrations.

CHAPTER 12

Approaching Christianity in the classroom

PETER DOBLE

Hasn't enough been written on this without adding yet another chapter? There is certainly plenty of good material around and there is more forthcoming as the last section of this chapter shows. But the question of Christianity's place in the classroom has been raised by the 1988 Education Act and much has been written in the popular press which is misleading. Consequently, a brief exploration of major issues will settle some doubts and start some new enterprises.

A legal requirement

Yes, the Act requires that those who prepare the Agreed Syllabus for an LEA must ensure that it reflects 'the fact that the religious traditions in Great Britain are in the main Christian while taking account of the teaching and practices of the other principal religions represented in Great Britain.' In fact this clause *requires* a multifaith syllabus but addresses itself to *balance* – and that is where we begin. The Agreed Syllabuses must be non-denominational – which confirms legally what has been worked out over many years, that RE is not induction into a Christian tradition.

What is the purpose of teaching Christianity?

Christianity is 'taught' as part of a programme of religious education. Nothing of the gains of the past 25 years has been lost in this part of the legislation. RE remains firmly an *educationally* justifiable exercise; it contributes to a child's development – in intellect, imagination and spirit. RE fosters an understanding of the world in its diversity and richness; it helps to face difference, conflict, doubt. RE's aim has been expressed in many different ways, but there is a wide agreement that it has to do with helping a child grow by encountering and increasingly understanding the religious traditions of humankind.

May only Christians teach Christianity?

Of course not. RE's purpose is to bring about understanding – in a rich, wide sense. To be religiously illiterate is to be as ill-educated as if one were restricted in numeracy or literacy. RE lessons are not an extension of the parish church; teaching RE does not make one a missionary. The distinction commonly drawn between nurture and education can be argued over for hours, but it remains helpful in emphasising that educators want children to grasp as well as possible what it must be like 'to stand in a believer's shoes'; nurture, however, intends to bring a child to belief.

Many teachers have personal relations with the Christian tradition, some positive, some negative; some are deeply-committed believers, others have either renounced connections or are indifferent. But if it is important that children grow up understanding the real world – which has a *very* substantial degree of religious motivation – then teachers can help understanding grow even if they are not believers or specialists themselves. Indeed, one of the features of the most-praised kind of educational practice is that the teacher is a learner alongside the child; the teacher is a specialist in children and their learning, not necessarily in academic disciplines. Teachers learn happily about computer programming and master the principle of *indeterminacy* if their children need it – they can also master the basic concepts, skills and attitudes needed for religious literacy.

Everyone can do it: it's all a question of intention.

Once it is clear that Christianity figures in the curriculum because it is *there* in the real world, because it shapes people's lives, because it features in the news, because it affects the environment, because it produces music and art and architecture and for a host of other reasons which *demand* exploration and understanding, then anyone interested in children's development can freely explore this religious tradition with them, not to convince or convert them, but to help them understand the world around them and so to grow themselves.

A place to begin

So where may one start? On the whole the answer is 'Wherever Christianity is seen as a *living* faith'. Some people start with 'origins', but that approach is fraught with difficulties connected with how one may properly use biblical material and anyway is more likely to be an historical study rather than religious education as described above. A helpful place to begin is by asking how a religious tradition helps to nurture its own children into faith. In this case, children frequently learn within their family what Christian faith is by the rounded calendar which brings to the forefront of their experience central features of faith.

'Christianity' doesn't exist

Someone may immediately object that this or that practice is not their experience of Christianity and their objection raises an important question for the teacher – what *kind* of Christianity is she or he to teach about? Even within Britain there is an immense variety of Christian churches – and variety is one of the features of this tradition which needs to be explored. Christians belong to a family of religious traditions whose differences are frequently so profound that it is misleading to speak of 'Christianity' without acknowledging at the same time that diversity is of its essence. The 'typical' Christian is a young Latin American Roman Catholic girl – and what unites her to all other Christians of whatever sort is that *they respond in life and worship* to Jesus's 'story'. This 'story' is usually brought to mind by a calendar of festivals and a lectionary, that is, an associated sequence of Bible readings. Orthodox, Catholic and Protestant may have different calendars, but their purpose is the same – to involve believers in responding to Jesus's story: this involvement is as much 'being' and 'doing' as it is 'believing'.

A developmental approach

If most Christian children grow up sharing in and responding to an annual re-presenting, a bringing to mind of key features of Jesus's story, this fact offers an entry point for a teacher who wants her children to begin to understand the Christians. One good educational 'fact' immediately stands out: *within* the tradition there is scope for a spiral curriculum. The calendar allows people to respond *at their own level* to this annual round and allows them to develop, to grow as year succeeds year and they discover new meaning in the story. A four-year-old at the crib will see things differently from a forty-year-old saintly scholar. So the calendar encourages a developmental approach and in the classroom a seven-year-old *should* be seeing different things in Christmas from an eleven-year-old's view of it; how can this be?

The calendar approach to understanding Christianity can be split into two parts; the first looks at key festivals, the second at how one may use the Bible in relation to those festivals.

Exploring festivals

If you want to grasp what a faith tradition believes is important about itself then attend to what it celebrates and Christians *celebrate* Easter both annually and each Sunday; it is their *key* festival. They say that without Easter there would be no Christianity. Consequently, this is a festival which needs to be explored in a spiral fashion.

As with most festivals one can explore what is going on in Easter celebrations by taking it to pieces:

- by asking what kind of celebrating takes place, where, with whom – and why *this* kind of celebrating
- by asking what stories Christians tell at this time, where, how
- by asking what symbols are associated with this festival, how they relate to the story/ies and to celebration
- by asking what meaning(s) are carried by the story and symbols and celebration. What a festival does for a believer is not something separate from the festival but part of its essence.

Celebrating a festival

The kind of celebrating to be reported depends on the Christians being looked at. From a very early stage in the Church's life the week leading up to Easter was given a special place; Easter made sense only in the light of the Cross which itself made sense only in the light of the life that preceded it and the Easter that followed it. (Here is a warning to us not to isolate a festival and 'do it' without allowing it to speak as *part of a whole*.) Some Christians make much of the week; their churches' decoration reflects the week's happenings; they mark sacred time and events, for example on Maundy Thursday they re-present both Jesus's Last Supper and its relation to his command 'to serve one another'; they may follow the path to the cross; they may keep watch during the three hours of Jesus's crucifixion on 'God's Friday'; they may keep watch through the Saturday night to wait expectantly for the rejoicing of Easter dawn. Easter is about far more than chocolate eggs, woolly lambs and new bonnets!

The stories of a festival

The stories Christians tell at Easter are those told by the Gospel writers. The Bible in a junior school is most safely used in relation to what Christians actually do with it. Questions about its historicity or about its puzzling aspects can be dealt with in the context of one's purposes in RE, not to convert or to defend a position but to foster understanding. Of course there are fascinating questions about the existence of four (or six) accounts of the Resurrection and persisting puzzlement about an empty tomb. These are matters about which Christians continue lively debate both among themselves and with others. Some of this can be handled at the top end of a junior school where a problem-solving approach to questions of Christian origins can have both an invigorating and liberating effect. What have the writers' accounts of the Resurrection appearances in common? What are their differences? Why? At a simple level answers to these questions can begin to show evangelists as writers with a distinctive story to tell, the central concerns of each and those they share. But far more importantly it allows the stories to emerge in their own right while at the same time giving them the context that Christians give them. All of this adds to a growing understanding of Jesus's 'story'.

Using 'Bible stories' in a junior school has often been problematic, starting with the problem of what to choose. Each festival has its own associated stories; here is guide enough to begin with. More importantly each story conveys central Christian concepts, usually in a concrete way. At the younger end of the school the stories can be told – but as Christians tell them and not in some way distorted by the teller's views. Just as descriptions of Easter celebrations can grow more detailed as children grow older – allowing them to explore why this, why that – so stories can be explored in greater depth and their concepts laid bare.

Symbols in a festival

Festivals usually have symbols associated with them – symbols are language without words. A cross somehow 'stands for' the events of Good Friday and carries a weight of meaning for Christians. Bread and wine are symbols exploited by Jesus at the Last Supper and a bowl and towel also carry a story and convey meaning. The brightly coloured eggs cracked open by Orthodox Christians symbolise the opened tomb of Jesus in a way that fluffy yellow chicks on a chocolate egg do not! And why is baptism strongly associated with Easter? Water symbolises not only much of Jesus's life but also that of his disciples. Of course, branches of the Church celebrate Easter in various ways, some 'weaker' than others, and this says much about the nature of the tradition, offering material for exploration – why is this so? What made these differences and why were they important?

The innerness of festivals

Festivals carry a weight of meaning for Christians – not something *added to* festivals but carried by them in the way they are celebrated, in the stories told to form and convey concepts and in the symbols that can renew themselves. This question of meaning is frequently misunderstood. An article in *Child Education*, December 1987, 'The Inside Story', was headed 'Religious observance is only an external display. If our teaching is to have real meaning for children, we must help them towards spiritual understanding too.' That is simply to perpetuate a gross misunderstanding of religious faith; the use of 'only' gives away a defective view. Millions of believers would have been astonished to learn that what went on inside them was divorced from their celebration. Of course, it *can* be, but is not necessarily so! One way of getting at what a festival means for a believer is to ask her or him to answer children's questions or to talk about it – but choose the visitor carefully and prepare well.

Another way is to look at the hymns they sing or the prayers they use; what this event (Easter) means 'for me' and 'my response' to it come across clearly. This puts the 'innerness' firmly into this approach to Christianity – and helps a child begin to grasp what it might mean to stand in a believer's shoes.

Which festivals?

If we begin where Christian nurture appears to begin, namely with a calendar of festivals and associated stories, then it simply remains to identify which festivals to explore. Easter, certainly, and Holy Week; Christmas, yes, but carefully detached from the secular hubbub which may well have infiltrated a school from its social context! Christians tend also to value Pentecost highly. A list of festivals can be gleaned from, for example, an Alternative Service Book; local Christians can be consulted to find their priorities. Using the four-fold model outlined above each of the festivals can be explored for its innerness as well as its shape and content.

Buildings also tell a story

That is not all. Christians worship in churches – both buildings and communities. Each has its own story to tell. As houses for living, faithful communities church buildings are frequently rich sources of symbols that tell the Christian story without words. What is the table or altar for? Why a lectern – and why *this* particular style? What do these windows say? Why a font here? Or why a baptistry here? A symbol search can also be rewarding. And don't forget the graveyard; what do its inscriptions tell us about Christian attitudes to life and death? It can be helpful to invite a member of the local community to share in sessions about the church; not necessarily the clergyman or minister – but certainly someone who relates well with children and has taken the trouble to be au fait with details. There are, at the other end of a Christian spectrum, meeting places devoid, or nearly devoid, of symbol or decoration – why? Which point leads us to the next – *use* local Christian communities, cultivate good contacts who can talk about their faith and its expression in worship and indicate how it *affects their lives*, both *communally* and *individually*, socially and liturgically.

Some gains

A teacher who is able to adopt a third-party stance, who can report what Christians do and feel and say, who can herself or himself go on learning alongside children will be able to help them to grasp the central features of

101

Christian responses to Jesus's story as it unfolds in celebration. A third-party stance or 'open' approach frees both teacher and taught from any hint of somehow *being* Christian; it may be that some teachers *are* Christian, but their task in a county school is to foster, not nurture, understanding of a larger Christianity than their own community's perception. Those with no religious commitment are freed from pretending to commend Christianity and are obliged to understand what it is to be a believer. Teachers committed to faiths other than Christianity are invited to hold dialogue with it and to share their growing understanding with those they teach. The letter of the 1988 Act can be enlivened by the spirit of the RE that has been patiently worked out over many years. If this hopeful message can be spread then educators can get on with helping children grow through good, open RE.

Bibliography

A. Brown, *The Christian World* (Macdonald, 1984)
A. Brown (ed.), *The Shap Handbook on World Religions in Education* (CRE, 1987)
P. Curtis, *Christianity* (Lutterworth, 1986)
Mary Hayward, 'Christian Festivals' in C. Erricker (ed.), *Teaching Christianity: A World Religions Approach* (Lutterworth, 1987)
Mary Hayward, 'Teaching Christianity: Process and Purpose' in the same volume of essays mentioned above.

All of these offer a great deal in an immediate way. Mary Hayward's essays focus on what might be done; Peter Curtis and Alan Brown offer two very different books, the former directed to a process of teaching, the latter an information book which well deserved its literary prize. Alan Brown (ed.), *The Shap Handbook on World Religions in Education* is a mine of information and should be in every school.

Clive Erricker's *Teaching Christianity* is essential for those who want to take seriously the business of 'teaching Christianity'. It is a collection of essays on a wide range of topics, theoretical as well as intensely practical. Among them these resources point to many others.

CHAPTER 13

Teaching Hinduism in the junior school

KEN OLDFIELD

Junior school children delight in Hinduism. It is not just the sheer kaleido-scope of colour and variety that dazzles them, they seem to identify intuitively with the notion of oneness or wholeness which lies at the heart of the tradition.

Junior school teachers seem far more hesitant. The variety intimidates and the sophistication and complexity of the mythology and the philosophy present apparently insuperable barriers. Behind it all, for many brought up in a protestant tradition, there is the fear of images and worries about the caste system. Shouldn't Hinduism really be left to the secondary school?

Why teach Hinduism?

In multifaith, multicultural Britain, Hinduism has an important place in the life of the junior school. As a foundation religion, Hinduism has given rise to and influenced Buddhism, Jainism and Sikhism and an understanding of aspects of Hinduism will enable our children to appreciate something of these other traditions, all of which are well represented now in the UK.

One attractive definition of Hinduism is that it is 'the rhythm of life of the people of India' and it is important that at some time in their junior schooling pupils study the largest democracy in the world which is home for 700 million people and which dominates the politics of South Asia. No study of India can ignore the Hindu tradition which permeates the life of all the people of the subcontinent whether Hindu or Muslim, Sikh or Jain, Parsee or Christian. As the ninth leading industrial nation in the world and one which has long had a special relationship with Britain, it must not be omitted from the curriculum of the junior school.

There are now about 380 000 British Hindus living out their tradition as part of British life. Introducing juniors to Hindu thinking and ways of looking at the world is an important part of our commitment to a multicultural, anti-racist curriculum. If this pluralist democracy, as Swann calls Britain today, is going to succeed, then it is essential that all our children leave school with some understanding of what it means to be a Hindu, Sikh, Muslim, Jew, Jain, Buddhist and Christian. That work cannot be left until secondary schooling. The foundations must be set in the junior school.

Understanding Brahman

But where to start? It is true that on the surface Hinduism appears complex and varied, and we have to acknowledge that we are never going to succeed in sharing fully with juniors the ocean of information about any major religious tradition. There is a great need for selectivity concentrating on the character, or if you like, the 'feel' and 'flavour' of the tradition, to set the foundations for more detailed study in the secondary school.

At the heart of the Hindu tradition is the concept of *Brahman*, – the Impersonal Absolute or World Soul which pervades the whole universe. Language like that hardly seems appropriate for juniors! Yet the concept is one easily shared with that age group, if expressed through the parables and images of some of Hinduism's most ancient spiritual writings – the Upanishads which have been beautifully translated by Alistair Shearer and Peter Russell. Hindus believe that there are four stages to life, and the first stage in which our junior children find themselves is that of the student. In the student stage, Hindus are obedient to their parents and teachers. In ancient times children not much older than our pupils went into the forest to learn the scriptures from brahmin teachers. They learned the Vedas ('The Knowledge') off by heart. The Upanishads relate the story of a boy called Svetaketu who proudly returned home having gained 'the knowledge' only to find when questioned by his father that he did not understand the nature of *Brahman*. His father (and we can do this in school very easily) called for a glass of water and told his son to put some salt in the water. The next day, he asked his son where the salt was. Svetaketu could not see the salt but he tasted it in all the water in the glass. That's how *Brahman* is in the world, the father tells his son. If before telling this story you have lit a joss stick and it has finished burning, the same illustration can be repeated in terms of smell. The whole room and even our bodies (well our lungs, certainly) have been permeated with a smell which cannot be seen, yet which is undeniably present. This is one of the ways that Hindus understand *Brahman*.

In another parable the father asks his son to cut open a fig, and again we can enact this with our children with almost any fruit. What is to be found inside? When one of the many seeds is cut open what can we find? In the Upanishadic story the boy sees nothing and the father tells his son that from the very nothingness a great tree has grown. That nothingness, that mystery which lies at the heart of all life is *Brahman*, the reality at the heart of the universe. There is an impressive piece of video called *The Fall of Freddie the Leaf* which celebrates the mystery of life and death through the life cycle of a leaf; this well serves our purpose in illustrating this idea more fully for this age group and helps young children appreciate the way Hindus see life as a cyclical process of birth, life, death and rebirth.

The final Upanishadic picture of *Brahman* which helps juniors to gain an understanding of what Hindus believe about the divine requires a pot of honey. Exploring where that honey has come from and the agents which have brought it into being can be very rewarding in all kinds of ways. Not just the bees and the flowers (How many bees? How many flowers?) but the people who have tended the bees and extracted the honey and how that honey becomes a part of our sweetness demonstrate the interlocking network of life which reflects the oneness or wholeness Hindus see binding us all together as part of *Brahman*.

Once the nature of *Brahman* has been established everything else follows on naturally. Hindus can find *Brahman* in the whole of life. Many gods, some in human form, some half human and half animal, some animal, rivers and seas, mountains and plants all display aspects of *Brahman* to be reverenced and respected. Exploring the images of the Hindu gods and looking at the cow, the river Ganges and the tulsi plant as symbols of the divine affords tremendous opportunities for art work, all giving expression to the unity of the universe (see *Hindu Gods and Goddesses: Aspects of the Divine One*). It also affords ways into talking about vegetarianism (the diet of most, but not all Hindus), non-violence and conservation, and the gentleness and reverence for all life which Hindus display.

Activities on a 'Hindu Day'

When a local Berkshire junior school approached me asking for help in arranging 'A Hindu Day' in their school, I was initially anxious about the possibility of tokenism in their approach. The staff assured me that the day would be a whole school experience which would form a foundation for future work, but that they needed some stimulus and outside help. We planned carefully and went ahead with the day which proved a great success.

All the children were asked to look at where their clothes had been made and if they had Indian clothes, to wear them on the day. Virtually everyone had some clothes that had been made in India. The teachers wore saris or kurta pajammas and throughout the day there was Indian music playing in the school.

A Hindu priest visited the school for the day, which fortuitously fell on Lord Ram's birthday. During the assembly we talked about the Hindu gods, especially Lord Shiva, The Lord of the Dance. We had a beautiful brass image of Shiva dancing and we talked about how this showed aspects of what

Brahman was like. Then the children sang 'The Lord of the Dance' for their Hindu priest visitor. In return he showed them how he worshipped Ram on the special day of Ram's birthday. He performed the *arti* ceremony. Then he made his prayer to Ram while the children listened and watched. It was a beautiful and moving prayer that all the children of the world and especially all the children of Colleton School might be blessed with the courage and the strength of Ram, stand up for good and right and remain loyal to their parents and friends. The children had learned another song about light which they sang as a way of saying thank you to the Hindu priest for showing them how he worshipped. To me this was a beautiful act of worship. The children had not worshipped Ram, and nobody's integrity had been infringed. Yet they had witnessed an act of worship and had expressed their thanks for that privilege in Christian songs which moved the Hindu priest as much as his prayer moved many present. Matters of worth were being shared.

After the assembly the youngest children spent time with me looking at slides of a day in the life of a young child in India. I have shown these slides many times, but never to infants before, and I have rarely experienced such rigorous questioning about every detail in the pictures.

The middle team spent time cooking. Some prepared Indian bread, chapatis, puris and paratas. Others cooked dal and a vegetable curry. They talked about the spices and the smells. When all was ready, they toured the school offering a taste of Indian food to everyone and asking for a response. The pappadoms were universally well received and the breads popular. The dal and the vegetable curry was a new experience for most children and not all responded well!

The older team split into three. One group set about producing a large map of India giving details of the mountains, the rivers and the towns. Others set to work producing group paintings of the Hindu gods, especially Ram, Shiva and Hanuman. The third group, working with their new friend, the Hindu priest, set about dramatising the story of Ram for the younger children.

After lunch we all joined together again. Jugnu Singh, an Indian storyteller, introduced his Indian puppets to the children and used them to tell the story of the Ramayana. (The Rani and Jugnu Singh Children's Theatre Company can be contacted through the RE Centre at the West London Institute of Higher Education, Lancaster House, Borough Road, Isleworth, Middlesex TW7 5DU.) As the story unfolded he gradually involved the children in it, with many joining the army of Hanuman whilst others enlisted in the forces of Ravana as the story moved to the great climax of the battle between good and evil.

After the puppets, the children who had produced the huge map of India talked about the vastness of the sub-continent. Then the painters of the gods showed their work, explaining what aspects of *Brahman* each picture displayed. Finally the older team performed their version of the Ramayana.

It was a marvellous day for everyone. One mother told me afterwards that her son had arrived home from school and for 25 minutes had recounted the great Indian epic, the Ramayana, in minute detail. The shared experience of the whole school and the atmosphere it generated served as a reference point for all the teachers, enabling them to pursue various aspects of it appropriate to their age group, especially in their language work, both oral and written.

This is but one example of how setting the foundations for studying Hinduism may be approached in the junior school. There are many more possibilities. Recently, I had the privilege of accompanying a group of junior children to a Hindu temple in north London. The questions asked and the answers recorded provided the foundations of a very different, but equally successful, approach to the tradition.

Resources

We now have excellent resources for developing programmes of work in this area, not least from the BBC *Watch* series which in autumn 1988 devoted five programmes to the Ramayana. The accompanying notes for the programmes and the book *The Amazing Adventures of Hanuman* suggest all kinds of opportunities for Indian storytelling. Perhaps the best book of Indian stories currently available is *Seasons of Splendour*, which with its marvellous illustrations by Michael Foreman, affords a beautiful selection of stories, many of which relate directly to the major festivals of Hinduism.

Whilst festivals can be used as a way into the Hindu tradition I have deliberately left them until last because they are very complex and can, if overused at the junior level, create a confusing impression of the tradition. Some junior schools are in danger of making their RE a calendar of festivals, which whilst being colourful and varied, often fails to penetrate the inner meaning which the outward celebrations clothe. Gaining an understanding of what Hindus understand by *Brahman* is more important than an annual celebration of *Diwali*, a festival which is in danger of being as little understood as Christmas or Easter! Do see *Religions through Festivals: Hinduism* however, which sets a range of festivals in their wider context and concentrates on Hindu children in Britain.

For teachers keen to think through their approach to teaching Hinduism in the junior school, a most comprehensive and detailed volume in the World Religions in Education series, *Approaches to Hinduism* is available with full resource lists and many creative suggestions for approaching Hinduism with younger children.

Capturing and sharing the richness of the Indian tradition with younger children can be a source of much delight and thoughtful reflection on the nature of life, death and the divine. Story, music, dance, drama, cooking, art and visits or visitors can combine to enrich our work not just in religious education but right across the curriculum.

Bibliography

Patricia Bahree, *The Hindu World* (Macdonald)

Robert Jackson and Dermot Killingley, *Approaches to Hinduism* (John Murray, 1988)

Robert Jackson and Dermot Killingley, *Moral Issues in the Hindu Tradition* (Trentham Books, 1990)

Robert Jackson and Eleanor Nesbitt, *Listening to Hindus* (Unwin Hyman, 1990)

Robert Jackson, *Religions through Festivals: Hinduism* (Longman, 1989)

Madhur Jaffrey, *Seasons of Splendour* (Puffin, 1985)

V. P. (Hemant) Kanitkar, *Hinduism* (Wayland, 1986)

Ken Oldfield, *Hindu Gods and Goddesses: Aspects of the Divine One* (CEM, 1987)

Linda Shansom, *Journey with the Gods* (Mantra, 1987)

Alistair Shearer and Peter Russell (trans.), *The Upanishads* (Wildwood House, 1978)

Rani and Jugnu Singh, *The Amazing Adventures of Hanuman* (BBC, 1988)

Rani Singh, *The Indian Storybook* (Heinemann)

Regional RE Centre, Westhill College, Birmingham, *Hinduism: Resource Material* (1988)

Posters on a variety of Hindu topics are available from Pictorial Charts Education, 27 Kirchen Road, West Ealing, London W13 0UD

The video *The Fall of Freddie the Leaf* is available from Educational Media International, 235 Imperial Drive, Rayner's Lane, Harrow, HA2 7HE.

Slide sets on many aspects of Hinduism are available from Bury Peerless, 22 King's Avenue, Minnis Bay, Birchington on Sea, CT7 9QL.

CHAPTER 14

Islam in the classroom

VIDA BARNETT

The beliefs, practices and stories of Islam help Muslims articulate and respond to universal questions – Who am I? Why should I? What can I do? Actions, symbols, artefacts, stories can all lead to relevant discussions which are very meaningful. Teacher and student walk a little way along their own personal journey or *Hajj*.

Shared discovery may entail a slightly different emphasis from one of commitment in mosque and home. The Muslim child will first learn the prayer positions, then the times and names of prayer which are fundamental to his or her experience as he/she watches and participates in ordinary family life. When sharing, however, the prayer mat will raise questions concerning prayer, invoke discussions about the meaning of short prayers, of everyone's need and source of help. The meaning of the act of washing, of standing close together in brotherhood, and the closing action of 'Peace' is more important than the learning of the five positions. Herein lies relevance, not in the acting out of the ritual. By the same token, objects and artefacts used in worship can trigger interest and enquiry among non-Muslims, but for Muslims they are never more than objects and aids: the spiritual intention comes first.

Relevant teaching depends on the use of actual prayers, quotations, reminiscenses, stories. For many teachers this will prove a problem and challenge. The short examples given here will, I hope, give a sense of 'first base' security and form the basis of an on-going collection of resources.

Where can we begin?

'Today, Muslim boys and girls all over the world are celebrating a festival.'

Assemblies on important days are a useful way of introducing a religion, but some teachers may prefer a gentler path, integrating the material with well-trodden themes.

Creation: the world about us

Television, sophisticated games, the microscope and beautifully illustrated books lead children to an awareness of the magnificence of space or an insect's wing. Who made the world? Who made us? Does it matter how we treat our world? The Qur'an frequently affirms the wonder of creation, insisting that it points to a Creator, that everything is a gift to humankind, His greatest creation.

> He raised the canopy of heaven . . . He laid the expanse of the earth, bringing forth waters and pastures therein He made the hills to be a joy to you.
>
> *Surah 5: 27–31*

A Muslim writer speaks of the earth with its people, skyscrapers, mountains, mines, plains, oceans whirling round its axis at 684 000 miles per hour – yet we do not feel movement – and don't fall off! 'It is easier to count the particles of sand on all the seashores of the world than count the numbers of heavenly bodies!' (Mohammed Zia Ullah, *Islamic Concept of God*). Carefully re-phrased, such occasional examples may stand beside a description of the birth of a baby kangaroo (Gerald Durrell, *Two in a Bush*), and Islam is absorbed into a meaingful, question-raising curriculum.

Who am I?

The Qur'an affirms that Allah created us – with a purpose. We are regents, the gift of the created world placed in our trust, to use wisely for the good of everyone, without exploitation. 'Whatever is harmful and is intended for a harmful purpose should not be manufactured or produced.' (Abdul Wahid Hamid, *Islam: The Natural Way*). The next topic follows naturally.

Caring: my neighbour: what should I do – and why?

Muhammad (peace be upon him)[1] often spoke of our treatment of animals. Whilst sheltering in a garden, he saw a camel tethered in the hot sun, obviously hungry and badly treated. 'Who is the owner? God gave this camel into your care to help carry your goods. As Khalifa, protector of God's gifts to you, you should treat it well.'

A woman who disliked the Prophet swept dust over him each morning as he went to the mosque. One day she was nowhere to be seen. Unlike his friends, he did not rejoice. 'Where is she?' He discovered that she was ill and had no one to care for her. Each day he brought her food and water and lit her fire before going to pray. He said:

> No man is a true believer unless he desires for his brother what he desires for himself . . . helping . . . guiding the blind, striving as far as your two legs can carry you . . . to succour him who asks.

The way is now clear for more specific topics.

Zakat and Sadaqah

If sources of wealth remain after normal everyday expenses have been met it is obligatory to give a proportion as *zakat*, charity – usually 2½ per cent (or more). They must give gifts to others as Allah has given gifts to them. Equally *all* Muslims should practice charity every day, helping others in any way they can. It may be a smile, or the giving of time. This is *sadaqah*, a sharing of all one has.

Should we all practise *zakat and sadaqah* – and how? Agency and newspaper materials can be collected, posters drawn, stories or poems composed. Organise a work experience project – invite the dinner ladies to a class concert, clear a piece of waste ground, take cards and cakes to children in a school for those with special needs. If money is collected, consider collecting it for a Muslim country where there is need.

Favourite Books

Why do people write books? What are our favourite books? Why? How do we treat them? For some people, the Scripture is the special book. Why? How is a Qur'an handled and why? To show its importance and difference it is placed above other books and kept wrapped. Washing hands before touching symbolises the hope that its reading will help 'cleanse' the reader's life, and the taking of time emphasises the desire to think about and care about its reading – as does the practice of some Muslims of placing it three times to forehead and lips before reading. We must emphasise that this is symbolism – not superstition. Water, wet tissues, a clean hankie, or sand in the desert are equally acceptable for washing, depending on the situation. The agnostic teacher will handle it carefully as a mark of respect, but perhaps only the teacher who believes in God, in Muhammad (p.b.u.h.) as a man of God, will demonstrate the kissing of the book.

Always recite a verse, an *ayah* when opening a Qur'an. 'God is light.' Look at beautiful pictures of Qur'ans, with geometric and arabesque designs (not people) and fascinating calligraphy. Why spend so much time? Let children select from a few simple verses – 'Guide us on the straight path', and copy and decorate them with geometric or arabesque patterns.

Visiting the mosque

After a little exploration of Islam, children can draw up a list of questions to ask their guide (often more useful than a 'work-card') thus giving the guide a relevant framework within which to speak. 'Do you sleep in a bed?' 'Have you got a Qur'an?' 'Why do you come to the mosque?' They may like to give gifts that they have made – decorated prayers, Qur'anic *ayahs*, cards, prayer mats. Some mosques might be persuaded to mount a small exhibition in the entrance hall! In the classroom, tell how Bilal, a freed Abyssinian slave, was chosen to make the first call to prayer from the roof of the newly built mosque in Madinah. What did he say? Why? How would he feel? (See *Bilal* by H. A. L. Craig.)

A visitor in school

Questions can be further explored with the help of a visitor to the classroom, but have such questions ready beforehand. Make them very specific. 'How did you say your prayers this morning?' 'What is your favourite Qur'anic reading?' A mother, bringing her baby into the classroom can describe his or her naming ceremony. Thus Islam becomes 'real', an everyday activity, not something strange. Now festivals and special occasions can take their rightful place.

Muhammad's birthday

Any stories relating to the Prophet are appropriate, but as we cannot draw the Prophet, illustrations should relate to other people acting in ways of which he would approve. Perhaps a description would be helpful.

> 'Anas' ibn Malik says that the Prophet of Allah had a moderate stature, being neither very tall nor very short. His person was finely symmetrical and the hair of his head was neither very curly nor very straight, his complexion was tawny.' Another follower said: 'In speech he was more truthful than all other men: by nature he was gentler than all . . . Whoever came to know him . . . could not help loving him.' He was called *Al-Amin*, the Trustworthy.

Ramadan/food and fasting/going without

Although *not* a festival, the month of *Ramadan* relates to the two festivals which follow. The children's discussions, posters, pictures, poems, can:

1   Explore what people don't choose to go without – houses, education, health care, playgrounds, food, clothes.
2   Explore what we *can* choose to go without and why: Muslims fast to

identify with the starving, to remind them of their responsibility to help others, and to learn discipline so that they can refuse to do other things, for example steal.

3   Explore what we do with the things we choose to go without, however small.

We can *all* give up *time* to help, visit, make things. It isn't good to ask our children to go without food themselves, but a five minute delay at 'breaktime', counted out by the clock, can help the younger ones understand, and everyone can be encouraged to make it easy for Muslim children trying to go without sweets, crisps, etc.

The Night of Power/special books

During *Ramadan*, Muslims give up their time to read the Qur'an more often. Many try to read it all before the end of the month. Again, short *ayahs* can be chosen and illustrated, the story of the first revelation on this night carefully told, and 'special' books discussed.

Eid-ul-Fitr/parties

If there are Muslim children in the class, remember to celebrate the following day when they are at school. All children can remember Muslim boys and girls throughout the world and wish them 'Happy Eid – *Eid Mubarak*,' just as they would wish their friends, 'Happy Birthday'. Dinner ladies will often make 'Indian' sweets (or the children can do so themselves). Design cards with a picture or message emphasising something *we* have given up, or tried to give up, for example our time. Visit the dinner ladies, the caretaker, thank them for giving up their time. Invite children from a special needs school for a party. Visit a school where there are Muslim children. Now the way is clear for an extended topic, gathering up what has been learned earlier.

Hajj/pilgrimage/journeys/doing without

A straightforward account of *Hajj* (pilgrimage to Makkah) is inadequate and may raise only superficial questions – 'Don't they get trampled on?' – or even derision and disgust – 'Stoning pillars! Killing all those animals!'

How do Muslims prepare for *Hajj*? Money must be saved, journeys planned, provision made for those at home. So much must be sacrificed even before they leave. Why? It is these sacrifices which form part of relevant shared discussion, not the ritual killing at the end. Pack a suitcase. This can remind us of work on prayer, prayer mats and beads, the Qur'an etc. as we pack these as well as our pyjamas. Different groups can explore different articles and mount a wall collage. Discuss the prayers said as you set out:

> Allah . . . look after the family, the property, the children. I do not start this journey because of hypocrisy, reputation but . . . seeking your grace, fulfilling my duty to Thee and following the way of Your Prophet, and the longing to meet Thee.

These can be calligraphically displayed over drawings of Makkah. Personal reminiscences are invaluable, but can also be culled from books:

> I walked on and on, all that had been bitter in my heart began to leave my heart . . . O Allah, Thou art Peace, from Thee Peace . . . Greet us Lord with Peace.

> On the far side of the courtyard, beneath the broad roof supported by hundreds of pale blue, green and gold columns were gathered thousands upon thousands of the faithful. Some were praying, some reciting the Qur'an, some meditating: others stretched asleep on the carpets or the marble.

A blank screen, then a slide suddenly filling the screen and a taped call to prayer can help children imagine the impact of the first sight of the city. Information can lead to 'What do you think a boy or girl of your age would feel? How and why is it important?' The well of Zam-zam can contribute to a theme on water and raise questions about the importance of souvenirs. Standing before the Mount of Mercy can introduce discussions of Forgiveness, the Special Book and the life of Muhammad (p.b.u.h.). An *Eid-ul-Adha* party can celebrate the lives of people who try to help others, people like Muhammad (p.b.u.h.), and can celebrate the ability to acknowledge wrong doing and the willingness to forgive. Cards echoing these sentiments made, and presented to parents and governors with explanatory words, may bring support for what we are trying to do. They might perhaps tell of the man who went to say good-bye to his neighbour, and found that he and his family were starving. The pilgrim gave him his hard earned savings and stayed at home – but fellow pilgrims *saw* him in Makkah! As the juniors complete their journey through the land of Islam may I wish them 'A Successful Hajj'.

Notes

Muslims repeat 'Peace be upon him' after the name of important prophets, for example, Jesus, Muhammad.

Bibliography

For teachers

Leila Azzam, Aisha Gouverneur, *The Life of the Prophet Muhammed* (Islamic Texts Society, 1985)

H. A. L. Craig, *Bilal* (Quartet, 1977)
Riadh El-Droubie, Islamic Correspondence Course: *Pilgrimage, Qur'an and Hadith, Fasting, Zakat* (Minaret's House, 9 Leslie Park Road, Croydon CRO 6TN)
Abdul Wahid Hamid, *Islam: The Natural Way* (Mels, 1989)
Richard Tames, *Approaches to Islam* (John Murray, 1982)
Ghulam Sarwar, *Islam, Beliefs and Teachings* (Muslim Educational Trust, 1984)
Mohammed Zia Ullah, *Islamic Concept of God* (KPI, 1984)

For pupils

Books suitable for lower juniors are indicated by L. Those for upper juniors are marked U.
Manju Aggarwal, *I am a Muslim* (Franklin Watts, 1984) U
M. M. Ahsan, *Muslim Festivals* (Wayland, 1985) U
Olivia Bennett, *A Busy Weekend* (Hamish Hamilton, 1984) U
Alan Brine, *Religion through Festivals: Islam* (Longman, 1989)
Gerald Durrell, *Two in a Bush* (Penguin, 1977) U
M. S. Kayani, *A Great Friend of Children* (Islamic Foundation, 1981) U
Khurram Murad, *Love at Home* (Islamic Foundation, 1983) U
Joan Solomon, *Gifts and Almonds* (Hamish Hamilton, 1980) L
Joan Solomon, *Shabnam's Day Out* (Hamish Hamilton, 1980) L
Jenny Wood, *Our Culture–Muslim* (Franklin Watts, 1988) L

Catalogues are available from:
Articles of Faith (Artefacts), Sacred Trinity Centre, Chapel Street, Salford, Manchester M3 7AJ
Iqra Trust, 24 Culross Street, London W13 0UD
The Islamic Cultural Centre, 146 Park Road, London NW8
Pictorial Charts Education Trust, 27 Kirchen Road, London W13 0UD
Slide Centre, 143 Chatham Road, London SW11 6SR

Many mosques have artefacts, cards etc. The British Museum has postcards of Qur'ans and calligraphy. Specific enquiries can be made to Shap Advisory and Information Officer, 81 St Mary's Road, Huyton, Liverpool L36 5SR.

CHAPTER 15

Judaism in the junior school

DOUGLAS CHARING

There can hardly be a school in Britain which has not included a component on Judaism. Especially in the days of 'comparative religion', many schools included such a section. In most cases this was nothing other than 'Judaism through Christian eyes' and in no way did justice to the richness and diversity of contemporary Judaism. Most teachers felt they were on safe and familiar territory when they tackled Judaism, or, to be more precise, 'Synagogue and Passover in the time of Jesus'. Thankfully a little progress has been made over more than a decade of teaching about world religions and a growing number of GCSE/A-level candidates have opted for the Judaism section within the Religious Studies paper. Teaching about Judaism has also become popular in junior schools and the purpose of this chapter is to encourage junior school teachers to look at aspects of Judaism in a wider context, thus offering a more lively and accurate classroom presentation.

First things first

Jews and the Jewish religion have been on the British scene for many centuries. In the late nineteenth century new synagogues were being opened almost weekly somewhere in Britain. Jews became the largest non-Christian religious group, a position now held by Muslims. At the same time, a host of Jewish institutions was founded. Welfare Boards, educational centres, cultural societies, trade unions sprung up wherever a Jewish community was established. Although the majority of these Jews hailed from eastern European countries such as Russia and Poland, it would be wrong to think of Jews as only white and European.

For many reasons the Jewish population is a shrinking one. Communities which once had synagogues no longer have them. Those that remain are much smaller and very often no longer have the services of a rabbi or minister. Of course, there are areas which have seen an increase in Jewish activity, but the world Jewish population is on the decline and Anglo-Jewry is no exception to this trend. Another point to note is the growth of Jewish day schools. They cater for around 20 per cent of Jewish children in this country. Thus a decline in the Jewish school population and a growth in Jewish denominational schools has meant far fewer Jewish children in the county maintained sector.

116

Where there is a Jewish child in a class, it is temping to make him or her a 'resource', but it should never be taken for granted that such a child either has a good knowledge about Judaism or has even a loyalty to the faith, since for some being born Jewish is as far as it goes.

What to teach

What aspects of Judaism should the junior school teacher pursue? Clearly many will prefer the topic approach. 'Food', 'dress' and 'buildings' are popular themes, as are 'Festivals of Light' when a class will look at *Chanukah* and *Diwali* as well as Christmas. Whilst most junior trained teachers are not RE specialists they can be helped by the many publications which exist, some of which are listed at the end of this chapter.

Topics and themes

Food: The most obvious Jewish foods to include would be *challot*, the loaves of bread used to welcome the Sabbath or Festival and *matzot*, the unleavened bread eaten during Passover. Other foods worthy of mention include the *charoset*, the mixture of apples, nuts and wine, eaten at the Passover *seder*, and *latkes*, the potato pancakes eaten during *Chanukah*. Recipes are easy to find and make, and children can easily help in the preparation as well as the eating.

Dress: The *kipa* (skull cap) and *tallit* (prayershawl) would be the most useful forms of Jewish dress to study. The children's tape, *Especially Jewish Symbols*, has two nice songs about these two items. See the bibliography for further details.

Buildings: A look at different synagogues can make an interesting study. There is also the possibility of looking at the *succah*, the temporary building used during the autumn harvest festival of *Succot*.

Language: What tends to unite Jews the world over is their use of Hebrew. Most Jews outside Israel have a limited knowledge, normally restricted to synagogue prayers. However 'learning' another language can be a lot of fun for young children, especially when the letters are so different from the familiar English ones. Children will enjoy drawing some of the letters, learning some words and even making coded messages. For example:

Hebrew		*English*
mi	=	who
who	=	he
he	=	she

There are many stories about the Hebrew alphabet and there is also a lively poster, so although you may not create many Hebrew scholars, RE can still be a fun period.

Celebrations: Children should be made aware that being religious is not all gloom and doom, as some parents (and teachers) believe. Judaism abounds with special days, most of which are joyful occasions. Clearly one has to be selective, but any of the following could be brought into the classroom. *Rosh Hashanah* is the Jewish New Year, which usually coincides with the beginning of the new school year. Children could make New Year cards to send to an imaginary (or real) Jewish friend. They could also join in with the custom of eating apple with honey.

Simhat Torah comes at the end of the *Succot* festival and is the time when adults and children dance in the synagogue with the Torah scrolls. Children often make their own flags and learn songs to sing whilst dancing. School children can also do these things. The books, *Let's Celebrate!* and *More Let's Celebrate!* can be of great help in making flags and other items related to all Jewish festivals.

Chanukah has become very popular in British schools in recent years. Here is an opportunity for children to act out the story, even writing their own script. A human *Menorah* can be created, the children representing the individual candles. *Dreidles* can be made or purchased and the children can learn to play with them in the Jewish fashion.

Purim may be a minor festival but it is nevertheless a very popular one especially amongst young children. Again the story can be acted out in true pantomime style. *Greggors* can be made and, of course, used during the reading of the story. It may make sense to alert colleagues to the abundant noise which will inevitably encompass the entire school, if you wish to remain true to the way the story is told. Another aspect of the festival is not recommended for the junior classroom, nor for that matter, the secondary – becoming drunk!

Pesach or Passover has not lost its popularity and its story of freedom has a place in the classroom. Again acting the story, writing a *haggadah*, as well as eating all the special foods and drinking wine (better play safe and only offer soft drinks) can make this beautiful festival come alive. Other forms of celebrations can include life cycle events. Jewish weddings are colourful affairs and Jewish marriage certificates are available as cards to show the children. Customs such as drinking wine and breaking a glass can be explained and children can draw the *chuppah* (canopy) as well as the bride, groom, rabbi, etc. Another event to consider is *Bar* and *Bat Mitzvah*. Should there be a Jewish child in the class, perhaps they have an older brother or sister who has celebrated the event and can tell classmates what happened.

Stories: For centuries, indeed since Bible times, Jews have enjoyed telling stories. A whole wealth of material exists much of which is now in book form. Every school should have at least one story book which can be used both in the classroom and also in assembly/collective worship periods.

Israel: Of course Jews in this country are British citizens, but most have a special relationship and concern for the state of Israel. A number of recently published books are available to create a classroom project.

Holocaust: Perhaps some teachers will be surprised to see this as a topic. Of course it is a most difficult area to treat and it is totally understandable if teachers wish to avoid this topic. However, even young children are aware of prejudice and if racism is not explored, it may be a little late in the day to begin to look in the secondary school, since prejudice begins early in all of us. Two excellent books are available for junior school children and are included in the bibliography.

Artefacts: Most children love to see and handle unusual objects. Jewish artefacts abound and are an excellent way of explaining aspects of Judaism. Some teachers, being non-Jewish, understandably are a little unsure as to whether they should handle them. Since they will hopefully handle them in a sensitive and sympathetic way, they should relax and feel free to use them as their own treatment of them will rebound on the attitude of their pupils. Since many Jewish artefacts are expensive to purchase, especially for junior schools, a visit to the local RE Resources Centre is a must since they all have kits which can be borrowed. Some Teachers' Centres also have kits available. However since these kits are constantly in demand it is advisable to book one at least a term in advance. Try to get your PTA to purchase one for the school, then at least you have use of it when you require it. If there is a Jewish pupil in the class, perhaps she or he can bring some items from home and explain to the rest of the class how (and why) they are used.

Visits and visitors

The last decade has shown a lively interest in school visits to places of worship. Pupils have gained much from such visits and there is no doubt that they will be on the increase in future years. Clearly many schools will be some distance from a synagogue. Others will find one or more within walking distance. For those who have never organised a visit the following ground rules may prove useful:

1   To track down a synagogue in your area may not be any more difficult

than consulting your local telephone directory or even the Yellow Pages. If you have no luck, do not despair, but visit your local Reference Library and ask to see the current *Jewish Year Book*, published each January by Jewish Chronicle Publications.

2 Decide whether you wish to visit for a service (Friday evening or Saturday morning) or during the week. Although it is best to see a community in action, most schools, especially junior, will opt for a weekday visit.

3 In large cities (London, Birmingham, Manchester, Glasgow, Leeds, Liverpool) you have a choice between visiting an Orthodox or Progressive (Reform or Liberal) synagogue. In other towns the local 'Hebrew Congregation' will be Orthodox, at least in name.

4 If you decide to telephone the synagogue, do it in the morning. Most synagogues run an office with only part-time staff. Please check that it is not a Jewish festival on the day you ring. Confirm any arrangement in writing. Should your first contact be a letter, enclose a SAE. In any arrangement make clear the age and number of pupils and the name of the teacher in charge and the telephone number of the school, and possibly teacher. Find out if the synagogue requires any special dress (for example head covering for boys) and make clear the area of interest you wish the speaker to explore (for example worship or festivals).

5 Make sure you know the name of your guide or speaker. The usual title for the spiritual leader is Rabbi, but a number, especially older men in the provinces, have the title Reverend. In some synagogues a lay person will speak to school groups. Not everyone can address themselves to children, especially young children, although they may not realise this. You may even find a visit therefore becomes counter productive. You will normally come to this situation through trial and error, but there is no perfect way to avoid an unsuccessful visit.

6 Although most synagogues will be pleased to arrange visits, there are some who may refuse to entertain a school. It may be that they have no rabbi or lay person who has the time or knowledge. Others will just not be interested. Do not feel too discouraged. Try elsewhere.

7 Share your visit experience with colleagues in other classes and schools. You may wish to follow up a visit by inviting the speaker into school either for a further talk or perhaps to show them how the children have learnt a song or made a scrapbook of their visit.

8 Beware! Some synagogues do not look like synagogues. They may look more like churches, and in some cases this was what they were prior to being adapted for Jewish use. Make sure you check directions, the name of the road when making travelling arrangements; and give plenty of travelling time, so you arrive on time to make full use of your visit.

9 For many schools, however, a synagogue visit will not be possible. These schools could be tempted to find a local Jew, but beware. Just because a

person happens to be Jewish it does not follow that they are able to speak on Judaism. Even those that can may be better suited to secondary children than junior.

10   Although synagogues and most visiting local speakers make no charge, it is strongly suggested that a donation be forwarded for a favourite Jewish charity. Also travel costs should be refunded for school visitors.

The above 'ten commandments' may seem daunting but many schools have had enjoyable visits and have entertained good speakers in the classroom, so do make every effort to follow these guidelines.

Schools in the Greater London and Home Counties areas may wish to plan a visit to the Jewish Museum in Tavistock Square, near Euston. Midland and Northern schools can enjoy a stimulating visit to the Manchester Jewish Museum, housed in a former Sefardi synagogue in Cheetham Hill Road, close to Victoria Railway Station. Whatever visit you finally plan, it will greatly enrich and enhance your teaching about Judaism.

Resources

There is no problem with regard to number and availability of good books and audio-visual aids for the teaching of Judaism. Most books are published by American Jewish publishers and intended for Jewish children or adults. They are, however, just as useful in British schools, and are normally presented in an attractive format. In more recent years, British publishers have produced good quality books on world religions, and these too will be most useful in the classroom. British published books are available from educational bookshops. The majority of the material listed here is American and can be obtained from the Jewish Education Bureau Book Department, 8 Westcombe Avenue, Leeds LS8 2BS (0532 663613). Request a current catalogue, but please enclose a SAE.

Bibliography

For teachers

Louis Jacobs, *The Book of Jewish Belief* (Behrman House, 1984)
Louis Jacobs, *The Book of Jewish Practice* (Behrman House, 1987)
Steven Rosman, *Sidrah Stories* (UAHC, 1989), These are stories based on the weekly Torah portions.
Peninnah Schram, *Jewish Stories One Generation Tells Another* (Aronson, 1987)
R. Siegal, M. and S. Strassfield, *The (First) Jewish Catalog* (JPS, 1973). This is perhaps the most exciting and lively book on a number of Jewish topics. They continue in:
R. Siegal, M. and S. Strassfield, *The Second Jewish Catalog* (JPS)
R. Siegal, M. and S. Strassfield, *The Third Jewish Catalog* (JPS)

Daniel Syme, *The Jewish Home* (UHAC, 1988). This deals with festivals and life cycle events.

Leo Trepp, *A History of the Jewish Experience* (Behrman House, 1973.) This is perhaps the best one-volume book on Judiasm ever published.

Beatrice Weinreich (ed.), *Yiddish Folktales* (Pantheon, 1988)

For pupils

Material suitable for seven- to nine-year-olds is followed by the letter J, whilst S is used for material aimed at pupils between nine and eleven. Do remember this is just a selection of the material available. New items are constantly being published and some older material goes out of print.

David Adler, *The Number of my Grandfather's Arm* (UAHC, 1987) S. This is a moving account of the Holocaust.

Greer Cashman, *Jewish Days and Holidays* SBS, 1979) J

Sophia Cedarbaum, *A First Book of Jewish Holidays* (UAHC, 1984) J/S

Douglas Charing, *The Jewish World* second edition (Macdonald, 1985)

Douglas Charing, *Visiting a Synagogue* second edition (Lutterworth, 1987)

Joyce Fischman, *Let's Learn about Jewish Symbols* (UAHC, 1969) J

M. Frankel and J. Hoffman, *I Live in Israel* (Behrman House, 1979) J/S

Barbara Genet, *Ta-Poo Ach Means Apple* (ARE, 1985) J. This is an introduction to the Hebrew alphabet.

Rivka Hadary, *Focus on Israel* (Hamish Hamilton, 1988) J

Jonathon Kendall, *My Name is Rachamin* (UAHC, 1987) S. This concerns an Ethiopian Jewish boy.

Clive Lawton, *I am Jew* (Franklin Watts, 1985) J

Clive Lawton, *Matza and Bitter Herbs* (Hamish Hamilton, 1984) J

Clive Lawton, *Passport to Israel* (Franklin Watts, 1987) S

Clive Lawton, *Religion through Festivals: Judaism* (Longman, 1989) S

Gemma Levine, *We Live in Israel* (Wayland, 1981) S

Bert Metter, *Bar Mitzvah, Bat Mitzvah* (Clarion, 1984) S

B. and C. Moon, *Israel is My Country* (Wayland, 1983) J

Jose Patterson, *A Happy New Year* (Hamish Hamilton, 1987) J

Miriam Schlein, *Our Holidays* (Behrman House, 1983) J

Sybil Sheridan, *Stories from the Jewish World* (Macdonald, 1987) J/S

J. Sugarman and G. Freeman, *Inside the Synagogue* revised edition (UAHC, 1984) S

Jenny Wood, *Our Culture: Jewish* (Franklin Watts, 1988) J

Michael Weisser, *My Synagogue* (Behrman House, 1984) J

R. Zwerin and A. Friedman, *Our Synagogue* (Behrman/Winston, 1974) J. Part A deals with the synagogue, Part B with the Sabbath and Part C with Festivals. There is also a teacher's guide to accompany the book.

Kar-Ben Copies is a small American Jewish publisher which has a growing list of excellent books on Judiasm for seven- to nine-year-olds. Some of the titles, all of which are available from JEB include: *Dayenu* (Passover); *Hannukkah Cat*; *Justin's Hebrew Name*; *Matzah Meals* (a Passover cookbook for children); *Modi'in Motel* (Chanukah); *Nathan's Hanukkah Bargain*; *The Mouse in the Matzah Factory*; *The Odd Potato* (Chanukah)

They also produce *My Very Own* series on all Jewish festivals and home. Also Ruth Esrig, *Let's Celebrate!* (1977) and *More Let's Celebrate!* (1984) – each book contains 57 holiday crafts for young children.

Another Jewish American publisher is Alternatives in Religious Education. Included amongst their productions are the following three cassette tapes: *Bible People Songs, Especially Jewish*

Symbols, Especially Wonderful Days. These sing-along songs are in English with Hebrew terms. Each tape comes with a booklet containing the words and music.

The Christian Education Movement has published a set of six colour posters by Douglas Charing, depicting synagogue and home celebrations.

CHAPTER 16

Sikhism: books and stories

ELEANOR NESBITT

Books introducing Sikhism and Sikhs to junior pupils are of several types. There are traditional Sikh stories, retold in English. Some have been published in India, some in Britain. Then there are books which focus on a Sikh family, usually presenting religious belief and practice in the context of daily life in Britain. There are also information books which aim to cover Sikhism as a whole or to portray one aspect of it. Since most information books are intended for secondary school pupils, they are not covered here but are reviewed in my article listed in the bibliography. A comparable range of publications is available for introducing juniors to other world faiths and to their adherents' daily lives. I hope that this chapter encourages readers to explore not only books on Sikhism but also the wealth of published material presenting other religious traditions. Many of the points raised apply to the resourcing and teaching of other religions as well as Sikhism.

The wisdom and history of Sikh tradition

> Once, long ago, Guru Gobind Singh saw the potter's donkey struggling under a heavy load. He thought how differently the donkey would have been treated had it been a tiger . . . When he arrived home the Guru looked for the tiger skin that had once been given to him . . . [and] . . . placed the tiger skin over the unsuspecting donkey's back. As the donkey walked into the village market place he was astonished to see the goats and sheep jumping out of his way in fear. However when the villagers beat their drums to frighten the tiger back into the jungle the poor donkey was terrified. He started to bray in panic . . . the tiger skin caught on a nearby tree and the skin slipped to the ground.
>
> *(Stories from the Sikh World pp. 54–7)*

Pupils in British junior schools are as good as Guru Gobind Singh's contemporaries at seeing the point that the Guru was making. Bravery must go deeper than one's uniform. The Sikhs' ten Gurus were brilliant teachers ('Guru' means 'teacher') and our pupils will enjoy the many vivid, thought-provoking episodes from the lives of the Gurus.

The tale of the donkey in a tiger skin (abbreviated above) comes from *Stories from the Sikh World* by Rani and Jugnu Singh. This collection spans four and a half centuries of Sikh history, beginning with Guru Nanak and ending with the courage of a Sikh who brought the Dalai Lama safely to India in 1959. Every story is beautifully retold, makes a clear point and is enriched by superb illustrations.

Thanks to this book and to Ranjit Arora's *Guru Nanak and the Sikh Gurus* junior school teachers and pupils can share a few great Sikh stories – Ranjit Arora retells, for example, what happened when Guru Nanak accepted food in the house of Bhai Lala, a poor carpenter, in preference to the lavish hospitality of Malak Bhago, a rich man. In 'What makes a true Guru' we can read the story of the humble, determined devotion which was shown to the second Guru by an elderly follower whom he then chose as his successor, Guru Amar Das.

These collections are a much needed addition to literature on Sikhism for juniors. But there is plenty of other material readily available for teachers to adapt for use with children. Published in India (but available, for example, from Books from India, 45 Museum Street, London) is a series of ten books entitled *Stories from Sikh History*. Teachers will need to select carefully from this rich source (for example, many stories of Sikh persecution by Muslim oppressors are not conducive to better relations between Sikhs and Muslims) and they will also need to simplify the language, especially of the later books in the series.

Amar Chitra Katha is an Indian series which every teacher should discover. Many libraries and some book shops stock it. For instance the series is available from Books from India (see above). In the guise of comic strips each issue recreates famous incidents from mythology or history. Many relate the life stories of heroes and saints. To date there are nearly 20 devoted to Sikh tradition. These are all listed in the bibliography. I would recommend particularly *Guru Nanak*, *Guru Arjan*, *Guru Tegh Bahadur*, *Guru Gobind Singh*, *The Three Gurus*, *Bidhi Chand* and *Ranjit Singh*. *Kabir* retells the story of a saint whose hymns are included in the Guru Granth Sahib (Sikh scriptures).

Two *Amar Chitra Katha* comics are devoted to brave Sikh women. These are *Sundari* and *Satwant Kaur*, which are based on historical novels by Vir Singh. Teachers need to balance the desirability of having stories about women against the portrayal of Muslim aggression.

For 20 years teachers have benefited from the generous provision of the Sikh Missionary Society. This was established in 1969 to teach Sikh children in Britain about their faith and provide English versions of traditional Sikh stories. Since the printing in 1969 for free distribution of 5000 copies of *Guru Nanak for Children*, many other booklets have followed. Teachers can obtain these by writing to The Sikh Missionary Society, 10 Featherstone Road, Southall, Middlesex. In the clear A4 format the new edition of *The Sikhs and Their Way of Life* combines line drawings, photographs, facts, and basic information about Sikh life, including recipes.

125

Sharing the lives of British Sikh children

This brings us to another valuable category of literature which should be in every junior school. These are the books which present in text and pictures the lives of Sikh children growing up in Britain.

For young children attractive introductions to Sikh family life in Britain are Joan Solomon's *News for Dad* and *Bobbi's New Year* and Olivia Bennett's *Kikar's Drum*, *A Sikh Wedding* and *Our New Home*. This describes the religious ceremony with which a new home is blessed. The boys in *Pavan is a Sikh* and *I am a Sikh* are nine years old but these books can be appropriately used with a wider age range. These two books provide background information on Sikhism – such as the way a turban is tied and the five symbols of Sikhism. With middle school children in mind Piara Singh Sambhi wrote *Understanding your Sikh Neighbour*. This is a more detailed account of a Sikh family, the Gills, in Leeds. (The pictures are black and white.) It includes a chapter describing a visit to Punjab. By reading this chapter, and enjoying the text and photographs of *Amardip and Rema: Two Sikh Children Visit India*, middle school children can share in detail in the experience of a holiday in Punjab. This is an excellent way of introducing children here to the lifestyle and history of Sikhs in India. Olivia Bennett's *Listening to Sikhs* includes substantial quotations from Sikhs in Britain and activities that could be attempted by many top juniors.

Other information books

There is also a growing number of junior books on Sikhism generally such as *Sikhism in Words and Pictures* by Sarah Thorley. Angela Smith's and Daljit Singh's *The Sikh World*, appropriate for older pupils too, is a rich source of information and colour photographs. There are also books on particular aspects, for example *Visiting a Sikh Temple* by Davinder Babraa.

In some areas local education centres have produced useful materials on Sikhism. For instance *Sikh Gurdwara: Visit to the Singh Sabha Gurdwara, Bristol* is available from Resources for Learning Development Unit, Bristol (see bibliography for further details).

Choosing and using books

In order to maximise the benefit of these books teachers should try to meet Sikhs. Apart from the pleasure of being welcomed into a community with which one may not have been previously familiar, it is important to listen to what Sikhs have to say. It is important for teachers to learn correct pronunciation of the names and Punjabi words in the books they are going to use with children. By speaking to Sikh contacts one is also better able to evaluate the many books on Sikhism.

Apart from examining the language level and assessing the visual impact, there are other factors to bear in mind when selecting books that portray Sikhs. Does the book show children in old-fashioned clothes? (Punjabi girls' suits date just as quickly as western fashions.) Are the Sikh adults and children shown with uncut hair or with short hair? (Sikhs may not like to see their community represented by individuals who have cut their hair.) Especially in schools with no Sikh staff or pupils the books will come to life if children can meet a Sikh visitor in school or visit a gurdwara. Books are helpful in preparing children for this experience.

In deciding which books to use with children and how best to do so, it is also helpful to do some background reading (see Chapter 9 by Owen Cole). Although Alan James' *Sikh Children in Britain* is now dated, describing children of a generation whose children are now entering school, it is still an excellent source of background material. Khushwant Singh and Raghu Rai's *The Sikhs*, a superb collection of photographs, and Sarah Lloyd's *An Indian Attachment* (her absorbing account of living with a Sikh villager) in their very different ways give one the feel of Sikh life in India. Expensive, but very attractive, is *The Golden Temple*, by Patwant Singh, available in Britain through Books from India (see above).

Fiction

> 'Harjit Singh, you have not plugged in,' said BOSS. Harjit's green turban appeared on the screen as the camera watched his head bobbing amongst the desks.
>
> *(Ali and the Robots pp. 30–1)*

Children will gain more, the wider the variety of the literature which they encounter. Fiction, involving Sikhs in Britain, though still scant, must not be forgotten. Contemporary stories like *Ali and the Robots* in which children of different cultural backgrounds appear naturally, with no sense of remoteness, are definitely to be welcomed. In her earlier books Jamila Gavin's Sikh characters are a little more distanced by their experience from their peers. For younger juniors *Kamla and Kate* introduces Amrik Singh, the new boy fresh from Punjab. (You may feel that this is too dated as Punjabi children in British schools now were born in this country.) For older children there is *Double Dare and Other Stories*, 'Double Dare' is the story of Terry Singh, an orphan in a children's home. His grandfather is at first a supernatural apparition:

> a somewhat odd character, who had a white turban wrapped around his head. He wore . . . white, wrinkling pyjamas, and he had a long, flowing, grey beard . . .
>
> *(Double Dare and Other Stories)*

127

Hari's Pigeon takes the form of a lively diary written by Hari Singh, a boy whose father has just married an English woman. Hari draws comfort from his pigeon. This book is primarily intended for older children but parts could be used creatively with juniors, for instance the description of how he names his pigeon. He remembers how children's names are chosen in the gurdwara and uses the same procedure, but substitutes a dictionary for the scriptures.

This is a reminder. In pursuit of active learning the teacher must never allow the Sikh scriptures or pictures of the Gurus to be used disrespectfully. Children can be encouraged to draw pictures of the Gurus from books (Sikh children often do this) and to copy some Punjabi words in Gurmukhi script. The stories of the Gurus can be read aloud, but should only be dramatised if impersonation of the Gurus is avoided. Traditional Sikhs would be upset by the idea of children acting the part of any of the Gurus in dramas. In discovering the wealth of material to engage pupils' interest in Sikhism we must never let our enthusiasm as teachers overwhelm our sensitivity to Sikh pupils and our respect for their parents' religious feelings.

Bibliography

Manju Aggarwal, *I am a Sikh* (Franklin Watts, 1984)
Ranjit Arora, *Sikhism* (Wayland, 1986)
Ranjit Arora, *Guru Nanak and the Sikh Gurus* (Wayland, 1987)
Davinder Kaur Babraa, *Visiting a Sikh Temple* (Lutterworth, 1981)
Davinder Kaur Babraa, *Religions Through Festivals: Sikhism* (Longman, 1989)
Olivia Bennett, *Kikar's Drum* (Hamish Hamilton, 1984)
Olivia Bennett, *A Sikh Wedding* (Hamish Hamilton, 1985)
Olivia Bennett, *Our New Home* (Hamish Hamilton, 1989)
Olivia Bennett, *Listening to Sikhs* (Unwin Hyman, 1990)
Jamila Gavin, *Double Dare and Other Stories* (Methuen, 1982)
Jamila Gavin, *Kamla and Kate* (Methuen, 1983)
Jamila Gavin, *Ali and the Robots* (Methuen, 1986)
Helen Griffiths, *Hari's Pigeon* (Hutchinson, 1982)
Steve Harrison, *Amardip and Rema: two Sikh children visit India* (Macmillan, 1986)
India Book House Education Trust (various dates) *Amar Chitra Katha* series:
    Banda Bahadur, Bhagat Singh, Bidhi Chand, Guru Arjan, Guru Gobind Singh, Guru Hargobind, Guru Nanak, Guru Tegh Bahadur, Hari Singh Nalwa, Kabir, Ranjit Singh, Satwant Kaur, Sundari, The Three Gurus
Alan James, *Sikh Children in Britain* (Oxford University Press for Institute of Race Relations, 1974)
Sukhbir Singh Kapoor, *Sikh Festivals* (Wayland, 1985)
Sarah Lloyd, *An Indian Attachment* (Futura, 1985)
Sean Lyle, *Pavan is a Sikh* (A & C Black, 1987)
Eleanor M. Nesbitt, 'The Presentation of Sikhs in recent children's literature in Britain' in J. R. O'Connell and others (eds), *Sikh History and Religion in the Twentieth Century* (Toronto, 1988)
Resources for Learning Development Unit, *Sikh Gurdwara: Visit to the Singh Sabha*

Gurdwara, Bristol, 'World Religions in Avon', Bristol (available from RLDU, Bishop Road, Bishopston, Bristol)

Gurinder Singh Sacha, *The Sikhs and Their Way of Life* Second edition (The Sikh Missionary Society, 1987)

Piara Singh Sambhi, *Understanding your Sikh Neighbour* (Lutterworth, 1980)

Daljit Singh and Angela Smith, *The Sikh World* (Macdonald, 1985)

Kartar Singh and Gurdip Singh Dhillon, *Stories from Sikh History* Books 1–X (Hemkunt Press, from 1971)

Khushwant Singh and Raghu Rai, *The Sikhs* (Lustre Press, 1984)

Patwant Singh, *The Golden Temple* (Time Books International 1988)

Rani and Jugnu Singh, *Stories from the Sikh World* (Macdonald, 1987.)

Joan Solomon, *News for Dad* (Hamish Hamilton, 1980)

Joan Solomon, *Bobbi's New Year* (Hamish Hamilton, 1980)

Sara Thorley, *Sikhism in Words and Pictures* (Religious and Moral Education Press, 1989)

PART FOUR

Religious Education and the Arts

Introduction

In her chapter on the role of art, Jo Price draws attention again to (Chapter 22) three of the elements of RE suggested in Chapter 1 – the sensitising, imaginative and expressive elements. Her suggested art activities follow the pattern of the basic awarenesses or sensitivities proposed by Edwin Cox as fundamental to the experience of religion. We find ourselves in the region of responses such as wonder and delight at the natural world, the sense of order, awareness of the individuality of others, the sense of right and wrong – and, as Jo Price points out, the experience of intense feelings such as anger, horror and pity.

The experience of encountering, expressing and 'giving form' to such responses is clearly close to the heart of religion. It is clearly also a central concern of the arts. When we bring the arts and RE together in the classroom, it is not just that the arts 'decorate' RE with engaging activities. Nor is it just that RE provides art, music and drama with useful topics or starting points. It is a shared concern for giving expression, shape and form to our experiences that brings the arts and RE together in the curriculum. Out of this comes another important point. The arts and RE have shared values. Art, music and drama do not indoctrinate or dictate. They explore. So does religion when it is most truly itself. And so, certainly, does religious education.

Awareness and sensitivity

We should take care not to assume that the arts have only to do with feeling, while RE provides the 'knowledge' component. To speak even more fundamentally, it is damaging and wrong to think that we have to spread the butter of feeling on to the dry bread of ideas. Surely the truth is more nearly this – that the very character and quality of thoughts and ideas is fired in the furnace of imagination and tempered by feeling? It is important that Edwin Cox talks of awarenesses and sensitivities, for these terms bridge the potentially disastrous gap between thought and feeling.

When David Self explains the use of drama in RE, he is describing activities that engage mind and body to explore responses, to bring ideas into consciousness and give them shape and clarity. Robert Green in Chapter 23 (as just one of his suggestions) shows how music can be used with the story of St Francis and the Wolf. This is not just a fun way to 'learn' a story. It is a way to possess those elements of human experience and their significance. But this brings us to questions that arise about stories in religion and in Religious Education.

Questions about story

Teachers are sometimes worried by the special status of stories drawn from the Christian and other world religions. Are they 'true' stories? Are all of them 'true' in exactly the same way? Our worry about the status of stories drawn from the world religions spills over into our concern for the treatment of stories in the classroom. If believers and non-believers hold a range of different opinions about the truth of particular stories, how is the teacher to be both honest in his or her own opinions and at the same time sensitive to the (perhaps) contrary judgements of others. And what about our use of the word 'myth'? Can it properly be used without assuming the untruthfulness story?

Jack Priestley suggests that there is more than one way to think about the truth of a story – and that furthermore we too often apply the wrong sort of test. He suggests that instead of asking, 'Is it true?' we should learn to ask, 'What truth does it convey?' Acting on his suggestion we might more easily be able to distinguish between historical and scientific truth. We might also open ourselves to truths that lie in fantasy and the dream-world – truths about human nature, human experience and the encounter with the divine. Jack Priestley's preferred question does not rule out the questions about the nature of the truth we are dealing with. It helps us to distinguish between them; and when we know more about that, we know more about what to teach, and how.

'What truth does it convey?' The suggestions made by other writers in this section are all concerned to help us apply this question with children in a lively and vivid way. There is far more to what children can and should do with story than is covered by simply recording or illustrating it, and this is where we can turn to the arts for help. Merlin Price, in Chapter 18, shows how children can be encouraged to relate stories to their own experience and reflect on meaning and values not only in discussion but in and through the various arts of exploration and expression. With Angela Wood, in Chapter 20, we see children in the act of expressing some fundamental responses to their own inner and outer worlds, and so sensitising themselves to the truths of those greater stories as believers discover them in the world's religious traditions. The relevance of the chapters by Robert Green and David Self has been already discussed.

The importance of stories

Properly speaking, stories are *events*. They occur as a three-sided exchange between the storyteller (who has a certain world-view and sensibility), the story-material (its characters, incidents and feeling for the world) and the reader or listener who has a certain life-experience on which to found a response. Probably all stories have 'religious significance' simply because they contribute to our understanding of life, communicating insights about the human condition and our experience of it. Of course we are more fully nourished by stories that are richer in character and incident, more sensitive to subtlety of the human situation; but nevertheless all stories have this potential to communicate and shape an understanding of life.

Philosophy and theology also communicate and shape an understanding of life, but perhaps stories are more immediate, more accessible to more people. We might say that stories are the raw material out of which philosophy and theology can be made. Human emotions and concepts (such as, for example, hope and love, jealousy and anger) can be subject matter for philosophy and theology, but in stories they appear with all the vividness of illuminated character, incident and context. Though we all reflect upon the significances of story (and in that sense are all of us theologians and philosophers) it seems that more people can be touched by story than by the work of the philosophers and theologians.

Stories from world religions

All 'great stories' acquire their following, can become 'cult' phenomena and be regarded as pointing to great truths. Stories that have been celebrated by the great religions of the world across time are not in these respects notably different. Importantly, however, they are the stories that have their marked significance for some particular religious tradition. Though we are of course free to respond to the stories immediately and in terms of our own experience, we miss something important if we at no stage hear them in the context of their native tradition. This remains an important consideration even where different religious traditions share what appears formally to be the same or a very similar story, for the story will hold a distinctive place in each tradition.

In that same native context stories from the world religions often communicate insights that reach beyond the human and everyday experience of human beings to represent facts and values that are timeless and in that sense 'beyond' or 'transcendent'. Illustrating encounters between the human and the divine, or between human frailty and human aspirations, such stories convey the ultimate values and beliefs of communities across time. We need somehow and at some stage to try and share in that dimension of response.

135

This is in essence what the scholars are pointing out when they refer to such stories as 'myth' – that they are cherished by a particular human community and tradition, and have been held to communicate fundamental truths. Believers have sometimes been worried by the use of that term, feeling that in ordinary usage the term 'myth' means an untrue story. Properly speaking, although the use of the term 'myth' does not endorse every story for all time and for all human beings, it does point to the great significance of those stories for believers and to the truths within them that believers hold dear. Myth is a term of honour among students of religion, and not a term of contempt.

Stories in religious education

Many teachers confess to feeling comparatively ill at ease with the classroom management of Christian stories. In his 'Stories from the Christian tradition' Jack Priestley begins by recognising that there is a genuine predicament. He investigates some of our unfortunate assumptions and practices, and argues against the fragmentation that too often characterises 'stories of Jesus'. He suggests that we need to see (and to teach) the unity and broad patterns of meaning to be found in what he calls 'the Christ Story' and 'the Jesus Story'. Only then can stories from the Christian tradition recover distinctively Christian values for the pupils and take their proper place in the classroom.

The importance of stories in any kind of religious education goes back to the importance of myth and the pursuit of truth. There are broad traditions of human experience, and there is the adventure of young hearts and minds recovering these for themselves, and testing their own experience alongside them. To communicate in and over the stories is to communicate insights about religion, religions and the religious dimension of human experience. The stories are gathered in the holy books; but also, the practices of religions such as festivals, pilgrimages and rituals can hardly be understood without exploring the stories which they recall and celebrate. Those whose contributions on classroom practice appear in this and other sections of the book offer practical guidance for that broad exploration of story.

CHAPTER 17

'It isn't true is it, Miss? It's only a story...'

JACK PRIESTLEY

The modern explosion in what we loosely term resources should not blind us to the fact that where the communication of religion is concerned the oldest resources are still the essential ones. Indeed much of our present day technology and techniques are designed to reinforce the traditional methods rather than to replace them. Chief among those methods lies the story. Not all religions have a developed theology but they do all have stories and those stories are absolutely central to belief. We might even say that belief means becoming identified with a particular story.

This is true of all religions. In this chapter I am going to illustrate my points mainly by reference to Christianity. I do this not from any confessional viewpoint but because it seems to me that nowadays a great many teachers have more difficulty with its central story than with that of almost any other major religion. Teachers who have become acquainted with the basic narrative of the Ramayana will happily tell of the exploits which led to the crossing of the sea to Lanka but still balk at the crossing of the Red Sea. Unless, of course, they are teaching Judaism, when the Red Sea story is recounted quite happily in the context of what happens at the Passover meal! However, although I want to deal with some of the particular problems associated in many people's minds with teaching Christianity and to pursue them more explicitly in Chapter 19, I hope that what I have to say is true of religious story as a whole.

Story and modern thought

The stories with which we deal as teachers of religious education are old. They have come down to us virtually unchanged over thousands of years. The Biblical narratives range from just over 3000 to just under 2000 years old. Hindu stories are even older. Why then is there a problem? Why today do we question their ability to be meaningful?

The answer, I think, is quite simple. The stories may not have changed but we have. A glance at the full Oxford English Dictionary tells the story of story. The earliest usage denotes a 'narrative true or presumed to be true'. It is the same as hi-story 'a branch of knowledge as opposed to fiction'. Gradually, however, the definitions become more and more qualified. Story is a 'recital of events alleged to have happened', 'a particular person's representation of a matter'. Finally, in the twentieth century, we reach the point where it is taken to convey the exact opposite of its original definition. Story can be a 'colloquialism for a lie', as in the phrase "you story-teller".

It is as if the whole history of Western thought since the Middle Ages is compressed within this one dictionary entry. What has changed is not the form of story but our notion of what constitutes truth. The question 'Is it true?' has become all important. It is a very limited question and allows for very precise and limited answers. A thing is either true or false. Every primary child knows how to ask it of any story but teachers do not always know how to answer it. The question which we should be encouraging our children to ask is not 'Is it true?' but rather 'Does it convey truth?' Put simplistically the first is the question of a scientific culture, the latter belongs to the world of the arts. But while the scientific way of looking at things has become compulsory for all of us the arts have become options. This does not mean that we have entirely forgotten the nature of story. Not even the most extreme literalists seem to be concerned about whether the Samaritan actually walked along the Jericho Road or not but when the Bishop of Durham suggests that 'What truth does it convey' is a more important question about the resurrection than 'Is it true' there is great excitement. What it does mean, however, is that we assume that direct statements are more important than narratives. That is, we assume that if we want to know what a story means we shall be nearer the truth if we use propositional language than if we continue with story.

Propositions give meaning to story

Barbara Hardy, in her contribution to *The Cool Web*, comments 'There is a widespread assumption that human beings begin by telling themselves fairy tales and end by telling truths'. In other words we see story as something for young children. Older children and adults get their truth in propositional statements (before rushing home to watch *Grange Hill* or *Dallas*). This was certainly the assumption behind the Goldman research of twenty years ago. Maturation could be plotted according to one's ability to make abstract statements from a narrative base.

Let me add immediately that there is nothing wrong with such an activity. All that we know as theology in any religious tradition arises out of just such an exercise. Theology has no language other than that of propositional statements. Theologians in their daily work do not sing, dance, paint or write poetry to express their ideas. They make statements. There is nothing wrong with that as long as we bear two things in mind. First, very few people, even amongst committed religious believers, become theologians or even engage in theological discussion. Perhaps it would be a good thing if they did but religions seem to survive without it. Secondly, when all is said and done, propositional statements can say very little. It is part of our western cultural assumptions to take it for granted that they are superior to the original story. That assumption is being increasingly challenged. Proposition *can* give meaning to story but the story is primary. Not only must we always return to it but, in the final analysis, it is story which gives meaning to propositions.

Story gives meaning to propositions

The idea that propositions not only can but must be transcended has a long history. Throughout the Socratic dialogues, for example, Plato constantly arrives at the point when explicitly or implicitly it is understood that the argument has gone as far as is possible and a stage has been reached where it is necessary to resort to story (mythos).

Another classic example, usually overlooked, is the New Testament. If modern Biblical scholarship has shown anything it is that propositional statements about the Christian faith, such as are contained in Paul's letters to Galatia and Rome, existed before the Gospels. They were not enough. The story had to be told. The reason is easy to grasp. Religion is characterised by its radical incompleteness. That is, at root it is never fully explicable. A key word in all religion is *ineffable*. The effable is, quite literally, that which can be drawn out of the fable or the story. Ineffability is therefore a recognition that there is more in the religious story than can ever be drawn out. That is what makes it *fabulous*. It is that which distinguishes religious stories from others. In the words of Ted Hughes, the present poet laureate, the religious myth is 'an irreducible lump of the world'.

Teaching implications

The implications of this for teaching immediately become obvious. If the whole meaning of the story cannot be brought out then teacher and taught are co-partners. The teacher by virtue of age, experience and learning may know more but will never know all. The child may well discuss insights the teacher has never seen. It was Cardinal Archbishop Hume who said at an educational conference I attended a few years ago 'There is not a man, woman or child in this world who cannot teach me something about the Christian faith'. But it is more likely to happen when a person is conversant with, or is part of, the whole story and not just isolated incidents. And this is where Christianity

139

seems to have a particular problem. For a long time now we who teach have assumed that we should start with the history and move to the other wider context, the realm of what we might call otherworldliness.

The question, of course, will be raised 'But how can you deal with the conceptual problems?' How can you teach Creation, Fall, Incarnation, Vicarious Suffering, Resurrection, Judgement and Consummation to junior children? It's too fantastic for words. Exactly. It is in fantasy that the answer lies, as C. S. Lewis showed us. All of those concepts are dealt with in the Narnia books, recommended for eight-year-olds and over.

Fantasy and religion

I am not suggesting that fantasy should replace the direct telling of the Bible Story. Nor am I saying that the Bible is just fantasy. But I *am* saying it is not just history. I am suggesting that the two belong together and that we could do worse than tell many Bible stories as if they *were* fantasy before, with great maturity, we explore their historicity. Fantasy allows us to evaluate our primary world from the vantage point of a secondary world. It is only in that way that the ideal of one can become the reality of the other. Space will not permit me to develop this theme further here but it is necessary to add that this is surely exactly what religion is and what religious education is all about. 'We live in two worlds' wrote John Navonne at the start of his book *Towards a Theology of Story* and when we try to live in one alone something goes wrong with us. The narrative keeps the inner and the outer world, the secondary and the primary world in harmony far more than the language of propositions can ever do. Religious story and tales of fantasy are not identical but they are not opposite either. In *Tales from Eternity*, Rosemary Haughton shows how close they can be and also asks us the very pertinent question 'Are we concerned with what life is *like* or what *life* is like?'

Religious stories are not scientific accounts. They are part of the biographies of those who try to live them out. In the end we cannot separate story and interpretation. At the beginning of his school text book *How to Read the Old Testament* Etienne Charpentier describes how he visited an old couple on the eve of their golden wedding anniversary. He flicked through old photograph albums as they talked. Suddenly he realised that without knowing the people the photos meant nothing and without the photos he would not see these old folks as whole persons once young and active like himself. So it is with religious stories. Divorced from a full community they lose their value. Likewise a community divorced from its story soon ceases to be a community in any real sense. A large part of our current difficulty in teaching Christianity is just that. We teach Hindu stories within the whole context of what it means to be a Hindu, but we largely separate Christianity from its whole story.

John Navonne further on in his book says there is no self without other selves. In religious terms too the individual needs the community as the community needs the individual.

The new problem in our multicultural society is that of finding out what our story is. I suspect it is in fact a larger problem for majorities than for minorities. Just what that majority story is is far beyond the scope of a short chapter such as this but I would be bold enough to say that Christianity plays some part in it. The danger for both minorities and majorities is that given in Laurens van der Post's comment about storytelling amongst Kalahari Bushmen. 'These people knew what we do not: that without a story you have not got a nation, or a culture, or a civilisation. Without a story, if you are to live, you have not got a life of your own.'

If that is anywhere near true then the story is and must remain a central issue of our work in schools.

Bibliography

Etienne Charpentier, *How to Read the Old Testament* (SCM, 1982)

R. Goldman, *Religious Thinking from Childhood to Adolescence* (Routledge, 1984)

Rosemary Haughton, *Tales from Eternity* (Allen & Unwin, 1972)

Ted Hughes, 'Myth and Education' in G Fox *et al.* (eds), *Writers and Critics and Children* (Heinemann, 1978)

J. Navonne, *Towards a Theology of Story* (St Paul's 1977)

M. Meck (ed.), *The Cool Webb* (Bodley Head, 1977)

C. L. Lewis' Narnia books are well enough known. For a very modern attempt at the same end see Fay Sampson's, *Pangur Ban* series (Lion, 1983–90). Six titles.

CHAPTER 18

Children exploring religious stories

MERLIN PRICE

Recent work in RE has tended to emphasise two key aims. One of these is to develop in children an understanding of religion (usually through the introduction of material from various religions). The other is to encourage them to explore at their own level some of the basic issues and questions with which religions deal. The Schools Council Working Party Paper 36 of 1971, and many of the recent Agreed Syllabuses all draw attention to these joint concerns of the subject.

In the past it would appear that too much RE curriculum material has dealt with these two concerns separately. Some children, for example, are taught simple information about religions without being encouraged to consider questions raised by their work. The two concerns are, however, closely interrelated and a careful selection and presentation of material will raise questions which children will be keen to explore.

Story is a key element in combining these two concerns. However the use in junior schools of explicit religious story, and particularly stories from the Bible, has rapidly declined since the 1960s. Nowhere has this been more apparent than in the early years. This decline has come about mainly as a result of an attack initiated by Goldman, whose research alleged that the primary school child was incapable of grasping the abstract concepts of which religious ideas are expressed.

A further argument against the use of such story material was that in most cases it was used in order to secure a single interpretation and furthermore was usually presented in a form almost entirely lacking in literary merit.

In the mid 1970s Brian Gates carried out an extensive investigation into the personal religious understanding of children. Part of this study examined children's responses to story. It argued that the category of scripture did not disconnect children's understanding from dealings with literature and expressive language. Story is understood as much by an act of the imagination as by a process of critical analysis. Over-emphasis on the cognitive understanding of a story limits both the story and the faculty of the imagination. The work of Margaret Donaldson also indicates that young children's thinking is far less limited than Piagetian assessments would suggest; and my own exploration of young children's understanding of story would appear further to substantiate the view that when children can make 'human sense' of a situation they can deal with it more competently.

If this is correct then the understanding of religious story depends as much on our constructing the correct language approach as on the factors of strict Piagetian development and the literary quality of the material.

The traditional means by which a religious story is explored within the junior school has usually placed undue emphasis on some forms of written response. Young children, however, may have difficulties in both the physical skills of recording and also in formulating a satisfactory response that is not influenced by the level of ability to manipulate formal language.

The superficiality of their response may well have more to do with these factors than their supposed level of cognitive development. As Jerome Bruner has said:

> Children can grasp the idea of tragedy and the basic human plights represented in myth. But they cannot put these ideas into formal language or manipulate them as grown-ups can.

The time provided by the teacher for such tasks is also often unrealistic. Gates quotes the following written response by an eight-year-old boy to the Maurice Sendak story *Where the Wild Things Are*:

> Q. What was the story about? Try to tell me in your own words.
> A. It was about the wield [sic] things.
> Q. Tell me why you liked or didn't like the story?
> A. I like it becose it had funye things in it.
> Q. What other stories did it remind you of?
> A. The heer and the tortoise.
> Q. Did it remind you of anything that had ever happened to you?
> A. Wen I went to Frans.

This response was classified at the Restricted Stage in terms of Piagetian assessment. By comparison, an oral interview I carried out with a child of four plus generated three pages of transcript. This included a careful and accurate retelling of the story together with a significant element of empathy with the characters and attempts to come to terms with their relationships with one another and the emotions that were involved. Such a response from a four-year-old suggests that the eight-year-old's response might have been sought in an inappropriate form and in too short a time limit, and that 'Wen I went to Frans' may well have concealed within its five words far greater insights and understandings of the way in which the boy related *Where the Wild Things Are* to his own personal experiences of life than would warrant such a 'restricted' classification.

The first factor then in constructing a more meaningful approach to religious story must be a greater emphasis on oral response and the provision of sufficient time for the child to explore and respond to the story in terms of his or her own experience.

If we consider the type of questioning used in much traditional follow-up material to religious story, there is a tendency for it to fall back on simple exercises which test only superficial comprehension, such as 'What was Zaccheus's job in Jericho?' Some material even manages to mutate the activity into a quasi-geography lesson by using the old standby of 'get out your atlas and draw a map of . . .'.

Too rarely are links made with other stories or common themes examined in stories from world religions. Nor is the form of questioning designed to develop skills of interpretation or empathy, or to relate the story to the child's own questions and concerns and the ways in which the story may help the child to come to terms with them.

Understanding of story then is dependent to some extent both on constructing the correct language approach to elicit the child's fullest response and in providing a framework of meaningful activities which will explore their responses to the full. This framework can obviously be initiated from the earliest years of schooling and should seek to:

- enable the child to put forward his or her own ideas in a non-threatening environment.
- encourage the child to respect and value the ideas of others.
- eventually enable the child to attempt to evaluate interpretations rather than passively accepting that there must be a 'right answer' which will be presented to them at the end of the lesson.
- provide experiences and opportunities which encourage the child to extend and develop his or her interpretations.

It is possible to suggest a set of initial guidelines which may promote the above aims:

1 Select material that is of literary merit and which contains a number of 'layers' of interpretation, thereby avoiding the establishment of the habit of 'guessing the right answer'.
2 Engage the child's faculty of imagination and develop responses linked to the creative arts.
3 Construct a language approach that makes 'human sense' of the exploration and interpretation of the story by its use and sequencing of carefully considered questions.
4 Provide activities, both linguistic, and through music and drama, that relate the exploration of the story to the development of empathy skills.
5 Use stories as a vehicle by which basic issues and concerns with which religions deal can be explored in a manner that is meaningful to the child.

Let us now look beyond these general guidelines and offer suggestions for a specific classroom approach.

In my own research straightforward narrative recall proved to be of a very high order even among the youngest children questioned. Sadly, it is this area which tends to predominate the way religious story is used in the junior classroom, all too often providing practice in a skill which the majority will have mastered, and to the exclusion of other skills which it is important to develop.

Bearing in mind an initial caveat as to the importance of sufficient time being allowed for the children's responses to be fully explored, and the dangers of too great an emphasis on written responses, then activities following the initial telling of the story can be divided into the following categories.

Developing empathy skills

Group discussions of insights into feelings and relationships between characters in the story should be an important activity. This could be further extended by allowing the group to develop and change story lines and the characteristics of individuals in the story.

Further oral discussion should also be developed where the child's own feelings and identification with the characters and situations are explored.

In the early years basic language development is inseparable from the RE aspect. Oral work where children are encouraged to identify words and phrases in the story that are evocative of feelings and emotions should be developed. Areas of specific language development should also not be ignored at this stage. Religious story, like all story, can be utilised in language development and teachers can find ways of using such stories for sequencing activities, story extension, 'what happens next/before' activities, and brainstorming.

Developing interpretational skills – eliciting interpretations and developing the ability to accept a plurality of interpretations

In asking children for their interpretations of a story the 'human sense' element is crucial. Interpretations beyond the literal are best elicited by questioning which relates to empathising with the characters within the story in terms of what those characters may have learned.

The sequencing of questions is also important. The most productive responses are provided when children have had an opportunity to work through the initial empathy questions (for example, How did X feel?) beforehand.

It is important too that children are provided with the opportunity to evaluate the responses of other children and adults in the group. Children can be presented with interpretations provided by other members of the class.

This is a rich area for development and a basis for discussion of the merits of each interpretation and why it might be meaningful to different individuals at

145

different times and at different ages. In the junior school an exchange of such interpretations between children in different age groups together with their justifications for their views would be of value, and would help to reinforce the idea that stories provide different ideas at different age levels and to different individuals. Older children may gain from creating stories of their own which serve to illustrate some of the interpretations suggested.

Relating story to the child's experience, questions and concerns

In examining the way in which children relate story to personal experience it may be necessary to focus on particular aspects of the story, examining it section by section, rather than expecting the child to be able to provide a matching of experience to the story in its entirety.

The way in which the story elicits questions and concerns must also be explored carefully. Responses to this line of questioning can indicate that the material is worthy of greater elaboration and discussion arising from the initial responses. Having identified questions and concerns the children need to be shown how a story may help in their resolution. Again framing questions which make human sense: 'How do you think that story would help so-and-so to sort out a particular problem?' may help children to explore the story in greater depth to try and identify any techniques, skills or attitudes suggested for resolving or coming to terms with such concerns.

Concerns raised by one story may also be resolved by reference to another. In one school used in my own research where questions about death were raised from the use of the story *The Garden of Eden*, children were presented with the story of *The Buddha and the Mustard Seed*, which suggests ways of coming to terms with death.

In many instances the stories themselves will not offer techniques and strategies for resolving or coming to terms with the questions of concern. Nevertheless this can then lead to approaches where aspects of religion, for example, rites of passage, may help deal with them.

This approach lends itself to combining the two issues raised at the beginning of this chapter, namely coming to terms with the issues with which religions deal, and understanding religion.

Developing responses from the creative arts

The junior school child should be provided with an opportunity to take part in art/drama responses after an initial telling of the story. Such activities provide an opportunity for the story to be internalised and developed and for the child to reflect upon it.

A particularly useful and productive exercise is for phrases identified as being particularly evocative within the story to be used as a stimulus for the following cycle of activities. Such a cycle allows the child time to reflect on the story and respond to it in a number of different media and over a period of time.

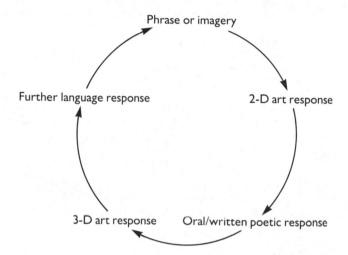

This activity has proved to be particularly effective prior to activities involving questions of interpretation described above.

Good story, be it religious or secular, contains the potential for the deepest insights. However the superficial way in which it has been dealt with in the past, particularly in the early years of schooling, has done much to devalue it. The traditional approach, leading usually to a single interpretation, has robbed story of its potential for growth. However, it is hoped that if the story's true potential can be transmitted by some of the activities outlined above, dealing in particular with empathy, emotions, ethics and language, then story will again become a resource to which the child may return time and time again, each time gaining new insights, and allowing story once more to become in the fullest sense 'a factory for understanding'.

Bibliography

J. Bruner, *The Process of Education* (Harvard University Press, 1978)

M. Donaldson, *Children's Minds* (Fontana/Croom Helm, 1978)

B. E. Gates, *Religion in the Developing World of Children and Young People* unpublished PhD thesis (University of Lancaster, 1976)

R. Goldman, *Religious Thinking from Childhood to Adolescence* (Routledge and Kegan Paul, 1974)

T. Hughes, 'Myth and Education', in Fox *et al.* (eds) *Writers, Critics and Children* (Heinemann, 1976)

L. M. Price, *The Role of Story in the Religious Education of the First School Child*, unpublished MA thesis, (University of Warwick, 1988)

Schools Council Working Party Paper 36, *Religious Education in Secondary Schools* (Evans/ Methuen, 1971)

CHAPTER 19

Stories from the Christian tradition

JACK PRIESTLEY

I once submitted an article on this subject under the title, 'Jesus Christ: What Story Should I Tell?' Fearing, I think, that readers might regard the title as blasphemous, the editors asked me to change it – rejecting my protests that the colon ruled out any possibility of such an interpretation.

In fact the rejected title pinpointed what I increasingly believe to be our central problem in teaching Christianity and so I draw upon it here again as an introductory comment. The fact is that many of us are confused both about what constitutes the Christian Story and the Christian tradition and confusion is not a good starting point for the effective teaching of any subject.

I want to deal with these in reverse order. First, I want to argue that, much as we like to think we are neutral and objective in our approach to teaching we are not, as the Muslim part of our community keeps trying to remind us. Within education, as much as within any other sphere of life, we are all social beings who have grown up within traditions, which, themselves, have been deeply influenced by particular forms of religion, in this case Protestant and Reformed Christianity, (see Edward Hulmes *Educational and Cultural Diversity*).

Secondly, I want to show that it is those particular traditions which lead many people to assume that by 'Christian Story' we mean stories from the New Testament. However, important though they may be, I want to show that they are by no means the whole Story and that our own mental picture of what does make up the whole Story determines how we select and teach the individual stories within it. I shall suggest that the central Story for Christians is that which I define as, 'The Christ Story': but I shall approach it by distinguishing first between 'Stories of Jesus' and then, 'The Jesus Story', both of which, I shall argue, have The Christ Story as their proper context.

Which Christian tradition?

There are, to start with, at least four major European Christian traditions: the Orthodox, Roman, Protestant and Reformed. Increasingly we are also becoming aware again of a fifth, which had seemingly all but died out, namely the Celtic (see *The Celtic Alternative: A Reminder of the Christianity We Lost*). With the possible exception of the first, all have played a major part in the development of the faith in Britain. Perhaps for just that reason a growing number of teachers have begun to use Orthodoxy as a means of teaching Christianity through unfamiliar phenomena but, interesting as such a development may be, it still avoids the major issue. Can we teach the faith which has been, and for a great many people still is, the traditional, historical faith of this part of the world? And can we do so in a way which we all can recognise as being both true to the subject matter and educationally sound?

To begin with, the problem is a cultural one, or, more precisely, it is the decline of the cultural usage of the word 'Christian' which causes many of our difficulties. One can be shot at in Beirut as a Christian, whether one believes anything or not, in exactly the same way as Europe's Jews were persecuted by the Nazis without any enquiry into their personal attitudes towards the Torah. Consequently we find ourselves still able to generalise about Jews, Hindus and Muslims in a way which is seemingly not possible for Christians. The nearest we come to it is in claiming that we live in a post-Christian society.

Historically, of course, it is the Protestant Reformation – itself a huge religious influence on cultural change and one of which any educated person should have some understanding – which slowly brought about this state of affairs. There are, I would suggest, some characteristics of this heritage which we should recognise if we are to resolve our difficulties about Christian stories in the classroom.

First, our Protestant/Reformed heritage simultaneously separated us from our deep history and ushered in the cult of individualism. Jews at *Pesakh* may refer, quite naturally, to the time, four thousand years ago, when 'We were in Egypt' but our Protestant inheritance has foreshortened our historical perspective, cut us off from a great part of our religious–cultural history such as the 'saints' and led to us not naming it, and, therefore, not teaching it, as our own.

In addition to this shortened historical perspective and the growth of an individualism which has broken down the societal and, therefore, the cultural use of the word 'Christian', there is a third characteristic which directly affects our classroom practice today. It is the Protestant and, more especially, the Reformed emphasis on the Bible as the over-riding authority of the Christian faith.

A title such as 'Stories From the Christian Tradition' will have been interpreted by many as heralding a chapter on Bible stories and so it largely is, but the question of Bible stories is only a part, albeit a fundamentally important part, of a more substantial problem. That problem is whether we can establish a broadly Christian perspective, recovering the tradition as a whole and discovering themes and approaches that reflect it. The ecumenical challenge (which has to be faced in the classroom as much as anywhere else) is to recover the positive unity of the Christian perspective and tradition. With all this in mind let me now turn specifically to the stories.

Which Christian Story?

The Christian Story is essentially the story of Jesus Christ. That sounds simple enough but the question of, 'Which story do I tell?' remains. There are three distinct approaches which I meet in schools, of which the first two are by far the most common. They may be summarised as:

1   Stories of Jesus
2   The Jesus Story
3   The Christ Story.

The Christ Story is by far the most important. It provides the framework without which the other approaches become meaningless or distorted. By coming to it via a look at them I hope to demonstrate this point.

The Stories of Jesus

The 'Stories of Jesus' approach predominates in our Agreed Syllabuses, especially for the early years. We are encouraged to select certain stories on the grounds of their conceptual simplicity and their relevance to early childhood, without any particular reference to their context within the whole narrative.

So we get whole schemes of work on 'Stories of Jesus as a boy' or 'Stories which Jesus told'. This seems to me to be fine if, and nowadays it is a huge 'if', it can be assumed that the basic outline of the whole story is known from elsewhere. Otherwise these are simply decontextualised fragments building up a picture which is positively misleading.

Storytelling begins with the teller. Nobody should attempt to teach the story of the Christian Gospel without first sitting down and reading it whole. Again we are victims of tradition, in this case that of the Bible study group which seems to have made it impossible for anyone to read more than six verses at a time. Teachers are very busy people but the whole of Mark's gospel, in a modern translation, can be read in one sitting of about half an hour. It is only by reading it as the author intended that one sees it as one story and becomes aware of the relationship of the parts to the whole. It can also reveal a central character whose total personality is easily distorted by any one isolated incident. The 'Stories of Jesus' approach often promotes a 'Gentle Jesus meek and mild' image, an image difficult to sustain if one has actually read the book!

The 'simple concepts' argument of educationists is also one to be treated with caution in this context. As anyone who has struggled with New Testament Greek will know, John's gospel is by far the easiest to read, being virtually monosyllabic, but by far the most difficult to comprehend. Parables are nice little stories, but the word literally means 'hurled alongside' as modern Greek peasants still 'paraballo' hay with a pitchfolk at the feet of a tethered horse or donkey. If we do not know the tradition they challenged we shall not understand their basic concepts, however simple the language. Far from being nice little stories they were pretty offensive to many who heard them for the first time and it was his parables as much as anything else which got Jesus executed. And next time you do a simple little nativity play it might be an idea to get your nearest professor of theology to explain it! It is of the nature of religious myth that simplicity of language, accessible to all, conceals profundity of meaning often inaccessible to the greatest minds.

None of this is meant to undermine the telling of 'Stories of Jesus'. For future development the one overriding necessity is that the stories should be known but it is equally important that no one has to un-teach what has been taught earlier and that applies to the context, the mood and the ambience of these stories as much as to the factual details.

The Jesus Story

To adopt a 'Jesus Story' approach is to be more systematic and to see it as one story rather than many. The parts are then linked together and, as with any story, the links become as important as the separate incidents because they often take the form of inner reaction and conflict over something which has taken place. Action is followed by reflection instead of being left to stand alone. The 'Jesus Story' approach also restores the balance of the original storytellers. Whereas 'Stories of Jesus' tend to emphasise the early part of the narrative a whole reading quickly reveals that one of the Gospel writers' main concerns was for the last week, which takes up no less than a third of their whole story.

Telling the 'Jesus Story' does not involve going into every detail. The story is perfectly capable of being transmitted in outline but it demands balance and a structure which ensures that certain key elements are not omitted. One could argue about how many but it would be difficult to do justice to it as a story without mention of Birth, Baptism, Teaching and Preaching, Palm Sunday, Last Supper, Trial, Crucifixion and Resurrection, although it has to be said immediately that St Mark managed to omit the first of these. Within such a framework any amount of detailed padding can take place. My own attempts at this are to be found in *Bible Stories for Today*. The period from Christmas to Easter lends itself, of course, both to the outline and to the Gospel proportions. As a core theme for a humanities project it can hardly be bettered over that period, bringing in all the social customs and historical associations of fast and festival.

The 'Jesus Story' approach is not, however, the full story of the Christian tradition. Just as 'Stories of Jesus' can sometimes assume a life and even a meaning of their own which distort the 'Jesus Story', so it too, in its turn, has often become detached from what is the real story of the Christian tradition, rather than simply a Protestant version of it. At the core of the Christian tradition lies the Christ Story, of which the Jesus Story is a part but by no means the whole.

The Christ Story

Most children, and unfortunately some teachers, still tend to assume that the word 'Christ' is little more than Jesus' surname. It is, of course, a title, and a highly significant one. Jesus-bar-Joseph, or Jesus Josephson was acknowledged by his followers not to be Joseph's son but rather the Son of God, the Messiah – in Greek, 'Christos'. He himself also used the title 'Son of Man'. The theology of all this need not bother us much here, save perhaps to point out that the phrase 'son of' is used in English, especially the American variety, as much as in Greek to denote, 'one who has all the characteristics of', as, for example, in phrases like, 'You son of a devil' in many a Hollywood Western.

What does matter is that the fundamental story of the Christian tradition is not a man called Jesus, who told a lot of nice stories, nor even of a martyr figure who roamed the lanes of Palestine two thousand years ago and founded a new religion. All the history and all of the teaching stand within the context of a story of cosmic scope which holds that He was God in human form, however we might interpret that. The Christ Story holds that that which was within the Son of God was there at the creation of the world and will be there at its final consummation. In the Christ Story, unlike the Jesus Story, we have all the ingredients of the cosmic myth, which is the basis of all religions.

What then does this mean in practice? How is such a story to be told? The answer is reasonably straightforward, and prior to the Reformation, it was well known. The model is there in the medieval mystery plays which, significantly, are now enjoying a resurgence of popularity in the world of drama, if not yet in the ordinary classroom. The form of those plays needs our attention. Their story begins, not with the babe of Bethlehem, but with the Creative voice or word of God (as does John's gospel, incidentally) and it ends not with the Resurrection, but with the Second Coming which still lies in our future. All of history is included within the story which gives meaning to the whole. That, in its full technical sense, is the nature of myth and the Christian religion possesses it as fully as any other.

Again, scope must not be confused with detail. The medieval mystery plays are extremely economical with the latter. Often one patriarch and one prophet suffice as representative of their kind but the basic framework demands that all the key structural points are included, however briefly. Detail can be added at discretion provided the framework is adhered to.

In the classroom this has immediate implications. It means first that the Jewish Scriptures contain an integral part of the Christian Story which is incomplete without them. Secondly, the one Story is still going on: we are in the midst of it. The common factor is that to which we give the name 'Spirit'. Perhaps the best analogy is that of the baton in a relay race. It is the runners who are immediately visible but without the baton there is no continuity and, once dropped, all else counts for nothing.

Certainly for junior schools the post-Biblical part of the Story is best taught through the small-scale local enquiry. Religious communities of all sorts are opening up their doors again for educational purposes from St Paul's Church in Jarrow (within the very walls where Bede penned his ecclesiastical history) to Buckfast Abbey in Devon – and no doubt there are similar initiatives in Wales and Scotland too. The saints, as the running heroes of this continuing story, are there to be explored after a long period of neglect.

Finally, a brief word on method. The scope of the Christ Story can seem vast and daunting. It is endless and yet, as Ted Hughes has reminded us in 'Myth and Education' in essence it is very simple and straightforward. What is needed is not so much a swotting up of detail as an appreciation of rhythm. It was A. N. Whitehead's contention that in education it was far more important to know the broad trend, the scope of the outline, than to know the bits and pieces. By the rhythm of education he meant the process of constantly referring to the whole. A balloon remains one balloon whether partially or fully inflated. It only explodes when too much is crammed into it without sufficient reference to the capacity of the whole.

Similarly Kieran Egan in *Teaching As Storytelling*, has argued much more recently that young children learn most effectively when they first grasp the parameters of a subject before filling in the detail. He also, perhaps significantly as a North American, exhorts us to draw on mythology much more than we do in primary education, even if his ultimate conclusions are somewhat questionable.

In the teaching of Christianity, as in so much else today, the danger is of fragmentation. Stories from the Christian tradition abound by the million. The basic elements can be, and often are, lost in the details. Unless their connection with the central holistic Christ Story is established they are mere dust in the wind, little moral tales of dubious educational value and scarcely religious at all.

Bibliography

K. Egan, *Teaching As Storytelling* (Althouse Press, 1986)

Ted Hughes, 'Myth and Education' in G. Fox *et al.* (eds) *Writers, Critics and Children* (Heinemann, 1978)

E. Hulmes, *Educational and Cultural Diversity* (Longman, 1989)

J. Priestley, *Bible Stories For Today* 2 Vols, (Religious and Moral Education Press, 1984)

S. Toulson, *The Celtic Alternative: A Reminder of the Christianity We Lost* (Century, 1987)

A. N. Whitehead, *The Aims of Education and Other Essays* (Collier MacMillan, 1967)

CHAPTER 20

Hide and seek: an approach to mystery and myth in the middle years

ANGELA WOOD

One day, in a playful mood, God decided to hide from all people the purpose of their existence. 'The meaning of life must be in the search for its meaning,' thought God. 'Now where shall I hide the meaning? At the bottom of the ocean? No, what if it were discovered by deep sea divers or – perish the thought! – washed up on the beach over a Bank Holiday! At the top of a mountain, then? Not there, either: there's too great a risk that it might be accidentally stumbled upon by rock climbers or even blown off and land in someone's garden while they're hanging out the washing! I know! I will embed the meaning of life in the human heart: they'll never think of looking for it there . . .'

And so it is that we can unlock our lives with the key of our own selves . . .

Learning by doing

The danger that religion will become a mere 'phenomenon' – a thing 'out there', an aspect of society in an abstract sense or, at most, of *other* people's lives – becomes very powerful as children reach their teens. But they can be helped to see for themselves that religion is also *within* them, part of the way they seek to make sense of life. I wanted to open up with a class the idea that religion is to do with being a full human being and part of that focused on myth, symbol and ritual that explore, express and perhaps extend our humanity . . .

Rumour has it in educational circles that children learn by doing and it's a rumour I'm always pleased to spread, so I didn't want to impose a definition of myth as a narrative form that encapsulates an agreed system of meaning, evolving in its transmission, and then distribute several well chosen examples. Even the popular comparison of Genesis 1 with an 'Aborigine/Eskimo/ whosever' creation myth would have been entirely inappropriate. I wanted, if you'll forgive the jargon, to draw from the pupils' own experiences and I needed to start much further back. It helped to spend quite a lot of time in eliciting the pupils' views of what makes a human being.

155

Inevitably, the pupils made unwitting comparisons with (other) animals, by saying, for example, that people 'light fires', 'can talk with words', 'have a sense of humour', 'get beliefs', 'do some worship', 'ask questions' . . .

Getting it out

We examined in turn each of the 'charges' made about people and found ways to express them as aspects of ourselves. Several pupils chose to 'ritualise' the essence of humanity in drama and role play. Others, like Nazma Qusar, wrote stories:

> **WHY DO PEOPLE HAVE FRIENDS?**
> Once upon a time there was a man. He lives alone. He have no friends. He had no wife and no children. There was no one to talk to him. He was very sad. He had no house and he sleep on the road. One night when he was sleeping, he had a dream. He saw that there were so many people in a big house. He saw many people are talking and laughing. He saw that people are happy. Then he wake up. He wanted to have friends. He went outside. There were many people. He talked to one of them. They were very nice to him. They asked to have a drink. They asked him why he was sad, he said he has no friend. They said they will be his friend. They said they will help him. So he was very happy to have lots of new friends.
>
> *Nazma Qusar*

Some chose to draw and/or paint their ideas – alone or with others – portraying the attributes in either iconic or symbolic form, and devising an overall shape in which to hold together all the component parts. One boy drew a 'mind' (like those nineteenth-century speculative diagrams of the brain); one girl drew a full red mouth with one tooth per attribute. The 'in crowd' of the class did pairs of feet on the move. 'It's how you go through your life!' they explained. Two girls – one dark-skinned, one light-skinned – traced round each others' hands and cut templates. Then they made hands of different shades of 'flesh', each one holding in the palm an aspect of humanity. The hands were linked and mounted. There were, of course, many variations on the 'gingerbread man' with buttons for 'can solve problems', 'changes through time and place' or whatever. One, in particular, was dubbed 'multi-person' – a very mixed up kind of kid! – on the everyman theme, I suppose, with a variety of ethnic features to make the point. The most striking and, for me, the most moving, was produced by a boy often thought of as tough, especially by himself. Yet through this it became clear that he had within him great powers of sensitivity and insight, and a capacity for tenderness that was not usually evident. He wanted to get across the idea that 'we're born with ways that we're all the same underneath . . . they come from somewhere'. The all-embracing shape for him just *had* to be a foetus: he carefully copied an unborn child *in utero* from a glossy, 'coffee table' book on the birth of a baby which the school library had on reference. That became the centre-piece of his picture and around it, as though also suspended in fluid, were human qualities depicted on womby shapes. It was the most elemental, almost archetypal thing and it also had the aura of a time capsule spinning in space.

Do you paint your toenails?

Looking at each other's pictures, watching each other's plays, and reading each other's stories prompted both curiosity and wonder. It also led very smoothly into some more conscious questioning activity – asking about each other – and then into asking questions about questions.

There were open questions that offered almost any response – 'What do you fancy for tea?'; closed questions that permitted 'yes' or 'no' or only a very limited response such as 'a quarter past eleven'; and those that we came to call 'locked shut' questions, such as 'I told you before, didn't I?' Then there are questions you're not supposed to answer at all, for example, 'What time do you call this?' and other non-questions such as the kind that teachers usually ask when they know the answer and are only checking if the pupils know! ('What is the capital of France?')

Quite the opposite of these 'educational' questions are the essentially 'religious' ones – those at the heart of the human response to life, the 'big mysterious whys'.

There are, of course, 'why?' questions which want – and can get – direct answers of an empirical kind: 'Why is it raining?' – 'Because the wind has passed over water and . . .'; or 'Why did he hit her?' – 'Because she called him names!' But these aren't at all the same questions as 'Why does nothing stay the same?' or 'Why is there violence in the world?'

'Drip torture'

Young children naturally wonder . . . What happens to it? Does it fall, or jump, or is it pushed? Or perhaps nothing happens and a certain awe endures within us all, needing only a ray of light or a drop of rain.

But when we are older, we can't just feel magical all the time: we have to live in the 'real' world and we have to do 'proper work'. The 'big mysterious whys' can often have enough respectability and sophistication to enable that sense of the numinous to mature and to reflect in a dynamic way on the issues of life.

The formulation of such questions is the hard part: a technique which certainly helped was to work with 'mirror partners' where A asks B an empirical question and B has to resist fiercely the temptation to answer the question by supplying evidence, and instead had to convert it into a big

157

mysterious why. So that the answer to 'Why did John Lennon die?' is not 'Because someone shot him' but 'Why don't people live for ever?' (or some such). Then it's B's turn to ask A . . .

It didn't come easily at first: for some it was like water dripping on a stone; for others, the penny suddenly dropped! But soon the class had devised so many 'big mysterious whys' that we had a big graffitti wall of sugar paper headed 'We wonder why . . .'

'There are more questions than answers . . .'

How long can we go on asking? Are there no answers? Certainly, no easy or tidy answers anyway but one approach is to imagine a time when whatever-it-is wasn't and to speculate what might have happened to bring about what-ever-it-is.

Some of them leapt up immediately, wanting to act it out with others, making the meaning as they went along and only later recording the narrative for blessed memory. Others wrote cold. Here are some of their questions and some of their answers:

WHY ARE THERE SO MANY DIFFERENT THINGS ON EARTH?

One day, centuries and centuries ago there was no people, no trees, no houses, no anything. Only one big ocean and the wind. One day the wind said to the ocean, 'Ocean, I am bored. I have lived on this place for billions of years yet never have I seen anything but sea and water . . . sometimes a bit of land when you have calmed down you move and the land from underneath you shows.'

'I am also bored, Wind, but I have an idea. If you agree, we could make a storm then my land staying underneath me would want to come up and I could make space for the land underneath me. Then we would have a new view. They did this plan and were very pleased with themselves and so they lived for many years. One day Wind said to Ocean, 'I am sure that I see tiny things moving on our land.'

'You must be going mad. Our land is completely still!' But Ocean was wrong. Wind saw bacteria changing and making moving things on land and that began to form different things. The Wind still saw things but decided he would not tell Ocean and maybe Ocean couldn't see because she was lying flat. As things formed they changed into creatures . . . that's when Ocean saw them. So the wind whose name was Bronto and the Ocean whose name was Saurus decided that, seeing as they made this world, this creature should be called Brontosaurus.

As years passed, other creatures were formed. One was named from the Wind's aunt and the Ocean's uncle, called Coelo and Physis; so the creature was Coelophysis.

As billions of centuries passed, these creatures changed very much and the creatures created other different things for the land. The Wind and the Ocean were pleased and proud and still are now because they have seen our land change.

Amy Lamont

WHY IS THERE A SUN?

Once upon a time, there wasn't a sun. It was just the moon and stars. The night was night and the day was night. There was no electricity so the only light they had was from the moon and stars.

One day about a third of the world decided to go to see the wise one and ask for light. The wise one was the wisest one on earth and he could do nearly everything. He could grow flowers from stone and fire in water. His name was Zwaziywaizi and he lived in the land of Zwazwaz.

The people set off, guided by the light of the moon and stars. When they got to Zwazwaz land they were very tired. When they got to the house of wise Zwaziywaizi, a man aged about 21 and named Mongru, stepped forward and said, 'Look, wise one. How are we supposed to go on living like this? We only have light in the night and none in the day. If there is a moon in the night time, there should be something like a moon in the day!' The wise one was just listening to their comments and thinking of what to do. A few minutes later, the wise one spoke, 'If you want light, you must make a deal!'

'Yes, yes!' they all agreed. Then the wise one said, 'I will need all the stone on land so you must grow all crops yourself in the ground and promise to look after them.' 'Yes, yes!' they all said.

'Go,' said the wise one, 'and by tomorrow you shall have light.' The people went back to their land looking very happy. The next day, by some power the wise one had, all the stone he needed was beside his feet; then, by another power, he was floating up in the sky (with the stones). Then the wise one was crashing the stones together which made fire which became a sun. And as for the wise one, he just settled high up in the sky.

Charu Chopra

WHY ARE THERE DIFFERENT COLOURS?

Once there was only white colour. The people, animals, trees, everything was white. Then everyone got bored with white. They all got together and think. After many days they saw a bird. Then the bird told them that there is a wise man far away in the mountains. He knew the secret and could help them. The next day, they started their journey. After many days, they reached the place where the wiseman was. Then they was sitting under a tree and the wiseman told them that far away there is a tree that's full of colour fruit and it's guarded by a dragon. The wiseman said, 'If you go and get the fruit for me, I will use the fruit to make different colours.' Then they started their journey. After three or four days, they got to the place where the colour fruit tree was. Then a dragon come and a person give some food to the dragon to eat. Then the dragon fall asleep. Then they pick the fruit up and went back to the wiseman. Then they give the fruit to the wiseman and the wiseman throw the fruit in the sky and colours shoot out over the sky and that's why there is different colours.

Chun Wah Mak

WHY DO WE DIE AND WHY ARE WE BORN?

In the beginning, Earth had a sister planet, Mondas. And it was a perfect life: no one died and no one was born. This went on for centuries and the people were happy and God was happy.

One day in a village on Mondas a farmer by the name of Sven shouted. 'I do not believe in God!' The villagers heard this and someone said, 'Maybe Sven's right!' and these few convinced the rest and told the next village who told the next village and so on. Soon everyone on Mondas was saying, 'There is no God!' When the people on earth heard this, they believed the Mondasians for they were very gullible.

Meanwhile in heaven, God was in his celestial palace when the Archangel Gabriel entered. 'O Lord, the people of Earth and Mondas have stopped worshipping you.' At this, God sprang into a mighty rage. He grasped Mondas and split it into two. He then scooped out the core and threw them into the farthest reaches of space. Then he grabbed the people of Mondas and squeezed until their blood filled the two halves of Mondas. From these he drank his fill.

After he had finished drinking, God was filled with remorse but he knew he had to punish earth as well. So he said, 'People of earth, you have an end to your life but so that the human race will not die out, children will be born to women. So that is why we die and why we are born.

Daniel Tetsell

WHY DO WE DREAM?

Once, long ago, when the world was still young, it was ruled by a powerful druid called Calamor. At that time, the world was perfect except for one thing: nobody had dreams except Calamor since that was his only link with the gods. But because the people had no dreams, when they fell asleep everything was black. This made them afraid to sleep and because they did not sleep they were too tired to do any work such as giving sacrifices.

So he prayed to his gods and so the gods gave the people dreams but these weren't ordinary dreams. In these dreams, the gods spoke to them so they knew what to do the next day.

But one night when Calamor was in bed, he thought that now the people heard the gods' wishes directly, may be they won't need him to tell them. And if they don't need him to tell them he wouldn't be a druid and if he wasn't a druid he wouldn't be the ruler. So all that night he made a spell and when at last the morning came, he cast it. The spell made the people have dreams which were meaningless.

But when the gods found out, they could not change the spell because it was so powerful. So they took their revenge by killing Calamor with a lightning bolt.

Ivan El-Minyawa

Why do we ask questions? I am reminded of the story of the children who kept pestering their parents to help them with their homework:

'Dad, what's 57 times 91?'
'I don't know!'
'Mum, do you know the population of Mongolia?'
'No, I'm afraid I don't!'
'What's the chemical formula for hydrogen peroxide?'
No answer.
'You don't mind us asking all these questions, do you?' asked the children sheepishly.
'Not a bit,' replied the parents. 'How else will you learn?'

CHAPTER 21

Living the story: drama in religious education

DAVID SELF

Those who write about educational drama can appear to forget that the classroom teacher's main worry is not how you encourage personal development within the group dynamic or even how you initiate a meaningful exploration of myth, legend and history to create a religious experience. What actually keeps teachers awake in the small hours is how to get 50 children on to a small stage in the week before Christmas, ensure they all face the right way and get them off again without knocking over the scenery and without offending an above-average number of parents.

For others, the combination of 'RE' and 'Drama' conjures up images and memories of two or three children acting out a fairly sterile scene in front of the rest of the class or in assembly:

> *Esau*: I think hunting's the best way to get food.
> *Jacob*: I think farming's better than hunting.
> *Esau*: I don't.
> *Jacob*: Well you're wrong. You don't know what you're talking about. Farming's much better.
> *Esau*: It isn't.
> *Jacob*: 'Tis.
> *Esau*: 'Tisn't.
> *Jacob*: 'Tis . . .

Then again, there are those who, on coupling RE with drama, immediately think of *Godspell*, *Joseph and the Amazing Technicolour Dreamcoat* or whimsical Christian entertainments staged by touring evangelists whose world is their minibus. Consequently, I should perhaps begin by defining what I mean (in this context) by the word 'drama'.

Theatre or drama?

I am not referring to 'theatre' which exists primarily for its audience but to 'participant-centred' activity, activity which exists for the sake of those doing it. Usually it will be improvised rather than scripted with the emphasis on 'being' or 'doing' rather than on 'acting'. I would also expect it to involve a mixture of movement and verbal activity and that the whole class would be active at the same time, working in separate small groups *for themselves*, rather than with any immediate idea of 'rehearsal' or presentation to an audience. If, with pupils experienced in this form of improvised group drama, I subsequently invite one group to show their work to the others, it is because I feel it will be useful for the whole group to have one particular improvisation as a common basis for subsequent group discussion.

This last point indicates a basic way in which improvised drama can be of use in religious (or moral) education. Experience through drama is a most valuable stimulus to, and sustainer of, discussion. All too often, classroom discussion of even a simple moral or social point can be flawed by prejudice, ignorance or lack of imagination. It may also be limited by a very natural lack of courage (in being honest) in those participating. But if a discussion is preceded by one or more short improvisations, then a 'world' is created (and experienced at first hand) which is safe to discuss honestly (because it is imaginary and because it involves other 'people').

How this can work in practice can be imagined by thinking of an actual example. Suppose the topic being studied is 'caring for younger brothers and sisters'. If there have first been improvisations in which the various situations have been acted out in role (for example 'babysitting' or explaining to a parent why a younger sibling has got very muddy or wet), then the following 'discussion' will be all the richer.

Drama and story

However, the main point of this chapter is to consider the value of drama in relation to story and religious education – and it is indeed in the junior school age range where the younger child's readiness 'to make believe' can be employed in drama activities to great effect. Not only is a story that has been improvised more likely to be remembered (because it has been, in a sense, *lived through*), but it will also be better understood and appreciated because of the simulated experience.

I would not go on, as some have, to suggest that drama itself provides a religious experience. Occasionally it can. Quite often, with repetition, some work does acquire an element of ritual; but its main value in my opinion is that it can be more effective than simply hearing a story or seeing a picture. For example, it is possible to hold up a picture and to say, 'Look at this vine-yard . . . Yes, they're all getting paid, but when did each of them start work . . .? So how do you think they feel about that?' Far greater will be the understanding if the details of the parable are recreated step by step, before talking about its implications.

Structured activity

One problem, felt by some junior school teachers, is that while their pupils may happily embark on movement work, they lack the vocabulary, language skills and knowledge to undertake useful verbal improvisation. As more than one teacher has lamented, 'My all-ability group of thirty are fine for the first three or four minutes but then lose all sense of characterisation'. Of course, if a story is merely read or told to a class once and then they are instructed to act it out, the result may well be as unimpressive as the Esau and Jacob dialogue. Drama, if it is to be an effective learning medium, must be structured.

Let us take an example. Suppose the topic to be covered is the story of the Exodus and in particular the wanderings in the desert. How do we ensure that any drama work is more than a straggling procession round and round the hall or room, punctuated by the occasional squabble about leadership?

One possible 'structured' sequence of exercises would be to begin with an introductory activity such as 'rock-climbing' – with the children working in small groups of three to five. Each group elects a leader. The groups are told they are going to be roped together, with two metres of slack rope between each of them. They lie face down on the floor, and start to 'climb' a steep, vertical cliff. It will be necessary to slow them down with reminders of its steepness, the lack of hand and toe-holds, the importance of using holds found by the one in front, etc. Although the concept of leadership is introduced here, the main aims are to establish atmosphere and a particular pace.

Next we can begin to focus on the subject area (in this case, the Exodus), but first there is a need for 'in-put'. By questioning and by the direct provision of information, make sure they have at least some knowledge of a desert climate (for example, midday heat, night frost), the rarity of oases, the effects of a sandstorm (dangers of choking), etc. With certain classes, it may be useful to 'rehearse' separately the effects of each of these – as well as the problems of walking in soft sand and on rocky surfaces. In their groups, again with elected leaders, they can now cross 'their' desert. The exercise should be repeated with additional 'problems' such as one of their group becoming ill or injured. Other strictures could be added, including discussions about, say, whether they go on or retrace their steps. At each stage, allow time for discussion or revisions and time for one or two repetitions. Allow leaders to opt out of groups and to pool tactics while the others assess their leaders and decide what they want to do. Next, allow two or more 'tribes' to team up under one leader. After this, they could usefully discuss how the situation had altered.

Now it is possible to introduce those sections of the Bible story to be covered, and allow the larger groups to improvise their versions of 'how they think it was', step by step. Again, allow time for repetition after discussion of how they could add to their version and make it more like the original – if necessary, reminding them of specific details. Note that verses 22–4 of Exodus 15 on their own can sustain quite a lengthy improvisation.

Following the drama work comes the important 'de-briefing' of discussion. 'What happened?' 'What was it like being a leader?' Then the all important: 'How must it have been for the Jews?' 'What were Moses' problems?' etc.

It is important of course that the teacher does not judge the work as 'theatre' performed for him or herself (fascinating or frustrating though it may be on that level). What matters is the involvement of the participants and the realisations it brings to them.

Illuminating a story

Sometimes the improvisation of a modern parallel may be a more helpful way into a story. For example, groups of four might represent a family (mother, father and two children; or, in single sex groups, father/uncle or mother/aunt and two children). They run a corner, newspaper shop. (Allow for development of the story at each stage, encouraging the invention of names, character foibles, etc.) Scene two involves the elder 'child' pointing out that one day half the business will be his or hers and persuading the older generation to advance that half share to allow him or her to leave home and to go to the big city. Scene three might involve the work being re-divided between the remaining three (and perhaps reading about the other in the newspapers). Scene four is the homecoming with joyful reception, etc. Subsequent discussion can analyse the emotions and reasoning of each character – and then the introduction to (and comparison with) the Biblical parable can be made. If all has gone well, the Parable of the Prodigal Son will seem to be as relevant and provocative as when it was first told. Those who have been involved in the project should also be on their way to appreciating the parable's relevance in its own time.

When writing in this vein, it is easy to imply that drama is the wonder drug that will solve every teaching problem. I would not for a moment wish to suggest that. It would, for example, be an unsuitable approach to the stories involving the Prophet of Islam, and some may not wish to encourage the portrayal of a Jesus-figure. However, as a group becomes used to exploring stories in this way, it can become a popular and efficient teaching aid.

Drama and RE

I am aware that much of what I have written could apply equally to the teaching of, say, history. I do however believe drama is especially helpful in religious education. It is a subject in which many favour an experiential approach and it is also a fact that many of the objectives of drama (as a subject in its own right) coincide with those of religious education. As any drama specialist will confirm, drama can develop sensitivity, personal awareness, tolerance of others, the gift of sympathy and, in some intangible way, it can educate the emotions. The list could be very much longer and suggest convincingly why drama deserves its own place in any school timetable. However, as I have suggested here, I believe it is too valuable to be 'only' a subject in its own right. It is a particularly useful way of exploring some of the areas that are part of a religious education. As the very experienced drama teacher, Dorothy Heathcote, says: 'Very simply it means putting yourself into other people's shoes and, by using personal experience to help you understand their point of view, you may discover more than you knew when you started.'

All this is not to suggest that children should undertake drama work only for themselves and never share their creativity with others. Indeed, while some may be quite happy to keep their improvised scenes to themselves, others will be eager for an audience!

What I would suggest is that we, as teachers, keep clear in our own minds the different purposes of 'drama' and 'theatre' and make sure that any audience beyond the class is aware which they are being invited to share.

In the case of drama, this may mean no more than making an announcement before the presentation: 'This term we've been learning about Christmas, about how we celebrate it today and about what happened on the first Christmas. What we want to do now is share with you what we have learned.' (Note: a group is *not* ready to share improvised work if the drama changes substantially when recreated in front of an audience – be that audience other members of the class, the rest of the school or parents. Provided they can remain in role, without 'opting out' to react to audience remarks etc., then they are perhaps ready to work in front of others).

Creating a 'play'

Once a tradition has been established of using drama as a way of exploring religious 'stories', then there is no reason why it should not be used in the *creation* of a Christmas 'play'. It must be stressed again that the audience should be aware that they are sharing in 'storytelling' (or drama) which exists for the sake of those involved in its creation and that they are not merely being invited to witness (and assess) a theatrical happening.

Once everyone appreciates this an awful lot of the producer's worries evaporate. Most of the rest disappear if you remember that only masochists tackle a scripted play with the under-eights and that only sadists dream of staging any junior age production on a conventional stage. If you do, it will end in tears. They deserve to be yours. Unfortunately, they are more likely to be those of a poor, confused, embarrassed mixed infant.

166

If your school is cursed with a school hall that has a stage, do not use the stage. If the head or tradition dictates its use, plead the chance to 'do different' for just one year.

The ideal arrangement is 'in the round', with the audience surrounding the acting area. Next best is a horseshoe layout. In either case, two or three circles of chairs will seat just as large an audience as will a conventional layout. Gone are the problems of straining to see from the back; gone are the worries of getting young actors to perform that most unnatural act of not speaking to each other but out to the audience; gone are the problems caused by the bunching of actors in one corner.

Gone too are problems of scenery. All you need are a few chairs and stools to serve as inn chairs, thrones, etc., a bale of hay (if possible) to announce the stable, and a manger. 'Journeys' become tours around the acting area.

The main point to watch for when staging a play in the round comes if you are using stage or directional lighting. Ideally such lamps should be mounted at an angle of 60 degrees to the floor, to avoid dazzling the audience.

The first rehearsal of an improvised play consists of your retelling the story (no matter how well-known it is) to those who will be presenting it. This retelling should be as vivid as possible: its richness and enthusiasm are what will fuel improvisations.

Divide the performers into groups of four or five. In early rehearsals each group will improvise every section of the story, playing all the parts. Note how many additional characters can be introduced into the story – Joseph and Mary must go to several inns, each must be crowded; servants are needed to carry in stools and chairs; the Wise Men visit Herod and his court must be populated.

After each improvisation offer encouragement, not criticism. Discuss what the events must have been really like. How did people feel? Further improvisations can be initiated to develop an awareness of Mary's weariness, Joseph's worries, the shepherds' awe, Herod's jealousy etc.

As improvisations become richer and more confident, allow groups to show their work to each other. Let this transition be as natural as possible. The emphasis is still on 'being', not acting.

Gradually, it will become clearer which group is most successful in each section and 'casting' can take place. From now on, a particular group will usually be the shepherds; another the Wise Men, etc. This should not preclude groups from improvising other people's scenes occasionally. As everyone comes to understand each section, there will be no problem when Melchior catches measles – except of course for Melchior.

Do not despair if the first run-through is either very short or very long. Accept it with encouragement. Provide time for group discussion and recollection of the story-line. Do not kill spontaneity by implying each scene must always be exactly the same.

In final rehearsals, discourage haste. Stress the need for 'eye contact' with the person being spoken to. Have at least two dress rehearsals, to allow the children to get used to their costumes.

After being involved in a project like this (which should not normally extend over more than four weeks), you may indeed discover that the involvement and sincerity generated by improvised drama result in a shared experience that is as educational and as moving for the parental audience as it is for your pupils.

And that, after all, is perhaps a kind of religious experience.

CHAPTER 22

The role of art in junior religious education

JO PRICE

The place of the visual arts in religious education is partly to stimulate the imagination and partly to communicate beliefs and practices.

In considering the questions and concerns with which religions deal we try to help children in their spiritual development. There is a potential for spirituality within every human being, and it is an area that can be nurtured and developed. HMI, in their publication *Guidelines 5–16* identify nine areas of learning and experience, one of which is the spiritual:

> This area of learning and experience points at its most general to feelings and convictions about the significance of human life and the world as a whole which pupils may experience within themselves and meet at second hand in their study of the works and the way of life of other people. Pupils can be helped to reflect upon those aspects of human life and the natural world which raises questions of ultimate meaning and purpose.
>
> *(DES, The Curriculum from 5–16, 1985)*

Through art we can help children use their experiences to externalise their internal thoughts and concerns. Knowledge and understanding too may be communicated through art.

Through religious education children can begin to learn how individual religious traditions resolve or suggest strategies for coming to terms with questions of ultimate concern. Accumulating facts and learning about a religious tradition is one part of RE, but we also need to address the area of developing an awareness of self, respect for others, and a sense of awe and wonder of the natural world that surrounds us. Art can provide a powerful vehicle in achieving this end. As Edmund Leach, in 'What Are the Arts For?' has said:

> If we are then to act as other than automata, we need from time to time to scrub out the programme, break down all the conventional categories, jumble everything together and start the sorting and ordering process all over again. That is what re-creating is about; that is what religion is about; that is what the arts are for.

We can see the results of man's involvement with religions through art all around us. Explicit architecture, artefacts, paintings, illuminated manuscripts, all speak for themselves, often labours of love and devotion expressing deeply held beliefs.

An artist's response to an awareness of the beauty of the natural world all around us or deep-felt human emotions can be viewed in any art gallery. The imagination may have been fired, a message communicated, or an experience reflected upon. Where words may be inadequate the visual image expresses all. Jack Priestley, in 'Teaching Transcendence', stresses the importance of young people encountering the 'beyond which always eludes'. However the teaching of RE does not always guarantee that the transcendent or the reflective elements are being pursued. We are too often preoccupied with the content of religions, with a closed approach concerned with questions and answers. The expressive arts are essentially open-ended and therefore a necessary vehicle in the full understanding of religion. Visual art work should link closely with other areas within the expressive arts such as dance, music and drama. Both the arts and religious education are part of the whole curriculum and it is necessary to plan for them in a cross curricular way.

The role of art

In order for art work to make a positive contribution to RE it is important to decide on aims and objectives. In Chapter 1 Robert Jackson identifies three elements pertinent to the use of art within the development of RE:

1   A sensitising element
2   An imaginative element
3   An expressive element.

Edwin Cox, in *Problems and Possibilities for Religious Education*, also suggests there are a number of basic awarenesses or sensitivities:

- A sense of continual change. An awareness that nothing in human experience is static, the natural world is in a state of flux, we ourselves are transitory. The world will never again be as it is at this moment.
- A sense of our relationship to the dependence on the natural order. Human beings are physically part of the animal kingdom and they rely for their food on the process of growth in other animals and plants.
- A sense of order in what we experience. An apprehension that the world in which we live and the experiences that come to us in it can be understood . . . it leads to the conviction that life too can be understood and may have some point . . . unless a person has the underlying feeling that the world has some kind of order, however dimly perceived, the questions of purpose that religions are concerned with will not seem worth discussing, and religions will not seem worth taking seriously.

- A realisation that there are other persons in the universe and that they deserve consideration and respect. Although I have to look at the world through my own eyes, I am not the centre of it, nor am I the only person living in it. There are other centres of consciousness, other individuals, and I have to take them and their ideas into account. We live in a complex of individuals and greatly mould and fashion each other.
- A sense of right and wrong. An awareness that perhaps actions can be divided into those that are desirable and good and those which are undesirable and bad, and that there ought to be some way of deciding into which particular category any particular action can be placed.
- A sense of the mystery inherent in life. A feeling of it, and a response to it, is perhaps one of the mainsprings of religions, which refer to it, in its most intense forms, as the 'numinous'.

Art activities

The following examples seek to demonstrate how art can provide an important contribution in addressing the above elements and sensitivities. The examples have been tried and tested in the classroom and it is hoped that they might stimulate thinking and inspire the reader to develop ideas that may be accommodated within their own topics and teaching styles. There is no intention of providing a comprehensive and exhaustive checklist of 'art ideas for RE'. It would be artificial to view each subject in isolation, and there should be considerable rigour applied in both ensuring a cross curricular approach and a view of the learning outcomes planned for each individual child within each area of experience.

A sense of continual change . . .

Towards the end of the junior school, children will often explore the topic of change, often related to a programme of health education. Using blue sugar paper, white chalk and charcoal children can depict themselves symbolically as they were when very young, as they see themselves now, and as they envisage themselves in ten years' time. A child's life unfolds on a single sheet of paper: perceptions of themselves, how they have changed as individuals, their aspirations and fears for the future. Often the three stages merge dramatically with one another.

This theme lends itself to work on Buddhism and the concept of impermanence. In order to appreciate fully how very slowly changes can occur the teacher may like to provide white paper, brushes, mixing palette, and white powder paint, plus one other colour. Beginning with a white brushstroke, the paper is slowly covered with gradations of the second colour painstakingly added to the white. No drawing is required, the pattern that is built up evolves from the starting point of the initial brush-stroke.

A sense of our relationship to and dependence on the natural order . . .

In order to begin to understand this relationship we must allow children to become involved physically with the natural world. Children can be taken to such places as the school grounds, a park, field or woodland area. Here, armed with boards, white cartridge paper, four primary powder colours, brushes and mixing palettes they can begin to observe colour, texture, and shapes.

Work on these paintings could continue over a period of two to three weeks, observing and recording changes which have occurred. Animals and pets can be used in the classroom, or observed closely outside. Observations can then be translated into clay, drawings, painting or collage.

A sense of order . . .

There is pattern and shape all around us. It is not necessary to focus merely on man-made patterns; collections of natural objects, such as a dried sunflower head, leaves, a honeycomb, or an ear of corn, collections of shells, or pebbles, can all allow children to explore their tactile properties, and can be arranged and rearranged into patterns of their own. All these may be drawn, painted, recreated in print or clay.

Rites of passage and festivals create order and ritual in religions. Children can be asked to make a personal response to their own experiences, for example a wedding they have attended, the arrival of a new baby in the family. What emotions are aroused? How can these be translated in terms of art?

Allow children to explore colour, shape and media in relation to feelings of joy, anxiety, etc. Festivals are brought to life throughout. Carnival is often neglected, yet children can be caught up in the creative element surrounding this festival. Masks can be constructed, and large paintings and collages on cardboard transformed into costume by the addition of shoulder straps.

A realisation that there are other persons in the universe and that they deserve consideration and respect . . .

We can begin by one child using another as a model for close observational drawing using black fine-line pens (or a selection of drawing pencils) on white cartridge paper. Roles can be reversed and the children might ask one another questions which will reveal aspects of their partner's personality. How are individuals seen by other members of the class? Portraits can be re-done, this time using different media such as oil pastels, paint or clay. Is the personality, an understanding of the individual, beginning to show through? In order to understand others we need to have a perception of ourselves. Allow children the use of materials such as discarded boxes, wood, or fabric, and allow them to make models of themselves that would indicate visually some aspect of either their physical appearance or perhaps personality or aspirations.

A sense of right and wrong . . .

Moral dilemmas may be explored from within, the feelings and reactions externalised through art before being verbalised. Religious story, events, familiar situations, may all be explored in this way. An extract from the *Diary of Anne Frank* can be used in considering aspects of Judaism. The extract may be read individually without discussion and may be backed up by a showing of the video *Dear Kitty* (This video contains some disturbing scenes, so care may be needed in selecting appropriate sections.) Such starting points may generate deep feelings and emotions. The teacher may wish to allow children to have access to a wide variety of art materials and to allow considerable freedom in how they respond. Intense feelings such as anger, horror, pity, will be involved and should children not wish to discuss their responses, then that wish should be respected. Once the children have externalised their feelings, an open-ended and sensitive discussion of the original material can take place.

A sense of the mystery inherent in life . . .

If we consider light and energy, we could look at great painters whose work exemplifies the emotional, sensual and intellectual implications of these mysteries. With the children, the teacher may like to look at the works of Rembrandt. All his work is lit from within and has no clear, identifiable source of light. His figures exude a spiritual light that illuminates the painting. There appears to be a searching for truth, honesty, and simplicity. *The Holy Family at Night*, and *The Crucifixion* are two such examples.

Dramatic effects of light and shade can be created by lighting a candle near a subject. This offers fascinating ways of responding to expression.

The sun is a source of energy, a life giving force. Looking at the paintings of Van Gogh we can see that yellow dominates. The sun was his God and provided him with the necessary energy to enable him to interpret the world. Notice a centrality of marks that revolves in his portraits at the centre of the face – between the eyes, rather like iron filings around a magnet.

The circle is a very significant shape in art. It also has symbolic characteristics across the major world faiths. Children can explore the source of circles within nature, making their own by cutting, tearing, painting and sculpting.

One of life's greatest mysteries is the creation. A creation myth, particularly one which stimulates visual imagery, can be read as a starting point and can then be developed firstly by exploring the language, and then by translating verbal expression into visual imagery using a variety of media. Suitable creation music can be provided, allowing children to respond freely, concentrating on colour, movement and form.

Using clay, children can 'create' something of their own relating to the myth. Having created they can then sculpt the 'creator', arms enveloping the creation.

Imagination is an important element in the religious education of children. Art is a potent vehicle for its development. Art is not solely for the accomplished artist. We can enjoy the artist's creation, but we can also be creative ourselves, expressing our feelings and using our own imagination.

Bibliography

E. Cox, *Problems and Possibilities for Religious Education* (Hodder and Stoughton, 1983)

E. Leach, 'What Are the Arts For?' (*The Observer*, 9 September 1973)

J. Priestley, 'Teaching Transcendence' in D. Webster and M. Tickner (eds), *Religious Education and the Imagination*, *Aspects of Education* No. 28, (University of Hull, 1982)

Acknowledgements

I should like to thank children and staff in the schools across Warwickshire in which I have worked for their co-operation and inspiration. Particular thanks go to Carole Etherington, Headteacher at St Andrew's C of E Middle School, Rugby, and Malcolm Wray, Art Inspector for Warwickshire.

CHAPTER 23

Music's contribution to junior RE

ROBERT GREEN

Very often music is used to serve other parts of the curriculum. It has, with the other expressive arts, much to offer on its own and in integration. The second aim of music education from those listed in *Music 5 to 16* (p. 2), 'to develop insight through music into areas of experience some of which cannot easily be verbalised', finds echoes in many statements about religious education: 'children can, for example, understand a good deal more about religion than they are able to express in language' (p. 3). RE is not just about children gaining knowledge of religions. To establish understanding, children need to relate the material to their own experience and make their own responses.

At this point RE and music are very close to one another. Keith Swanwick, in *A Basis for Music Education*, summarises music and the arts' role:

> The crucial concept here is not creative self-expression, or social relevance, or technical skill, it is *responsiveness*. To respond means to make an answer to, to show sensitiveness to and to correspond with. The ability to respond adequately to another person, an object, a life experience or whatever is a fundamental and crucial human attribute. To feel a lack of it is to go hungry, to find the world grey and bleak ... An aesthetic experience is primarily and always an intensified response raised into full consciousness. Aesthetic means to feel more powerfully, to perceive more clearly. Its opposite is *anaesthetic*.
>
> *(p. 112)*

It seems that music, like RE, has influence over the more serious and real parts of our lives. Culture and religion are inseparable. But also music should be *fun*, and *joy* is found in all religions. Creativity can help us to a personal understanding of the issues faced by individuals and by society. Responses which would be highly complex if expressed in verbal language can be made easier by the creative arts. Indeed I am constantly surprised and delighted by the sophisticated responses made to the arts, and music in particular, by younger children.

There is no doubt that music and RE together can help children towards an understanding of moral and religious issues. The aim of this chapter is to suggest some ways of using music in junior RE. Both curriculum areas will benefit and others may be added even further to enrich the experience. Various strategies will be proposed, some for the less skilled in music, some requiring help from the music consultant or specialist.

There are three musical activities: **Composing, Listening** and **Performing**. Ideally a good music scheme (even the individual lesson) should include the three ingredients.

Composing

For those that consider themselves 'unmusical' or who feel that music is a mystery, composing may seem a daunting proposition. Yet it is no more so than exploring with colour and paint or devising dramatic role play for drama. Any organised sound is an exciting musical event. The following suggestions are fairly easy to use. How angry art teachers become when told, 'I can't draw, Miss'. The same applies for music. The important thing is to have a go, to go on a mutual voyage of discovery for pupils and teacher alike.

A musical collage can use any sounds, natural, vocal or instrumental. They can be put together at random or directed by signs, either written or gestured. Many 'musical' shadings may be added, for example, loud(f), quiet(p), faster, slower, higher, lower, more emphatic etc. Methods for notating this are best invented by the children. Figure 1 is an illustration of a simple graphic score. Inventing their own symbols with colour and shape will add another creative activity.

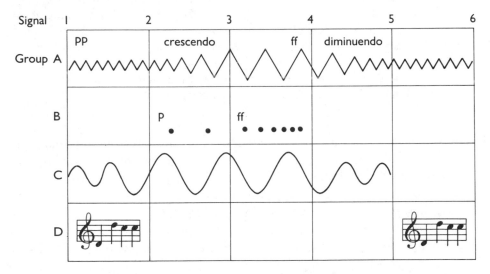

Figure 1
pp = very quiet   crescendo = get louder   ff = very loud   diminuendo = get quieter
Groups A–D may be played on any suitable sound maker, for example C might be voices wailing or violin glissandos, D might be pitched percussion, recorders or electronic keyboard. The signals are not necessarily given at regular intervals. The whole improvisation can be allowed to develop its own mood and texture under the direction of the conductor, who gives the signals.

This sort of composing is used to illustrate stories, poems and drama and can lead to subtle moods and atmospheres. The results should be recorded to enable everyone to hear the complete piece. Use as much space as possible with antiphonal groupings. The sounds will include vocal, natural, instrumental (classroom and orchestral) and electronic (keyboards and computers) examples and may lead to the addition of words. Sometimes this work includes fully notated tunes or rhythms.

Children enjoy writing their own tunes. Working in pairs with a prepared instrument they can construct a good melody, which may be a setting of words. The scale (series of notes) that they are given will influence the final result. The following selection of scales (Figure 2) are fun to use. It is best to suggest initially that the composers start and finish on the first note of the scale. Some accompaniments are added in the form of *ostinati* (repeating patterns). Where these accompaniments are similar, they can be used as easy links between the different moods created by the scales. As in the collage, there are many subtle nuances in the scales themselves; these can be further coloured by the choice of instrument. Contrast a tune played on electronic keyboard, flute, metallophone, trumpet, old metal bar or tin tray.

Some of these scales immediately open doors to music from various cultures; further avenues to explore are Gamelan, African Drumming and Blues, Jazz and Rock. Refer to Vulliamy and Lee – *Rock, Pop and Ethnic Music in Schools* for very practical help. Try creating your own ritual chant; see the listening list below for Gregorian and African chants.

Listening

It is even more important that children have the opportunity to widen the palette of sounds and music that they hear. More exposure to music has not meant that variety has gone hand in hand with quantity. But listening is not solely going to concerts or listening to a record, cassette or compact disc. It is also listening to your own composing and performing and being aware of all the sounds around you.

Ideally children should experience as much music as they will story, technology or fine art, for example. Listening needs to have variety and provides a good opportunity for integration with other parts of the curriculum. There is a mystery about the response we make to communal artistic experience. Blacking in *How Musical is Man?* describes it as 'being alone in company', a nice phrase that is not far from some responses to religion. Linking composed music to stories and experiences in religions is exciting and relevant. The following chronological list is *very* selective and is intended as a starting point. It covers aspects of 'religious music' over a number of centuries. A personal choice is always the best; music that you find powerful and stimulating will be easier to convey to the children. This list will, it is hoped, jog memories and start discovery. All music is 'suitable' for young ears. Play short examples and encourage discussion and language development. Maybe one short excerpt every day for a week might be followed by time for playing the favourites again. A live performance is much preferred when possible. A visit to a church, temple, synagogue or gospel hall is made much more exciting with some live music. How many children hear a first-class cathedral choir in the resonance of a huge building?

Figure 2

Note: Any groups of notes chosen from the Pentatonic (1) and the Whole-tone (2) scales will make good accompaniments for tunes using those scales.

The rhythm of the suggested accompaniments may be changed to suit the metre and the mood of the tune.

Add untuned percussion to supply rhythmic accompaniment. Start with chanted word rhythms. For the Raga add a Tala rhythm, for example:

X = Main beat
O = Silent wave

Listening list

Gregorian Chant

Twelfth century organum

Mediaeval and Renaissance Polyphony – an enormous field to explore. Try these English composers – John Dunstable, John Sheppard, Thomas Tallis, William Byrd, Orlando Gibbons

Giovanni Gabrieli: antiphonal motets with instrumental accompaniment, for example *In ecclesiis*; *Hodie completi sunt*

Monteverdi: *Vespers (1610)*

Vivalidi: *Gloria*

J. S. Bach: *Sanctus* from *Mass in B minor*; *St Matthew Passion*

Handel: *The Trumpet Shall Sound* and The *Hallelujah* Chorus from *The Messiah*

Haydn: the opening section of *The Creation*

Mozart: *Dies irae* from the *Requiem*

Berlioz: *Te Deum*

Verdi: *Dies irae, Libera me* from the *Requiem*

Walton: *Belshazzar's Feast*

Tippett: *A Child of Our Time*

Britten: *War Requiem*

Messiaen: Organ Music

Missa Luba – based on music from the Congo

David Fanshawe: *African Sanctus*

Spirituals

Russian Orthodox choral music

Lloyd Webber: *Jesus Christ, Superstar*

Stephen Schwartz: *Godspell*

Gospel Choirs – numerous recordings are now available

The Resource section (p. 183) in *Festivals* has good lists of recorded music from around the world and includes a cassette. Each chapter of *Rock, Pop and Ethnic Music in Schools*, lists relevant recorded music

Indian Music by Leela Floyd includes a cassette

Performing

Performing or sharing music is often the culmination of much creative work. All music making is a social event in which we enjoy working together. In performing we can extend this communal pleasure to include an audience. In the context of RE this aspect is particularly useful. Through music-making we can together express a whole range of emotions.

Choice of material for performing is always difficult since there are new compositions emerging daily. Nearly all songs reflect a range of experience which will lead towards an idea to extend the curriculum. For example, 'Jack and Jill went up the Hill' suggests the history of water supply, carelessness, the development of modern bandages, regret, pain and sympathy! Specific material from world religions is becoming increasingly easy to find. Two books which use festivals as a starting point are *Festivals* by Jean Gilbert and *A Musical Calendar of Festivals* by Barbara Cass-Beggs. In both cases the openings for further work are tempting and both books contain background information and ideas for cross curriculum work.

The pressing need in performing songs or hymns is that the experience should be fun and that a good standard of performance be aimed at. Nevertheless it seems a pity if we always go for the immediate catchy success. Cultural heritage is important. For today's child to know 'Prepare' from *Godspell* but not to have enjoyed, for example, 'When I survey the wondrous cross' might be a loss in future years.

Music can unite contrasting religious festivals simply on technical grounds. 'Taffta Hindi', in *A Musical Calendar of Festivals*, (p. 78) for the Hindu festival of *Onam*, uses a similar scale to 'O Hanukkah' (p. 102) for the Jewish festival. (It is basically the Dorian mode – see Figure 2.) 'Hari Krishna' (p. 93) uses a similar scale and is sung by a leader followed by the congregation in the same way that Gregorian and African chant make use of the antiphonal effect. This links well with the composing element described above.

Performing a story through music

To illustrate in more detail how a music response may enhance and intensify a child's experience, the story of St Francis and the Wolf at Gubbio is given some suggestions for musical presentation. This version of the story is taken from *St Francis and the Wolf* illustrated by Masahiro Kasuya. Key moments only are quoted from the story.

Introductory music: Dawn
Ravel: *Daphnis and Chloe* (Suite No. 2) – opening
Mahler: *Symphony No. 1* – opening

> It was very early in the morning. Dawn had begun to break but still there were no signs of life . . .

Sound Collage – the Silent Village
Each note of the whole-tone scale is played on the chime bars at random, or when directed, by seven players while other sounds are added on untuned percussion or with the voice.

> A huge wolf, starving and ferocious terrorised the neighbourhood . . .

Wolf music
Untuned percussion or a strong tune of three or four notes. Try the Dorian mode (Figure 2).

Just then St Francis of Assisi reached Gubbio. Known by everyone, he walked from town to town . . .

St Francis theme
Use words suggested by the children to create a simple verse which can be set to music using the gentler pentatonic scale (Figure 2).

. . . Next morning St Francis set out for the forest in search of the wolf . . .

St Francis confronts the wolf
A threatening repetitive drum beat represents his determined walking – add the St Francis theme. A gradual intensifying of the atmosphere is improvised introducing more instruments, getting louder, adding electronic effects from a keyboard or synthesiser and, perhaps, a vocal chant, until a sudden climax as the wolf leaps out.

. . . Suddenly on the edge of the forest the wolf, growling horribly . . . But St Francis was not afraid. Standing quite still . . .

A sudden silence followed by quiet, static music, perhaps Vaughan Williams: *Fantasia on a Theme by Thomas Tallis.*

. . . 'How wicked you have been, Brother Wolf . . . Now come with me and apologise to the poor villagers of Gubbio' . . .

A gentle walking rhythm with the St Francis theme and the Wolf's theme, this time quiet and calm.

. . . Next day the sound of children laughing and birds singing could be heard again, and the villagers, too, sang at their work.

An opportunity to sing a song about animals, creation, service or kindness. Also a recording of bird-song might be mixed with the children's own collage compositions of sounds of the village and the countryside. Finally a piece of exuberant dance music might be played of any style, any period.

These outline suggestions take a fairly conventional view of the story. The whole is easily modernised to include current important issues, for example, the 'green' movement, the World Wide Fund for Nature. A more modern approach would be matched with modern music to set the scenes and mood. The whole presentation should combine art, movement, drama, creative writing and environmental studies.

The musical ideas described in this chapter will all contribute to the school assembly, using it as a useful time to share class activities, to give children the satisfaction of perfecting something for sharing and to heighten the impact of a topic or story. The usual communal singing and playing at assembly are quite compatible with this, and if combined with focused listening, add much to the artistic environment of the school.

Music is one of the subjects included in the National Curriculum. If it is used in an imaginative way it will benefit everyone, children, community, the less musically confident teacher and increase the understanding of different cultures. And, of course, it is fun.

Bibliography

J. Blacking, *How Musical is Man?* (UOWP, 1973)
B. Cass-Beggs, *A Musical Calendar of Festivals* (Ward Lock Educational, 1983)
L. Floyd, *Indian Music* (OUP, 1986)
J. Gilbert, *Festivals* (OUP, 1986)
HMI, *Music 5 to 16* (HMSO, 1985)
R. Jackson (ed.), *Approching World Religions* (John Murray, 1982)
M. Kasuya, *St Francis and the Wolf* (J. M. Dent, 1983)
K. Swanwick, *A Basis for Music Education* (NFER, 1980)
G. Vulliamy, *Pop, Rock and Ethnic Music in Schools* (CUP, 1982)

PART FIVE

Methods and Issues

Introduction

Religious education is a constantly renegotiated activity. It is sensitive to developments in our understanding of religion, to freshly perceived social needs, even to the prevailing understanding of 'childhood' and to the way 'learning' is understood from one generation to another. It is thus full of 'issues' and, to the extent that we think we have resolved them, it ought also to be full of 'methods'. The situation is one of perceived needs, more or less firmly resolved responses, and some remaining questions. The contents of this section reflect that situation. They capture a stage in the development of RE which is divided here into common concerns (our governing aims and objectives), combined and integrated studies, fieldwork, and school worship.

Common concerns

Consider first the ground rules by which we now operate. Jill Davies writes about a rather specialised operation in her chapter on special needs; but her ground rules are certainly not unique to special schools or to the Agreed Syllabus from which she in fact drew the objectives for the Primary Phase:

- to foster children's feelings of awe, wonder, delight, joy and mystery.
- to encourage in children a recognition of their own value and importance as individuals.
- to help children consider their personal response to moral issues; to assist them in their early exploration of the meaning of life and to help them face and learn from painful experiences which they encounter, such as fear, suffering and death.

Activities appropriate to those particular children are both vivid and direct. For example, we see children with learning difficulties celebrating the fact and the sense of community by hanging leaves on a tree (named for each person present) and by lighting a candle for each person in the group. Perhaps programmes in other schools (where there is not the same specific dedication to providing for special needs) will be more elaborate in range and content. But one has a sense that 'special needs' pupils might in some senses be getting the best of it, and that for all of us there is the challenge to touch the hearts and minds of children with the sense of meaning, mystery, celebration and individual worth within a community. These are things to be celebrated in the lives of children and shown to them as a key to the appreciation of religious forms of life. Eleanor Nesbitt and Robert Jackson add another dimension to this by reminding us that children often come to school with experience of religion. We need to be sensitive to this, to learn about it and to learn from it.

Combined and integrated studies

Although the basic curriculum is defined in terms of subjects, the organisation of teaching and the delivery of the curriculum does not have to take place within subject boundaries. Indeed, it will be regrettable if methods so suitable to the expanding awareness of the young child are ousted by the formal requirements of subject accountability.

With the advent of the National Curriculum, Rachel Gregory's chapter on topic work is very timely. It demonstrates the advantages that accrue to RE and to other subjects in an integrated curriculum. But at the same time, we are shown how to distinguish between various kinds of topic work, how to recognise a badly conceived topic and how important it is to work within an overall scheme for the school so that there can be due balance and progression.

Fieldwork

Dennis Starkings describes some visits to places of worship. Such occasions are special opportunities to experience the meaning of religion – opportunities too easily lost or thrown away if visits serve merely to 'illustrate' things already attempted in the classroom. The theme broadens with Robert Jackson's account of the exciting things that can happen when children become ethnographers. It is amazing what junior children can do and comprehend if our sense of possibilities is large enough to let them get on with it!

School worship

The chapter on 'Worship in the junior school' is written by a Chief Producer for BBC Radio who has needed to make educational sense of the Education Reform Act's provisions. Geoffrey Marshall-Taylor's reflections will be welcome to teachers who face the same challenge.

CHAPTER 24

Topic work and junior RE

RACHEL GREGORY

When I inherited my first classroom I discovered that each seven-year-old in the class had a drawer bulging with dog-eared exercise books: books for the 3Rs, of course, but also grey books for History, orange for Geography, green for Nature Study, dark red for Religious Education (or was it 'Scripture'?) and so on. A look in the teacher's drawer revealed a syllabus that clearly laid down what should be taught each term in each subject, and each exercise book was obviously expected to absorb its appropriate weekly dose of writing-plus-picture. I dutifully followed the system – although it soon became clear to me that the goal as far as many of the children were concerned was to finish a book and experience fleetingly the sensuous delights of a new exercise book.

By the time talk of teaching through topics and themes filtered through to me I was already asking myself whether teaching young children about cavemen and continents, jaguars and Jesus, all in the same week, made any sort of sense, let alone educational sense! Some kind of integrated approach using topic work seemed to be the answer. So it was out with the exercise books and in with the topic folders and home-made books, and I began to experiment.

The RE dimension

At first RE remained on the sidelines, seemingly too different or difficult to rub shoulders with the rest of the curriculum. It seemed safer, and easier, to stick with the weekly Bible story and put an unequivocal tick in my record book. But gradually RE crept into the topics. After all, it was easy enough to choose the Bible stories to fit in with the current topic. By selecting two or three Bible stories to suit the topic title I assumed I was adding a religious dimension to the topic. When several topics later I stopped to reflect on my experience and take stock of my approach, I wasn't so sure. Is Noah's Ark really a story about 'Weather'? Does Jesus walking on the water help to deepen and enrich the children's understanding of 'Water'? Has Joseph's coat anything to do with learning about 'Colour'? Is the story of David and Jonathan the best story I can find to develop young children's understanding of 'Friendship'? If the answer to these questions is 'No' then what *is* the nature of an appropriate RE contribution?

Finding myself becoming more and more interested in RE, perhaps because of its challenging questions and general lack of answers, I began to look at some of the more recently published agreed syllabuses and books about RE. I became aware of the breadth of RE's horizons. I discovered that primary RE was about personal identity, relationships with others, the natural world and ways of conveying meaning, as well as the more explicitly religious people, places, objects, practices and stories. Obviously all these could be explored through topics and themes, and how much richer the topics would be if threaded through with some of these strands. Exploring the various different elements of the junior RE programme through topics and themes provided an exciting and satisfying way of working, but it soon became clear that it was also very challenging and demanding. There are many factors to consider in the selection and planning of topics and many issues to be faced in determining the most appropriate RE contribution to the topic.

The place of RE in a topic

The scope for including RE varies, according to the nature of the topic. There are three main types of topic in relation to RE:

1   Topics which give opportunities for work in a number of different curriculum areas including RE. RE is only one of a number of contributing disciplines, for example Water, Food, Spring
2   Topics where RE is the central discipline, for example, Who is Jesus? Prayer, Festivals, Places of Worship
3   Topics where the RE contribution is minimal or incidental, for example Castles, Transport.

Most teachers work with all three types at different times. An RE-centred topic may be followed by one where a historical perspective is the main focus. A long-term cross curricular topic may be suspended for a couple of weeks to allow a short-term RE-centred topic to take over – for example, as the school develops the theme of Harvest or *Diwali* and celebrates the festival. It is important to plan for a balanced curriculum over the term, and over the year as a whole. The topics chosen should provide opportunities for each child to encounter appropriate experiences and content from the whole range of curriculum areas.

A school policy for topic work

The individual class teacher will be able to plan a balanced programme of topics over one year for his or her class, but a school programme will also be necessary to ensure overall progression and avoid needless repetition. Many schools plan an outline programme suggesting topics to be explored in each year, but there is usually enough flexibility to allow teachers to adapt the programme to follow their own interests and enthusiasms, and those of the children. Such flexibility would also allow the introduction from time to time of a whole-school topic, where each class contributes to a common theme in its own way and at an appropriate level. This happens naturally at festival times, but can be extended to cover other more wide-ranging, long-term topics as well.

Building up understanding in RE is a slow process. Ideas which may be partially grasped at one stage need to be reinforced and developed later. The topics chosen will need to offer opportunities for building on previous learning and laying foundations for later understanding. Most of the topics commonly encountered in the junior school can be explored with any age group, but without overall school planning and record keeping there could be unnecessary repetition of material or a lack of appropriate foundation experiences. Some topics may deliberately feature more than once in a child's school life. Teachers avoid mere repetition of material by varying the approach and encouraging a deeper level of study.

Selecting a topic

When selecting a topic there are many factors to consider – some of a general nature and others specifically related to RE, teachers may find themselves addressing some of the following questions:

Is the topic broad enough to give scope for work in a number of different areas of the curriculum?

RE emphasises a whole view of life. It has natural links with the creative arts, the humanities, language and literature, environmental studies and science. It is in topics where the subject matter can be looked at from a number of different viewpoints that RE fits most naturally and makes a distinctive contribution. In cross curricular topics the components from the different disciplines enhance and enrich each other, interact and set each other off to advantage, giving a satisfying, harmonious 'whole view' of the particular topic being explored.

Is this topic too broad to be manageable?

A very broad topic can lack focus and encourage shallow treatment of the material. For example 'The Oak Tree' might be chosen as a topic in preference to 'Trees'. Knowledge, awareness and appreciation of trees in general can be built up through the detailed focus on one particular species rather than a broader, and inevitably shallower, study of all the commoner trees. Similarly, a topic on 'Spring Festivals' or 'Festivals in which light is a dominant symbol' might have a clearer sense of purpose than the broader 'Festivals'. An understanding of the common and distinctive elements of festivals and celebration can be developed through looking in detail at a few carefully chosen examples.

Is the topic genuine?

Some topics seem to be a hotch-potch of unrelated ideas held together by a somewhat tenuous connection – a sort of 'hat-stand approach'. A topic entitled 'Black and White' which dealt with crossword puzzles and zebra crossings, badgers and race relations would seem to lack the real coherence of a genuine topic. A topic on 'Founders of the Faiths' also raised questions about topic validity. Did Jesus, Muhammad, the Buddha, Abraham . . . actually 'found' a faith? In using the umbrella term of 'Founders' are we trying to fit rather different experiences into a pre-determined mould?

What is the potential of this topic for RE?

Topics where RE is the main discipline such as 'Places of Worship' or 'Sacred Books' have an obvious potential for RE – or at least some aspects of it. However, even in such explicitly religious topics, care must be taken to give a distinctive emphasis to the material or even a topic like 'Our Church' can remain merely a historical or sociological study. It is perhaps some of the broad general topics that have the greatest potential for junior RE: the great universals of Light, Bread, Water, New Life . . . and topics of everyday human life like Food, Clothes, Journeys, Books, The Seasons, Myself, Family and Friends. It is through topics such as these, which provide opportunities for reflection on experience, that religious understanding can be developed: questions are raised about the meaning and purpose of life . . . What does it mean to be human? Why suffering? Skills necessary for understanding religion are developed . . . the ability to enter imaginatively into someone else's experience, an understanding of symbolic language; and attitudes essential for religious understanding are fostered . . . respect for the views of others, reverence for life. Many of these topics – particularly those where ordinary, everyday objects and universal human experiences have become deeply embedded in religious tradition as powerful symbols or rituals – also provide prime opportunities for exploring aspects of religious beliefs and practices.

The selection of material within a chosen topic will be determined largely by the ages and stages, abilities and interests of the children. Learning will start from their experience and create opportunities for reflection on that experience and discussion of thoughts, feelings and ideas.

How do you know it's RE?

Whether RE contributes to a topic or provides its central focus, the basis for selecting material will be the aims and objectives, or skills, attitudes and concepts outlined in the appropriate Agreed Syllabus. These should be a reminder of the breadth of RE and point to the inadequacy of an approach which covers RE merely by including a seemingly appropriate Bible story – often chosen purely on the basis of a loose work association, for example the parable of the sower in a topic on 'Farming', the story of Noah in a topic on 'Animals'.

One of the paradoxes of junior RE is that it seeks both to focus on concerns shared by the whole curriculum, life and ethos of the school and to retain its identity. Topic work which emphasises not separateness or integration but interrelation, enables RE to have both a whole view of life and a distinctive identity. Learning in RE takes place through many channels and teachers will look for opportunities to introduce a variety of stimulating approaches which are as important as the content of the courses. Topic work provides scope for direct, first-hand experience so material can be selected that can be explored through visits, visitors, celebrations, handling artefacts, etc. Attractive, up-to-date books and audio-visual resources will also be used. Teaching RE through topics and themes is not a matter of following a manual of well-tried and tested ideas but rather of being committed to a quest which involves sensitive, thoughtful consideration of the issues, and a willingness to explore new pathways.

CHAPTER 25

Visiting places of worship

DENNIS STARKINGS

A visit, of course, is a very special opportunity to bring the experience of religion to life in the imagination of children. The question is how to maximise the opportunities and contain the disappointments. Most of this chapter describes actual adventures in the art of visiting. Partly these derive from work done (or contributed to) by other people. Some are drawn from an article previously published in *Resource*. Other activities described here derive from the writer's own work with students in teacher-education, and from activities jointly organised by the writer and Gwen Nodder for both university students and children working together. (Gwen Nodder teaches at Bilton Church of England Middle School, Rugby. The shared projects involving school pupils and teacher – education students have been based on the Primary Teaching Centre set up by the Department of Arts Education at the University of Warwick.)

Let's take a first look at the raw materials. Even when worshippers are not present, buildings dedicated for worship are never 'empty'. At the very least they will have an atmosphere of some kind – possibly distinctive, perhaps even overwhelming. And then there is the furniture of religion – the layout of the building, the presence of objects significant in worship. All these things are clues to the human experience of religion. Moreover we normally cannot get into the building unless a responsible priest, minister or layperson is present. This person just *might* be a helpful expert with an understanding of children, or perhaps not. In any case, it is the teacher's job to see that aims are met as far as they can be; and the job is too potentially rewarding to leave in anyone else's hands!

Knowledge and the sense of place

Knowledge of religion is very important. Without it, feeling remains unrefined and ill-educated. But 'mere information' should never be mistaken for knowledge. 'Mere information' is a dead thing. By contrast, knowledge and understanding thrive only in association with the imagination. They depend on some sympathy for the context in which things have their meaning and value. The special opportunity afforded by visits to places of worship lies in the stirring of the imagination – pinpointed here as 'the sense of place'. It is a context for the expansion of understanding and the refinement of our responses.

The particular atmosphere of a sacred place, and the fact that places of worship arouse expectations for many believers, is something for us to notice and to think about. As the lady at the airport said to Rabbi Blue, 'Young man, certainly God is the same everywhere, that is well known, but I am not and I need a chapel'.

Of course, religion happens under the open sky too, and perhaps more often there than in some of the buildings one knows! Nevertheless these are buildings made, adapted, and cared for under the inspiration of some kind of religious feeling. To invite children to make and to share their own responses to such places is to encourage at least one step in learning about themselves, about other people and about religion. For its educational and religious integrity, such an exercise depends on honesty. What Lionel Blue eventually found at the airport proved to be merely a 'chic, gaudy chapelette'. To the extent that religious education is about recognising the religious sensibility, it must also be about detecting the bogus and the vulgar.

Sights, sounds, smells and feelings

The experience shared by three teachers of their visit to a local parish church illustrates how this sort of encounter might be managed. A class of seven- to nine-year-olds took their materials with them. Their theme was 'Feelings', and the emphasis was upon the feelings that come through the senses. They sat in the church quietly while some organ music of Bach was played. They were invited to write down how they felt. They were sent about the church and asked to notice smells:

> 'Smelt like burnt fireworks.'
> 'I think it smells like dust.'
> 'Fresh, dusty, cold, sneezy, misty air.'

They were asked to touch and to find words for their sensations. Pretending that they had a blind friend, they described what they had seen. They wrote down brief descriptions. They made drawings in a variety of media related to the theme of the senses.

Back at school that same afternoon, they began with a class-discussion on feelings associated with their own experiences of christenings, weddings, funerals, and church services. They thought about the role of the church in the community. One way of making this real for the children is to think first about why people meet together, for example at school, at the Brownies and at parties.

With the class divided into three groups, one group wrote poems or prose based on feelings of happiness, sadness, fear, anger or wonder. Another group engaged in direct and spontaneous painting in response to feelings evoked by music. Using large sheets of paper, they were encouraged to paint as freely as possible. The third group (inspired by the church's newsletter) made use of the word processor to compile their own broadsheet. It contained their own ideas for ways in which church and community might work together.

Going in fresh

When these same writers came to their visit to a Hindu temple (following the same theme) they chose deliberately to limit the preparation. They announced the visit and explained that everyone would be required to wear suitable clothing – trousers or ankle length skirts for the girls and women, and modest clothing for everyone. There are of course sound reasons for careful thought about all sorts of preliminaries, and no visit should happen without the kind of preparation that deals with apprehension and copes with possible prejudice; but in this case the goodwill of the class, and its previous adventure in the church were an existing and sound basis. For another account of a visit to a Hindu temple see *Approaches to Hinduism*.

The children went straight into their experience of the temple – removing their shoes before entering the shrine room, sitting cross-legged on the floor, embarking directly on their encounter with pictures and images of the gods, the smell of incense, the use of bells and lights. They observed *puja* and then they wandered about asking questions of the priest and their teachers. They received the customary *prasad* – the gifts of blessed food. It was afterwards that their own responses were developed through class activity. They heard the story of Rama and Sita. A display of Hindu artefacts was set out for them to investigate. They developed art work from their own remembered impressions and draft sketches. Written work was developed from the feelings aroused by the visit. Later on they saw the CEM video, *Hinduism Through the Eyes of Hindu Children*. Given the aims they had in mind they had taken care in this case not to prejudice the children's direct response but rather to develop it afterwards.

Exploring the space

'Mere information' about the layout of the place of worship treats it on a level with the bus station. So how can we sustain the vitality of real exploration and discovery and manage the information that is necessary? There are some tips that people have found useful. So far as the layout of the building is concerned, or the meaning of its contents, make it a problem-solving exercise for the children while they are actually there. For example, the altar in a Christian church is likely to be prominently placed. It is useful to have the Eucharist vessels already placed on it – the wine and wafers (or bread) ready at hand. Look at the altar. What have you got at home that looks something like this? So it's a table. What do we see on the table? This can get us into simple but central meanings of the Eucharist itself – the shared meal celebrating the fellowship of Christ with his people. At home we sit round the table. Can everyone do that here? This can get us into a discussion of the most suitable arrangement for worshippers, and perhaps pupils could go on to design their own. In some modern churches the altar is central and many others have modified their seating to get as near to this as possible. All of this teaches a great deal about contemporary Christian community values. If the place and the objects have *human meaning* for the children, their later researches into books, their subsequent art and modelling and photographic work will have so much more meaning for them.

There is one possible project that serves admirably to remember the visit and the atmosphere of place. It consists of arming a few expert young photographers with respectable automatic cameras for indoor and outdoor shots. The slides are then arranged in order so that you have a photographic conducted tour of the place of worship. With a tape recorder, you play one continuous sound (hymn singing, or organ music perhaps?) fading it in as your slide show approaches the building and fading it out as you come away again. A more elaborate approach would be to have sound appropriate to the picture – such as the voice of a sermon as you come to the pulpit, or the key words of consecration as you come to the altar. There is the added advantage that once this sort of material is in your hands it can also be used to convey these responses to other classes who might not be making that visit.

The distinctive tranquility of a Buddhist monastery in the heart of the Warwickshire countryside has been captured in a slide sequence taken on a glorious summer's day. The sound of monks chanting is faded in as we move from the garden to the house, and faded again as we come back to the garden and distant view over the fields.

Explaining expert matters

There are some topics where the children cannot do so very much to puzzle things out for themselves – topics perhaps where meanings have their origin deep in history or related to some particular story. We must not leave it to the priest or minister. He might be a brilliant communicator but he might not, and in any case we are the ones who know that the children should get out of the experience. On the other hand he is likely to be more of an expert on the knowledge we need – so it's a matter of arranging carefully to share expertise in a joint enterprise.

If the priest's Eucharistic dress is to be explained, for example, there is not much the children can puzzle out for themselves beyond the recognition that we do wear special clothes for special occasions. This is worth establishing, but we need much more. Perhaps the answer here is to agree a *style of conversation* with the priest. The teacher can help the priest to maximise the children's involvement and give him clues as to what to say! The teacher opens up conversation with the children about special clothes for special occasions. She brings in the priest to say why the Eucharist is a special occasion. Why will he prefer to wear special clothes anyway? (He will perhaps explain that he wants people to see him as a priest and not as Mr X.) So begins the process of dressing in one garment after another. 'What does this help you to remember from the Christian story?' the teacher asks. She asks supplementaries when she thinks the children need them, and encourages the children's own questions and comments. She draws attention to things the children can do or explore further back at school. 'Shall we make drawings now, and then make a cardboard figure when we get back to school so that we can fit it up with the priest's garments? And we could write down what all the garments mean, perhaps?' Don't let them make notes while the priest is talking, at least not the younger children. The teacher can make notes, perhaps. So far as the children are concerned, let them recall it all later on in school.

Looking for special opportunities

Just down the road from the University of Warwick there is a delightful Greek Orthodox church. But what might the children actually *do* that they have not already done in connection with their own parish church? One idea we have pioneered and mean to develop makes use of the numerous and beautiful icons that are actually in the church.

First, the *idea of the icon* needs to be explained at a level the children can grasp. The key idea to put across is the use of ordinary things – wood, paint, brushes – to make something extraordinary and beautiful out of them: it's a key idea in the Christian approach to life. But when we ask the children to think about why Christians should want pictures of these holy men and women – and animals too (as in St George and the Dragon) – this really does tie in with their own experience. Children have photographs at home, photographs of aunts and uncles, pets and friends. We all have these pictures because we care about others, because they belong to us and we to them. That is why these icons are in church. They are pictures of the Christian family, of things that have happened and of things (one thinks of St George again!) that just might have happened.

The children are equipped with a summary of the story attaching to as many icons as can be managed: some of the icon figures are local saints (special to that particular community) and so more difficult to cope with in the reference books, such as, *The Oxford Dictionary of Saints*. Groups of children are asked to puzzle out pictures so that they can explain how their picture tells the story. They learn about really *looking* at things; and they learn about the deep history of the Christian family. They learn a great deal about iconographic representation. The test of this is that they have to explain the icons and the stories to the other groups.

First find your bhikkhu

The Venerable Ajahn Khemadhammo is senior *bhikkhu* (or monk) at the Forest Hermitage, which is a Buddhist monastery in the Theravadin tradition. (It was at the Forest Hermitage that we made the slide sequence previously described.) The Venerable Ajahn has welcomed numbers of children there over the past few years, and in turn has visited them at school.

All sorts of things have happened in that time – at first simple talks about the story of the Buddha, and quiet wandering about the place. (It actually exemplifies the tranquillity which lies at the heart of *samatha* meditation.) Children were able to question the Ajahn about the monastic life and his own experience. Then, and because trust had been built up between teachers and parents, children were able to practise a very short period of guided meditation and discuss their experiences with the Ajahn. One rather nice exchange was about suffering. The Ajahn asked whether children suffered at all. The children told him of course they did, and agreed that something should be done about it. 'That's what I think too,' the Ajahn said. The matter was then allowed to drop, and we were on to the more familiar subject of vegetarian food.

It was food that brought us to a real adventure. Monks in the east go on alms-rounds through the villages for their food; but this does not normally work very well in Warwickshire, so we decided to do something about it. The children had discussed vegetarianism and its relation to the first of the Five Precepts of Buddhism. They knew something about the monastic life and that the one meal of the day had to be taken before noon. One of their teachers was there early, preparing rice and heating up a beany crumble. (Something hot was thought a good idea.) At about ten the school and University buses brought some thirty children and a teacher laden with plastic pots and mountainous contributions of food from the children. From the kitchen door the food was distributed to the children who then took up their allotted places around the Hermitage grounds. Ajahn Khemadhammo and the Venerable U. Lokanatha then came out barefoot with their almsbowls and walked about to receive the food offerings.

197

It proved to be a feast-day at the Forest Hermitage. There was at the same time an edition of the class newspaper to prepare – all about the Forest Hermitage and its life. About half the class was transfixed for a while by the invitation to sit with the monks while they ate from their bowls, to talk and (if they wished) ask questions. An interview with the Ajahn was, after all, to be the main feature in the newspaper. The rest were already about the place, drawing the symbolic lions (for example) and the newly-built English Shwe Dagon Pagoda, or photographing the *Buddha-rupas* (images of the Buddha) and innumerable other things.

The photographs of the alms-round – so carefully taken by a couple of expert young photographers – were lost in the dark room that afternoon. It was not their fault. The materials were defective. Never mind, we had other photographs which survived. And as the Ajahn pointed out, it was a valuable lesson in the impermanence, the transitoriness of all conditioned things which is close to the heart of the Buddha's understanding of life!

Some tips about organisation

Finally, a few words about organisation. Of course all those things one has to do under the regulations of the LEA or the Governing Body need to be checked in each case – such matters as insurance, the ratio of teachers to pupils, the parental consent forms. For general advice see *Beyond the Classroom: Guidance from the National Union of Teachers on School Visits and Journeys.* There are however some special considerations relating to visits in RE. Here are a few of the major ones:

1   Long before consent forms have to be signed, do take parents into your confidence. They should be aware of the school's RE policy, so that they will understand *why* you are going as well as where. The aim should be also to get some willing parents to join in the trip – or at least know that they would be welcome. Converted by experience of their children's enjoyment, parents make the best ambassadors for RE.

2   Get to know the person who will receive you at the place you are visiting. Ask deliberately about any special requirements as to dress or deportment. Talk to him or her about what you wish to do so that you can form an impression of the expertise available to you. Fundamentally that person must show understanding of your *educational* aims and not assume (for example) that this will be an opportunity for evangelisation. At best you will have someone who will work with you to achieve your goals, but simple helpfulness will do nicely. If neither seems likely, rethink your aims or go elsewhere.

3   Confirm agreed date and times in writing. Write to say thank you

afterwards – or preferably get the children to do so in overwhelming numbers! It is often worth a phone call immediately before the visit just to be sure that events such as funerals (or indeed any other business) will not get in the way of your visit.

Happy visiting!

Bibliography

Rabbi Lionel Blue, *Bolts from the Blue* (Hodder & Stoughton, 1986, p. 92)

Margaret Chapman, Anne Elsmore and Jo Price, 'We're off on a Visit' (*Resource*, Volume 11 No. 1, Autumn 1988)

David Hugh Farmer, *The Oxford Dictionary of Saints* (OUP, 1978)

R. Jackson and D. Killingley, *Approaches to Hinduism* (John Murray, 1988, Chapter 4)

NUT, *Beyond the Classroom: Guidance from the National Union of Teachers on School Visits and Journeys*

CHAPTER 26

Children as ethnographers

ROBERT JACKSON

The term 'ethnography' is used in a variety of ways by social anthropologists and other social scientists. This chapter uses the term to indicate the methods and techniques used in fieldwork, and suggests that, in suitably adapted forms, they can be very useful tools for children studying religious education.

Many agreed syllabuses, school books and audio-visual materials stress the importance of studying religion as it is lived and practised by people. The 1988 Education Reform Act, in legitimising the study of different Christian denominations and in stating that new agreed syllabuses must reflect Christian 'religious traditions' and also take account of the 'teaching and practices' of other religions in Britain, reinforces this view. The importance of understanding contemporary practice of religion is also affirmed by DES Circular 3/89:

> The Government believes that all those concerned with religious education should seek to ensure that it promotes respect, understanding and tolerance for those who adhere to different faiths.

The activity of attempting to grasp someone else's way of life raises interesting questions of method. How do children from a secular background set about understanding religious ways of life? How do children from one religion grasp the faith of people from other traditions? Just as importantly, how do children from one denominational background gain an understanding of others within the same religious tradition? It might be just as hard for a Methodist child to gain an understanding of a Catholic mass as to grasp the significance of Muslim public prayer.

A sensitising element

Ideas associated with ethnography can provide tools for children to be sensitised to traditions other than their own and to suggest methods for making sense of religious practices, beliefs and symbols. They can reduce the tendency to superimpose familiar concepts and categories on to unfamiliar rituals and practices and can help children to overcome the negative or even hostile feelings that can be provoked by new and initially strange beliefs, rituals, customs, art and languages. The following activity, reproduced from *Religions through Festivals: Hinduism* has been used with older junior children in order to arouse their interest in studying unfamiliar religious traditions and to help them identify appropriate methods for doing so:

> Get into a group of between three and five friends and sit facing one another. Have pen and paper ready. You have to imagine that you are aliens from another planet. You are very clever, you have X-ray vision and you are friendly. But you don't know anything about planet Earth, the beings that live on it, or the languages they speak. Your mission is to look for signs of life near your ship and to report back to your base commander with a short message describing what you think is happening. Your craft silently lands near the dwelling place of some earthlings. Using your X-ray vision you look through the walls. The scene you see is the one in the picture (two children placing parcels beneath a decorated Christmas tree). Now, together with your friends, write a short message to your base commander describing what you think is happening. Spend about five minutes preparing the message. Don't read any further until you have written your message.
>
> If other groups in your class have done the same task, take it in turns to read out the messages from the different groups.
>
> As you listen to these messages, in your group, do the following tasks:
>
> - make a list of the observations that the alien got wrong
> - make a list of the observations that the alien got right
> - can you think of some things that the alien would need to do in order to understand what is in the picture? Make a list of them.
>
> You may not have looked at someone else's way of life before. Look again at your lists. What things do you need to do so you don't make the mistakes that the alien made when he observed the earthlings?

The messages written by children are often very imaginative (for example the Christmas tree is the superior being, being worshipped by minor beings or visitors from yet another planet) and humorous (for example written in Martian, with or without an English translation). Discussion following the activity can establish an awareness that more than intelligence is required to understand another way of life. Children may point out that the alien needed to spend a much longer time observing the earthlings, and would have to establish some way of interviewing them about what they were doing — perhaps by learning some of their language or by using an interpreter. They may also point out that the alien could have contacted his home base to find out whether there were any records of earlier explorations of Earth which included an attempt to explain the ritual that had been observed. The exercise can establish that attitudes (such as open mindedness and not jumping to conclusions), as well as appropriate methods, need to be used to reduce the chance of making serious mistakes when trying to interpret some aspect of an unfamiliar way of life. Often the children themselves suggest the standard ethnographic methods of close observation, interviewing and the analysis of documentary and other source materials such as artefacts and pictures. These methods can then be employed in studying new material from religious traditions.

Incidentally, once children have realised the limitations of the intellect in trying to puzzle out what is happening in a ritual or the symbolism of a piece of religious art, the activity of 'puzzling' can be very absorbing as a starter, before new information is fed in by the teacher or from other sources. During a visit to a Hindu temple one group of older juniors was given the task of 'puzzling' the symbolism of the various images and pictures in the central shrine. After the project, the student teacher wrote:

> This activity really sparked off an interest which continued long after the visit. Each child wanted to find out more about the shrines and pictures they had seen. None of them was satisfied with just the basic answers needed for the questionnaire – they wanted explanations. They found the method absorbing and of all the groups they were the best informed.
>
> Also they wanted to discuss issues arising from the work, even questions like 'Who is God?' and 'Why do different people think there are different Gods?' These children were a good source of information for the other children and were keen to explain points from the photographs and pictures. Also they were keen to explain things to children in other classes and I found groups at break and lunchtime showing other children photographs and objects on display – a real question/answer activity in progress!

Observation

Ethnographers use participant observation as a method to help unravel the meaning of artefacts, spaces, symbols, terminology, roles, and so on within different ways of life, placing varying emphasis on the amounts of 'participation' and 'observation' in relation to one another according to the kind of investigation being undertaken. It is unlikely for practical reasons that children will be involved in sustained studies requiring an element of participation (but see 'Elements of Religious Education' in Chapter 1 and 'Learning from the religious experience of children' (Chapter 27) on how children might report their own experience of religion). They can, however, learn skills of observation which will help them to collect material systematically during visits to places of worship and which may assist them in interpreting slides and videos of acts of worship or rites of passage such as baptism or bar mitzvah. They can apply the same techniques to personal experiences of religion, such as acts of worship or other religious ceremonies attended with their families, or even acts of collective worship at school.

For practical reasons, most visits to places of worship will take place during school time and usually when the building is not in use for worship. Observation thus focuses on the building itself, its setting and its contents. By way of preparation, some general work can be done in school to enhance children's experience during a visit. With slides and pictures features of the exterior and interior of the building can be introduced. Parish churches are set in ground which is consecrated, and there will be a boundary between the consecrated and unconsecrated ground. Children can guess why this boundary exists, and try to spot differences between consecrated and unconsecrated ground (for example burials are only on consecrated ground). Parish churches are generally oriented with the sanctuary at the east end so that the congregation faces east towards Jerusalem. Similarly mosques are built with the qibla wall towards Makka, so that Muslims face the holy city during prayer. The shape of the building may be significant. One of the more ornate Hindu temples of India can be seen as a complete world in which the peak indicating its ritual centre represents the mythical mount Meru at the centre of the world (see *Approaches to Hinduism*, Chapter 11). In contrast, most Hindu temples in Britain are not purpose built and may be modifications of former schools or churches. Some parish churches have a cruciform shape, with its obvious symbolism. Without getting bogged down with too many architectural details and terms, children can consider the age of the building, that it may have been added to or adapted over the years, they can discuss the materials used to build it and they can look for other external features.

Children can draw a simple plan of the interior of the building, indicating the main spaces. A parish church usually has a hierarchy of spaces – the nave where the congregation sits, the chancel and the sanctuary – with the boundaries between them marked by the chancel screen and the communion rail. The spaces may have their own symbolism. 'Nave' is from *navis*, the Latin word for ship, suggesting the church's protection of the faithful from the storms of life. There will be furnishings associated with ritual activity within the building. In a parish church the font may be towards the west end near the doorway – worshippers enter the church building through the door; the faithful enter the church through the sacrament of baptism. There may be a pulpit (why is the preacher elevated above the congregation?), a lectern and a range of furnishings associated with Holy Communion, including the altar and the communion rail.

Windows are often sources of knowledge as well as pieces of art work. Why do the beautiful patterned windows of the El Aksa mosque in Jerusalem have no representation of people or animals? What does the bapistry window in Coventry Cathedral signify? In parish churches stained glass windows often illustrate bible stories, and a study of them can lead to an introduction to the biblical text and to issues raised by it. A nineteenth-century window illustrating the text 'Lord now lettest thou thy servant depart in peace' (Luke 2 verse 29) introduced the story of Simeon and a discussion of why this text is often used on memorial windows. Key incidents in the Gospel story are common, from the Annunciation to the Resurrection appearances, and can all lead to further reflection and study. Churches and other sacred buildings may also contain other works of art that may be replete with symbolism.

Parish churches are usually well provided with memorials from stone tablets and tombs to statues and war memorials. As well as reflecting conditions in earlier times (death in childbirth, high infant mortality, death in battle) these often raise questions for discussion about mortality and life after death. Gravestones in the church yard have the same effect, and children will often draw attention to the graves of children of their own age.

Even in an empty building there may be indications of its contemporary use. The altar in the sanctuary may not be the one in common use. This may now be nearer the people in the nave. Why should this be so? The notice board may reveal much of the life of the parish and its relationships with the wider community.

On video, or by using a sequence of slides, children can study the temporal as well as spatial aspects of religious worship. What are the roles of the people taking part? What are the stages in the ritual or the act of worship? Is there a view of sacred time in which the ritual is set – for example the Anglican liturgical year? What can be found out about the reasons for the worshippers being there, or about their feelings during worship? What beliefs are implied by the worship? What terms, symbols and gestures are used by the worshippers in their speech and movements? Gradually children can build up accounts of devotional acts, using as far as possible the terminology of the people taking part.

Interviewing

Ethnographers make extensive use of interviewing as a research tool, whether chatting informally or using semi-structured or structured interviews requiring the use of interview schedules. Junior school children can make excellent interviewers, but they need help in drawing up schedules of questions and in practising the techniques of interviewing. The idea of interviewing a vicar about his job or a visitor about her practice of religion can be exciting until the task of formulating questions comes around. Without help children may produce a random series of questions which may miss key areas of experience. When the children come to analyse the interview and make use of the data they may realise that the most important questions have been left unasked.

One useful technique is to classify questions under subject headings. In this way the general subject can be broken down into some specific areas which will suggest to children a range of questions. During a project on the 1950s one class of fourth-year juniors prepared an interview schedule to use with parents and grandparents about their memories of the period. Initially a long list of questions was suggested by the children and it was only when these were reviewed in detail with many prompts from the teacher that it was realised that there wasn't a single question about life in the home. The children were then asked to think of broad areas of experience on which they could focus more detailed questions. After discussion in small groups and reporting back the class settled on the areas of home, school, work and leisure. Groups then divided these areas into narrower fields. Home included types of house; ownership of houses; parts of houses; family relationships. 'Parts of houses' in turn suggested topics such as furniture, electrical appliances ('did they have fridges?'), diet and nutrition. 'Leisure' prompted groups of questions on fashion, sport, films, TV and so on. Children then arranged their questions in groups under main and sub-headings before reviewing the whole exercise to check whether important areas had been omitted. A similar approach when interviewing the local parish priest about his job might generate specific areas such as 'to do with services' (liturgical); 'visiting people' (pastoral); 'to do with the church building' (administrative/fund raising); what he thinks/believes/ enjoys (personal). Each of these headings should suggest narrower topics and specific questions.

Using a tape recorder, asking questions with confidence and flexibility (for example, following them up with supplementaries, adapting the question order to fit the way in which an interviewee is responding and slipping in an extra question prompted by a response from the interviewee) are skills which need practice. One group of eleven-year-olds, in preparing to conduct interviews during a visit to a Hindu temple, practised their interviewing skills with the school secretary, the Deputy Head, the Head Teacher and the cook before venturing into the field and recording an interview with the President of the temple committee.

Analysing documents

Another standard ethnographic method is the analysis of documents that are produced by groups of people being studied. Children have analysed the contents of a parish magazine, for example, as part of a study of a church community, classifying the contents into different literary types (letters, diary, reports, articles) and types of content (especially noting how much of the magazine was concerned with religious or spiritual matters). It was also noted that although part of the magazine focused on the local community, there was also material about the diocese, and about the church in the wider world (in this case an article, a letter and a map concerned with the visit of Anglicans from Nicaragua, Barbados, China, South Africa and the USA to the diocese and the deanery). This stimulated discussion about changing ideas of what 'being a missionary' means. Other relevant documents might include pamphlets about the history and furnishings of a church or other religious building, or even notices or posters.

Using the data

The analysis of data collected can be a rewarding experience for children as long as it is well-managed. There is no need, for example, for a complete transcription of recorded interviews. By setting the counter at zero at the beginning of a tape, children can listen to an interview and divide it by topic, noting down the counter number at the beginning of each section. In this way they can easily find information or extracts for quotation.

The aim of collecting material systematically using ethnographic methods is not to reduce RE to a social science. The elements of religious education outlined in Chapter 1 can all be drawn on using the information. We have already seen how the activity of puzzling with one group of children led to the analytical activity of their raising and discussing theological questions. Two further examples illustrate the imaginative and expressive use of information collected by interview and observation.

The children who interviewed the President of a Hindu temple committee made use of some of their material in an assembly which they presented to mark the end of their study of two places of worship – the local parish church and the Hindu temple. The assembly, held in the presence of parents and guests, including the vicar and the President of the Temple, included the raising of moral issues about race relations, an explanatory guide to some of the pictorial work done by class members and a dramatised television news broadcast. Here is an extract from the script which draws on the interview with the temple committee President:

> On Friday 14 February we visited the Shree Krishna Temple in Coventry. There we interviewed the President, Mr Lad. The temple was a school room before it became a temple in 1966. Mr Lad came to England in 1968. Mr Lad usually eats Indian food every day, but he has tried English food and he said he likes vegetable soup, bread, chips and cake. Mr Lad is a happily married man and he has six children and nine grandchildren. He lives in a terraced house in Coventry. He was married in India. He says: 'My marriage was like a king's procession!' Mr Lad goes to the temple first in the morning to wait for the priest, then in the evening for the evening *arti*, a service where they make offerings to the God. They decorate the temple like we decorate our houses at Christmas. The Hindus at this temple have five main festivals. *Diwali* is Mr Lad's favourite. Although most Hindus are vegetarians, Mr Lad eats some meat, but not meat from the cow because it is their sacred animal.

Although the material is principally factual, it is very different from the kind of information that would have been gleaned from many school books. There is a strong personal element which brings the piece to life as well as showing understanding of some features of contemporary Hinduism. Incidentally, note the reference to the President's liking for cake. On going to the staffroom for coffee after the assembly, he was presented with a cake made by the children and a scrapbook of work based on the visit.

The poem reproduced below was written by a child as a follow-up activity after a visit to a parish church. It makes use of information acquired through observation, but that knowledge is transformed by the child's imagination and reflection, showing a sense of sacred place and an attempt at some simple theology.

Inside Wroxton Church

The porch like a stone cave.
The saint's niche in the wall like an empty shell.
The stoup, where people may wash off the outside world.
Many have passed through the entrance,
sad and happy feet over the same stones.
The organ pipes pointing fingers of music
up to where people believed Jesus was.
The stairs going up to the pulpit
like an entrance to heaven.
The front with colours greyish brown and crusted yellow
The screen being guarded by a lion and a griffon,
The cold stone, unseeing faces.
In the morning
the sun shines through the east window
on the carvings in the chancel.

(Reproduced on a transparency as part of Religious Education in Primary Schools: In-Service Training Kit.)

Bibliography

Olivia Bennett, *People*; *Buildings*; *Worship*; *Signs and Symbols*, four books in the *Exploring Religion* series (Bell and Hyman, 1984)

Robert Jackson, *Religions Through Festivals: Hinduism* (Longman, 1989)

Robert Jackson and Dermot Killingley, *Approaches to Hinduism* (John Murray, 1988, especially chapters 3 and 4)

Lawrence Jones, *The Observer's Book of Old English Churches* (Warne, 1965)

E. Nesbitt, ' "My Dad's Hindu, My Mum's Side are Sikhs": The Religious Identity of Valniki and Ravidasi Children in Britain,' Arts Culture Education Research Papers 2 (National Foundation for Arts Education 1990. Available from NFAE, Dept. of Arts Education, University of Warwick, Coventry CV4 7AZ

Susan Tomkins, (ed.), *Christian Objects* (CEM, 1977)

NUT (n.d.) *Beyond the Classroom: Guidance from the National Union of Teachers on School Visits and Journeys*

Religious Education in Primary Schools: In-Service Training Kit (Schools Council/Macmillan Education)

CHAPTER 27

Learning from the religious experience of children

ELEANOR NESBITT and ROBERT JACKSON

Chapter 1 referred to a 'sharing element' in Religious Education, the idea that pupils' and teachers' personal experiences of religion can make a very important contribution to the process of RE. Michael Paffard's book, *Inglorious Wordsworths*, is one source that shows children's capacity for spiritual experiences and insights which can enhance RE. A minority of pupils is likely to have a more formal and regular experience of the practice of religion which is also potentially source material for RE, though, as Leslie Francis' research on Anglican young people shows, they may not adhere to a predictable series of orthodox beliefs. Brian Gates' work on religion in the developing world of children and young people shows children's ability to understand religion before they can think in an adult fashion, while Edward Robinson's book *The Original Vision* has accounts by adults of the importance of childhood religious experience for their later development.

Unlike Gates' work, which was done largely in schools, and Francis', which was based on questionnaire returns, we conducted an ethnographic study of a group of eight- to thirteen-year-old Hindu children in Coventry, spending time observing children in the home and community over a period of a year. The research involved detailed fieldwork among local Hindu families, semi-structured interviews with 34 children and detailed case studies of 12 children. Gujaratis and Punjabis (boys and girls aged 8–13) of various castes and sectarian orientations were included. Some of the research data has been converted into curriculum materials (see 'Religious Education: from Ethnographic Research to Curriculum Development' for an account of this) while a detailed account of the project is to appear as a book entitled *Hindu Children in Britain*. The short account which follows is meant to show how we as teachers can become more aware of the rich and complex religious background of some of our pupils, and that, if we can get access to it, pupils' experience of religious life can be a rich source of material for study by other children.

Nobody knows exactly how many Hindus live in Britain but a scholarly estimate sets the figure at over 350 000. Over 40 per cent of people with a South Asian background in Britain are below the age of 19. This means that there is a significant Hindu presence in our schools and in society generally.

This is one reason why teachers, particularly teachers of RE, need to be better informed about the experience of Hindu children.[1]

The three Hindu Nurture Projects, based at the University of Warwick, have attempted to provide such information, partly in order to produce material for use in the training of teachers and partly as a basis for devising curriculum resources for pupils. Children from the second project participated in four radio programmes in the BBC Radio Four School Series *Quest* and one in the series *Contact*.[2] Some of their experiences of festivals appear in *Religions through Festivals: Hinduism*, while some of their reflections on stories, pilgrimage, worship, symbols and ceremonies are included in *Listening to Hindus*. Using these books other children and their teachers can share in the rich cultural experience of these Hindu children in Coventry.

We used the word 'nurture' to describe the process by which Hindu children developed characteristically Hindu behaviour and belief or some adaptation of these. The second project looked at nurture both of a formal and an informal kind. 'Formal nurture' refers to supplementary classes run by faith communities for their children and our first project looked exclusively at such classes. In Coventry the Gujarati Education Society, which has close links with the Shree Krishna Temple, runs weekly classes in Gujarati language. The content of these classes and in particular of the annual Parents' Evenings cannot be separated from Hindu prayer and myth. In the Ram Mandir, a temple largely frequented by Punjabi families, children attend Hindi classes. From local Hindu organisations teachers in many parts of Britain can learn of the existence of such classes in their own area. The children who attend these often contribute short items of drama, song and dance to parents' evenings or to celebrations held at festival times. Teachers who are interested would be warmly welcomed to such occasions and gain enjoyable experience of how Hindu adults are passing on to their children parts of their cultural heritage.

Apart from the distinct cultural identity of Gujaratis and Punjabis, supplementary classes reflect other factors. One is the existence of thriving religious movements of which teachers may not be aware. These movements influence the lives of many Hindu families. In Coventry, for example, the Sathya Sai Baba organisation runs weekly, graded classes (*Bal Vikas*) in two venues and holds immensely popular annual camps. Followers worship Sathya Sai Baba, as a living incarnation of Shiva-Shakti (God in both male and female aspects) and of the saint Shirdi Sai Baba. The *Bal Vikas* ('child blossoming') classes are conducted in English. The children (who in Coventry are all Gujarati) wear white clothes to attend. They learn *bhajan*s (hymns) and *sloka*s (Sanskrit verses) and their meaning. They hear stories intended to inculcate the 'human values' of love, non-violence, right conduct, truth and peace. Many of these stories recount inspiring episodes in the lives of great people – not necessarily Hindus – when, despite difficulties they showed honesty, forgiveness or some other 'human value'. In *Bal Vikas* the children are introduced to meditation ('silent sitting'). This means sitting cross-legged, eyes closed without fidgeting or speaking, imagining something beautiful such as a flower. The children also perform *arti* (a ritual in which a light is circled in front of the focus of worship – in this case a framed picture of Sathya Sai Baba) followed by distribution and eating of a small quantity of *vibhuti* (a powdery ash with a sweet taste). Teachers could encourage children in school to practise 'silent sitting', not only as a way of sharing a distinctive experience, but also as an aid to relaxation and concentration.

During the period of our research another devotional group, the followers of ISKCON (the International Society for Krishna Consciousness), otherwise known as Hare Krishna, gathered each Saturday evening for *kirtan* (congregational hymn singing) and a homily. During this the children would stay in another room where they learned about Krishna, wrote on such topics as 'why we need a guru' and coloured in religious pictures which had been duplicated from colouring books published by the movement. Hindu parents who are not involved in ISKCON appreciate the attractive literature produced by the movement and are glad if their children learn stories of Krishna from them. (Interested teachers can obtain materials suitable for classroom use from Bhaktivedanta Books Ltd, PO Box 324, Borehamwood, Herts WD6 1NB.) However, Hindu children learn most as a result of 'informal nurture', in other words by their participation in family worship, rites of passage and festivals in the temple and above all at home. Our project recorded the many other intertwined strands in the transmission of Hindu culture.

In this chapter attention can be drawn to only a few aspects of the findings. Fuller reports of the projects appear elsewhere. One discovery is the cross cultural communication barrier which makes it hard initially, at least, for teachers to capitalise on Hindu pupils' sometimes very rich knowledge of their heritage. Not only concepts but also the actions and items central to Hindu ritual have no English equivalents. Children resort to gesture, to words from their mother tongue and to (often misleading) renderings, for example, 'candle' for *diva* (a small oil lamp used particularly in worship). Teachers need to familiarise themselves with such key words as *mandir* for the temple or the domestic shrine, *puja* for worship involving offerings, and with *arti*, *diva*, *rakhi* (see below). It is also helpful to learn the names in popular use for deities. For instance two children interviewed used the names 'Kanaiyo' and 'Lala' respectively instead of 'Krishna'. For Ganesh the alternative name Ganapati was used. Children could often give a description of a deity's appearance without remembering the name. The goddess was often 'the one on a tiger' – for Punjabis 'Sherwalimata' or 'Sheranwalima'. If teachers have the opportunity to talk to children at home, and ask them or their families about religious pictures displayed in the home, they quickly encounter the titles in use for well-known deities.

It is all the more important for teachers to increase their knowledge of

Hindu mythology and festivals (including accurate pronunciation), since schools are to varying degrees playing a significant part in the transmission of Hindu tradition. The books by Jamila Gavin and Madhur Jaffrey are excellent collections of mythological stories retold for children, and the latter gives clear guidelines for pronunciation of Indian names. Teachers' questions prompt children to discover the name for their religious identity and to elicit information from relatives. In one child's words:

> I just found out that I'm Hindu – well my mum told me because the teacher said . . . 'Are you a Hindu?' and I said, 'I don't know'. When I told her . . . she wanted to know about *Diwali*.

Teachers may tell the story of Rama and Sita, for example, or involve children in a dramatic presentation for *Diwali*. In this Hindu parents are happy to assist them – often by helping to dress the children appropriately, by pronouncing the characters' names accurately and so on.

In order to understand their pupils and their families, teachers also need a sympathetic awareness of the values of Hindu society. Parents are more hurt if their children grow up without certain values, such as respect for elders, than if they are unacquainted with myth and ritual. Children are expected to use relationship terms to convey affection and respect. Depending on the relationship, whether real or honorary, it is felt either rude or excessively formal for a child to refer to or address someone without using *bhai* (brother), 'auntie', *masi* (mother's sister), etc. In our research experience children show awareness of family bonds (regarding cousins as brothers or sisters for instance) and of responsibilities. In particular boys indicated that as adults they would care for their parents while their sisters would look after their parents-in-law.

Children participate in marriages and in festivals which reinforce family ties and the distinctive role of different family members. *Raksha Bandhan* annually celebrates the brother–sister relationship and makes no distinction between siblings and cousins. All the Hindu children interviewed participated as did their older relatives. The girls tie an ornamental thread (*rakhi*) on their brothers' or male cousins' right wrist and receive some money from them. The fast of *Karwa Chauth* expresses the married woman's sacrificial concern for her husband's welfare. By observation and imitation children learn their future role. Young girls often try to copy their mothers by fasting on that day, and they decorate their hands with designs in henna paste (*mehndi*) as they would for a wedding. A child's abstention from lunch or the designs on a girl's hands can be cues to the teacher for sensitive sharing of the underlying reasons.

Some children are not simply observers or even imitators but are participating fully in ritual activity or, on occasion, playing a leading part. A child may perform the *arti*, rotating the lamp in front of a religious picture in the domestic shrine, or distribute *prashad* (blessed food) in the temple. A child may sing solo, leading the congregational hymn singing. Even toddlers are helped to play the cymbals and they enjoy the *prashad*.

On some occasions the child is of focal importance. A boy will probably see photographs of the *mundan* ceremony – his first haircut. (One East African Gujarati mother's recollections of rites of passage in her own family is a case study in Robert Jackson and Dermot Killingley, *Approaches to Hinduism*. A *mundan* ceremony of a Coventry Punjabi boy is featured in *Listening to Hindus*, a book for children.) Such photographs can be brought into school and form an excellent basis for discussion of ceremonies that mark new stages in life. Pre-adolescent girls are given food and a gift at the culmination of worship of the goddess whose purity and power they embody. If a girl says she has been a *goyni* or a *kanjak*, she is referring to this widespread custom, although she is unlikely to understand it in these terms.

Children learn stories of the gods from relatives and teachers, from books and through watching dramas and taking part in them, often miming to a recorded soundtrack. They see them on video too. The video is arguably the most powerful single channel of cultural transmission. It is thanks to watching videos that many Hindu children can with confidence describe the colour throwing in India at the festival of *Holi* or the adventures of Rama. As a product of modern technology the video predisposes children to view its message in a positive light. Relatives' marriages and other religious events are recorded on video and played at home. Imported Indian movies provide popular family entertainment. Children become more familiar with their mother tongue and/or Hindi, see scenes from their spiritual homeland and share in the same escapist world of Indian cinema as older relatives and as Hindus in India. Some families play videos of a specifically devotional nature – such as the Ramayana recitations of Morari Bapu, who draws large audiences when he visits British cities, or the miracles of Sathya Sai Baba. Families are quite likely to be willing to show teachers such videos or lend them for (edited) viewing by other pupils as a stimulus for topic work, for example on marriage.

Hindu adults often assert that Hindu children are growing up in ignorance of their religion and culture and teachers may be influenced by such pronouncements. Fieldwork indicates that this is far from universally true. Instead we have found a complex Hindu environment in which diverse traditions are thriving and many processes come into play. Our Hindu parents and children frequently comment on the interest in their religion shown by individual teachers in school. We hope that our project and the curriculum materials based on it stimulate the interest of pupils, whatever their background, and encourage teachers to draw sensitively on the experience of children.

Notes

[1] Of the Hindu Nurture Projects, based at the University of Warwick, the first project (1984–5) was a study of the provision of formal teaching of the Hindu tradition in supplementary schools around England. The third project – Punjabi Hindu Nurture in Coventry (1988–9) – involved research on the religious lives of children from two Hindu sectarian Punjabi communities in Coventry. The second project – The Hindu Nurture in Coventry Project (1986–7) – is discussed in the present chapter. The second and third projects were funded thanks to the generosity of the Leverhulme Trust. All three projects were directed by Robert Jackson with Eleanor Nesbitt as Research Fellow. The work on Hindu children has been extended into the Ethnography and Religious Education Project which is funded by the Economic and Social Research Council and is studying Christian, Jewish, Muslim and Sikh children in Britain.

[2] The following 20-minute programmes for BBC Education (Radio 4 VHF) drew on material from the Hindu Nurture in Coventry Project and feature members of families who contributed to the Project: *Hindus and Sikhs in Britain* (Radiovision); *Celebrating Holi*; *Celebrating Navratri*; *Celebrating Diwali* (all January and April 1987, repeated in Autumn 1989); *A Day in the Life of a Hindu Family* (November 1988). A filmstrip which accompanies the radiovision programme is available from BBC publications (School Orders) 144–52 Bermondsey Street, London SE1 3TH.

Bibliography

L. Francis, *Teenagers and the Church* (Collins, 1984)

B. Gates, 'Religion in the Child's Own Core Curriculum' (*Learning for Living*, Autumn, 1977)

J. Gavin, *Stories from the Hindu World* (Macdonald, 1986)

D. Hay, *Exploring Inner Space* (Penguin, 1982)

R. Jackson, 'Religious Education: From Ethnographic Research to Curriculum Development' in R. J. Campbell and V. Little, *Humanities in the Primary School* (Falmer, 1989)

R. Jackson, *Religions through Festivals: Hinduism* (Longman, 1989)

R. Jackson and D. Killingley, *Approaches to Hinduism* (John Murray 1988)

R. Jackson and E. Nesbitt, *Hindu Children in Britain* (forthcoming)

R. Jackson and E. Nesbitt *Listening to Hindus* (Unwin Hyman, 1990)

M. Jaffrey, *Seasons of Splendour* (Puffin, 1985)

M. Paffard, *Inglorious Wordsworths: A Study of Some Transcendental Experiences in Childhood and Adolescence* (Hodder and Stoughton, 1973)

E. Robinson, *The Original Vision* (Oxford, Manchester College, 1977)

CHAPTER 28

One step at a time: RE and children with special needs

JILL DAVIES

Some years ago when the Inner London Education Authority's Agreed Syllabus for religious education was being planned, I was asked to extend my work to include support for schools catering for children with special educational needs. This was a great challenge, for, like many people who have experience only in mainstream schools, special education seemed to me to be a very different and difficult area. Wondering if anybody would be interested in introducing religious education into an already over-crowded curriculum, I plunged in. What follows is an attempt to convey some impression of the exhilarating experiences which ensued. For the sake of brevity I have used the term 'schools' in referring to schools for children with special educational needs.

I would like to start by giving some examples of the kind of work being done. Although the schools were a new experience for me, religious education was by no means new to the schools. One of the first schools which I visited invited me to its Christmas celebration. The hall was brightly decorated with scenes from all over the world. The pupils entertained parents and friends of the school with music, song and a play which used the whole hall's decorations as a backcloth. They had devised the play, with a Christmas theme, themselves, and acted it out with tremendous gusto and considerable danger to the audience as they charged around the world looking for their 'Christmas Guest'. Adults and children alike explored the meaning of Christmas as well as the wonder and fun of the occasion.

Later we met the performers and shared the tea which the pupils had made. Perhaps many of the adults present, like myself, were given a new insight into questions about the meaning and purpose of life, for all those children were severely physically handicapped and were confined to wheelchairs. Later I grieved to hear that one of those lively pupils had died during the holiday.

At another school, I spent an afternoon with a group of children with severe learning difficulties where, through carefully planned activities, they were to experience something of what it means to be a valued person and a member of the community. We started the afternoon by sharing orange squash. As the visitor, I was greeted by, and greeted, each child by name. We played a game to help us remember each others' names, using a song to celebrate the name. We hung a 'leaf' bearing each name on a tree and lit a candle for each person in the group. At the end of the afternoon we said goodbye to each other. A simple enough process, but one containing many ways of assuring the children of their importance, their membership of the group and their responsibility to the group. Simple enough, but effective, and one advisory teacher left feeling wanted and stimulated.

As time went on, teachers began to approach me for help. One teacher, working with delicate children, most of whom also had moderate learning difficulties, embarked on a project concerning Judaism. He arrived in my room to look at resources – books, posters, artefacts – and left festooned with lists and useful addresses. Later, I was invited to see the results. The room was decorated with pupils' work and the 'caps' they had been given while visiting the Jewish Museum. I heard of the sights they had seen, the stories they had been told and all the books which they had used in their work. They came to look at my Seder Plate and Scroll. 'You mustn't touch,' said one small boy, 'it's Holy, so you must be very careful.'

They had learned of the scapegoat story and were rather taken with the idea of 'getting rid of their sins' and making a new start. So teachers and pupils together had inscribed their sins on a scroll which was solemnly handed to the scapegoat (me) to be taken away into the wilderness. After all that we needed a song and the special bread which they had made for the occasion.

In many schools in those early days, religious education was sporadic, perhaps linked to important festivals or to the pupils' questions about the meaning of life. Sometimes, one teacher's enthusiasm for the subject proved to be infectious, so that other teachers – and hence more of the pupils – became interested and involved. Gradually, structured programmes were introduced, though there is no shortage of memorable occasions. In one school where the pupils are registered as blind or are partially sighted, the academic year culminates with an occasion which lasts for two days. The theme of Pilgrimage provided an ideal opportunity for learning about the history of, and reasons for, pilgrimage. Pupils made their own pilgrimages to local places of worship and, through story, poetry and their own experiences of school journeys were able to appreciate some of the hopes and fears, the loneliness and togetherness of pilgrims.

One group researched the journey – the cost and famous places to be seen *en route*. For practical reasons, the teachers decided to concentrate on three religions, Christianity, Islam and Judaism – and a common destination, Jerusalem.

On the day, the pilgrims set out in three groups and made their way through the grounds to the school hall, encountering storytellers, music-makers, markets, appropriate refreshments and even a small zoo as they went. In the hall, the other children played the part of hosts, welcoming the children to Jerusalem. The day ended with each pupil being given a certificate to show that they had taken part, and candles were lit for each pupil.

An aim and some objectives

These schools have different approaches to religious education, dictated in part by the needs of the pupils. All, however, are a valid response to the aim of the Agreed Syllabus:

> The aim is to help young people to achieve a knowledge and understanding of religious insights, beliefs and practices, so that they are able to continue in, or come to their own beliefs and respect the right of other people to hold beliefs different from their own.
>
> *(Religious Education for Our Children, The Agreed Syllabus for the Inner London Education Authority, 1984, p. 7.)*

They also demonstrate some of the objectives for the Primary phase.

- to foster children's feelings of awe, wonder, delight, joy and mystery . . .
- to encourage in children a recognition of their own value and importance as individuals:
- to help children consider their personal response to moral issues; to assist them in their early exploration of the meaning of life and to help them face and learn from painful experiences which they encounter, such as fear, suffering and death.

(ibid. pp. 8–9)

Each school needs to decide the order of priorities which will best serve the pupils' needs. The starting points for schemes of work in religious education are many and imaginative. For some, as in the second school mentioned, the religious education is implicit and experiential. Other teachers may be faced with responding to important questions about the meaning and purpose of life. Children in one group who had watched the gradual deterioration and eventual death of a classmate, asked if it was their turn next, and why they should bother about living and learning if life was going to be short. 'I don't want a God who put me in a wheelchair', said one pupil.

Sometimes the pupil's curiosity is sparked off by a visit to a place of worship. One pupil started a whole chain of questions when she noticed a fellow pupil was not eating any pork. Another group were very confused about what it meant to some of their friends to be Roman Catholics. Sometimes lack of understanding breeds prejudice. A group of boys declared their dislike of Sikhs 'because they are always armed with huge swords'.

Some key topics

Again and again in working with teachers, I have been forced back to basic ideas which are very simple, yet at the same time capable of being developed in depth. The topics which seem to correspond both to religious education criteria and to pupils' needs include:

- **Personhood** – identity, valuing and being valued
- **Special places and special objects** – from the 'den' and the 'personal box' to Holy places and objects
- **Special people** – friends, family, relationships, caring and being cared for; important figures
- **Special actions** – music, dance, drama, gesture, ritual, worship, pilgrimage
- **Special feelings** – love, joy, awe, wonder, anger, fear
- **Community** – belonging, giving and receiving
- **The idea of the holy** – God
- **Suffering and death**
- **Rites of passage**

All these areas raise profound questions and pose dilemmas for teachers when some pupils are experiencing the content of the teaching. For example, how can we teach about belonging when many of the pupils are not regarded as belonging to any part of the community outside the school which they attend? We need to think through responses which preserve the integrity of the pupil and the teacher, which do not patronise, which admit dilemma, which keep open the lines of communication and which do not distort the claims of the religion we are trying to teach.

We also need to preserve the integrity of the subject. For the non-specialist teacher, religious education has obvious links with other subjects, for example, English, social studies, health education and moral education. Support must be given to help teachers identify and gain confidence in developing the distinctive contribution of religious education to the curriculum. Here too, there is a need for care. If a project includes an activity like hatching out chickens, the awe and delight which follows can only be part of a religious education programme if the teacher intends it to be so and does some follow up work to make the intention explicit. In the same way, it is valid religious education when teacher and pupils plan a garden so that children can use the experience of working together, of valuing each other's contribution, of having a special place in which to be quiet, as *part* of their religious education syllabus.

Resources

An Advisory Teacher is a resource. Part of my work is to provide ideas and resources for class use. Together with many teachers it has been possible to build up a collection which includes dolls, posters, books and artefacts so that pupils can see, touch, listen to, smell and sometimes taste the objects which they see on visits or hear of in story.

Religious education in schools for children with special needs is not essentially different from that in mainstream schools. However, the pace of the work and the methods used may be different. I am continually amazed at the imaginative and creative approaches used by teachers in special schools, and am convinced that the more we try to improve the quality of religious education for children who are not mobile, cannot see clearly, cannot hear clearly, have difficulties in making relationships and in understanding abstract concepts, the more we shall enrich religious education for all children.

CHAPTER 29

Worship in the junior school

GEOFFREY MARSHALL-TAYLOR

To those who have never tried to organise daily collective school worship, it often seems straightforward enough. After all, you just choose some combination of readings, hymns and prayers from the range of anthologies on the market. It would indeed be easy if the teacher's only objective in assembly was to go through formalities in order to comply with the law. Whatever their views of legislation on collective worship, most headteachers want their assemblies to be worthwhile occasions for all the children present; they also want them to reflect things which are 'worth-full', as the term 'worship' implies. But what does this involve? What sorts of ingredients are appropriate for the junior school child? In what senses can worship take place?

Child centred

The starting point for collective worship in schools must be the children themselves. Too often children's worship has resulted in the force-feeding of young people with the indigestible and inappropriate food of adult thinking and experience. This is not to say that children should never be presented with a world beyond their own experience. Rather, it is to emphasise that worship is essentially about expressing and sensing what is within us. The Education Reform Act makes it clear that teachers are not to suspend their professional skills when devising worship. It should take account of the 'ages and aptitudes of the pupils involved'.

School and church

There are those who think that what is expected in school worship is a distillation of what goes on in churches, mosques, gurdwaras, temples or synagogues: all that is needed is, in the Christian context, to provide a selection of the readings, hymns and prayers drawn from adult church worship. The Hertfordshire booklet on collective worship puts another view this way:

> rituals such as prayers, hymns and readings from the sacred writings of any faith are the means to religious worship, not worship in themselves.

Of course some material from church worship may be suitable for a school assembly. That is not the point. It is fundamentally the wrong approach. A school is not a church. In a school only a small proportion of children may be from homes where religious worship is a regular part of life.

A theistic event

'What about God?' asked a bewildered and exasperated teacher after a morning's INSET on collective worship which had explored ways of giving expression to matters of human worth and value, but which assumed that any reference to God was entirely inappropriate. It is curious that God should be left out of school worship in a society where theistic belief (not commitment to a faith) and religious rites of passage are part of the experience of most people. It is possible and appropriate for school worship to have a theistic basis whilst at the same time being sensitive to the needs and experiences of all the children present.

Growing with worship

It is important to stress that a sense of worship does not begin in individuals when they have either a convinced commitment to a particular faith or a developed notion of God or an ultimate being. Belief in God often grows from deeply personal or spiritual encounters, sometimes related to responses such as awe, wonder, mystery, fear and joy. Even in formal religious buildings, acts of worship can be less to do with ideas than with shared experiences which light a touch paper in individuals and in the assembled community.

In a school, there will be at least three main groups of children in any group gathered for collective worship: some, from religiously active families, who are at home with worship; some who will be looking in on worship for the first time; and some who, with a developing sense of the transcendent, will be crossing what John Hull called the 'threshold of worship'. It is possible to provide an occasion of worship in which all three groups feel involved, but often at different levels of response: an assembly within which worship is one possible outcome.

The BBC's *Together*

For many years this range of responses has been catered for in the BBC School Radio's weekly junior assembly series, *Together*. It is one possible model of achieving collective worship of a 'broadly Christian character', which is not narrowly confessional. The published introduction to the broadcasts explains the approach: 'the broadcasts create a context in which worship is possible but not demanded. They are, however, presented in a way which recognises that many participating children have no explicit awareness at all of religious beliefs and responses, let alone any commitment to a personal faith ... Worship is one level at which response is possible. It is hoped that children will feel involved and stimulated, both intellectually and emotionally, by what they hear.'

Themes

In the junior school, as at any educational stage, the themes chosen for assembly will be those to which the children can relate. Some examples may be helpful:

- **Life themes** focusing on elemental symbols such as light, fire and water; exploring metaphors such as 'building', 'giving' or 'journeying'.
- **Relationships** the problems and possibilities arising from mixing with family, friends, neighbours and strangers. From this may come greater openness, empathy, self-confidence and appreciation in dealing with other people.
- **Self-knowledge** through a greater awareness of our distinctiveness and of our shared humanity.
- **Values** examining human behaviour and attitudes; the making of moral choices.
- **Religious ideas** reflecting on ideas about God and on themes, such as forgiveness and caring drawn from the great world faiths.
- **Issues** responding to events in the news and issues which are important to the children themselves.

Participation

It is important that children feel that they are participating in an assembly. To do this they do not have necessarily to be presenting it themselves. Class-led occasions, which invariably express a great deal of classroom thought and activity, can be very powerful. At times they can make more impact on the performers rather than the observers. Even more vital is for all children present to feel participants by being drawn into the presentation. Sometimes a story well read by an adult can achieve this better than drama or dance. The means is not as important as the sense of involvement and the response generated.

Often the theme or situation of a story is so compelling that children participate by being totally involved in the unfolding of events and in creating the imaginary scenery and characters for themselves. One way of achieving participation in considering values is in devising stories or dramatised situations in which a moral dilemma is unresolved: children are then actively sharing in the decision-making and their resulting thoughts could form a sequence of further assemblies. From time to time all the children present can be drawn into storytelling by allowing them to provide sound effects for the narrative; for example, by making the noise of rain (with their nails on the floor) or of wind. Most of all, they will feel participants if the subject matter echoes their experience.

Take one theme

As an example of providing occasions for worship in the junior school, the 'building' theme provides many possibilities. There would be several assemblies extending over several days. Presentations will explore the theme both in the external, physical sense and in the metaphorical, internal sense. For instance, the story of Rahere, the court jester, who built St Bartholomew's Hospital in thanksgiving to God, has many layers to it. Intrinsic to it, is the idea that Rahere is doing more than putting stone on stone: it is an achievement of courage and determination; it is for the benefit of others, a benefit still seen today; and it is an expression of his belief in God's care for him.

There are also insights into worship in the story. For example Rahere's thanksgiving is demonstrated in praise and practical achievement. For him action was itself worship, a theme echoed in all the major world faiths.

A story such as Brian Sibley's 'Building barriers and bridges' has the qualities of a comic-strip adventure in which two communities recognise their interdependence. Oscar Wilde's *The Selfish Giant* poses questions about our relationship with other people and the world around us: what are the consequences of building a wall of selfishness? The biblical parable of the 'House on the rock' poses another question: on what are we building our own lives? It allows the possibility to look at individuals from different faiths, past and present, known and unknown, whose beliefs have been the basis for caring and other positive action. Some assemblies could be news-based, examining the sort of world we are building, allowing children to express their own hopes, fears and disappointments.

The 'building' image can be further explained with the help of stories from religions other than Christianity. Each year at Passover Jewish children remember how as slaves in Egypt, their ancestors made bricks for the Pharaoh's building programme. The mixture of chopped apple, nuts, cinnamon and wine which Jewish families eat in the Seder meal symbolises the mortar which the slaves had to mix. Sikh children learn that the beautiful Golden Temple in Amritsar has an entrance on each of its four sides and that this is to emphasise the equality of people, whatever their caste and social background. Local religious buildings – churches, mosques, gurdwaras, synagogues and temples – can be a rich source of information and experience. They are more than places for worship: they are themselves an expression of worship. As a visual focus, at the front of the assembly a 'wall' could be built over several days made up of boxes, to each of which children could attach their own labels describing the qualities or influences which are affecting the way they are building their lives: friends, family, school, sport, music, fashion, etc. The presentation could include drama, dance, mime or single-voice storytelling. What gives the topic a distinctive junior approach is the openness to explore questions and metaphors rooted in the junior child's experience.

Assembly story checklist

In any school term, it can be worth taking stock of the assembly stories or presentations covered. How varied are they? The DES Circular 3/89 on collective worship makes it clear that when a school pursues a policy of worship 'mainly of a broadly Christian character', material from other traditions may be included and that, providing the majority of acts of worship are of this sort, some may reflect other religious faiths.

During any year, how varied are the assembly stories at your school?

Historical	Contemporary
Biographical	Biblical
Children's fiction	Folk tales
News-based	Anniversary-based
Drama, dance, mime	Musical
Community-based	Values-based
Environmental	Seasonal
Class-led	Teacher-led
Visitor-led	Radio-led
Christian	Jewish
Muslim	Hindu
Sikh	Other faiths
Multicultural	Allegorical

Questions

It is essential that worship for junior children acknowledges the stage of development which they have reached. Their questions need to be acknowledged and given voice. It is therefore right to refer to religions without conveying the impression that there is consensus in society about them. In the weeks before Easter, for example, it is more appropriate to refer to what 'Christians believe' rather than use the phrase 'we believe'.

Prayer

For the same reason, many schools are unhappy about using the phrase 'Let us pray'. They feel that it assumes a level of religious commitment which is not present. In the BBC's *Together* broadcast referred to earlier, a time of reflection is often introduced by these words: 'Now, a moment of stillness: a chance to think or pray for a while.'

The prayer which follows allows a religious response and also allows assent at other levels, as in this reflection:

> We think of all those who were involved in the Lockerbie air disaster.
> To those who are injured, give healing;
> To those who are sad, give strength;
> To those who are lonely, give friendship.

Often prayers can be used which express particular insights. In an assembly about the destruction of the rain forests, a prayer was read out which had been written by an Indian from Central America. It was introduced in this way: 'Here are some words written by someone who lives in a rain forest that's being destroyed. A prayer of an Indian from Honduras'.

There is renewed interest in the use of reflection or directed silence in worship. A moving example of this was an assembly which followed news reports of suffering and starvation in an African country. The teacher had put Save the Children Fund posters on a display board. The children talked about their feelings on seeing the television pictures. Then the teacher led a short time of directed silence in which she worked through the images of deprivation, gave thanks for our comforts and expressed the hope that those who were suffering might soon have food, money and shelter to build their own lives. It was a moving occasion, more powerful than any formal prayer. What happened here was an opportunity for worship.

Songs

The same principles apply in the selection of songs for assembly use as in the choice of other material. Theistic items cannot assume the commitment of hymns like 'Fairest, Lord Jesus'. But then, realistically, only a handful of schools choose such items. The popularity of the BBC's *Come and Praise* book

(2½ million sold in ten years) indicates a desire to find songs which echo the experiences of children. For juniors these cannot be childish. Few of them express personal religious devotion. Their style and content has, in most cases, roots outside formal church worship. The themes are those which are suitable for collective school worship: they include caring for the world, the seasons, festivals, the human family, the journey of life, peace, day by day, and the life of Jesus. Again, the aim is to include all children at some level of interest, while allowing a religious expression for those with a developing sense of God.

Worship in isolation

When an assembly has made a powerful impact often the last thing anyone wants to do is to rush off to write or draw about it. But no assembly is an island: children bring to collective worship their own experiences in and out of school. Increasingly teachers are looking for ways of linking what happens in assembly with the rest of the curriculum. The theme of 'building' outlined earlier is a good example of a topic which can readily be related to class activity, each feeding the other with ideas.

Successful worship

The notion of 'successful' worship has a distasteful flavour. School worship works in the same way as any good educational experience. It must enable children to be themselves and to relate positively and creatively with one another and the world around them. In an atmosphere which is open and caring, it will allow a range of intellectual and emotional responses of which worship can be a part. It can play an important role in a child's personal journey of discovery. That may or may not lead to a belief in God. Whatever the outcome, the challenge is to make the journey worthwhile.

Bibliography

Collective Worship in Hertfordshire (Herts County Council Educational Department, 1989)
Geoffrey Marshall-Taylor (ed.), *Come and Praise 1 and 2* (BBC, 1978 and 1988)
John Hull, *The Act Unpacked* (CEM, 1989)
Geoffrey Marshall-Taylor (ed.), *The Johnny Morris Story Book* (BBC, 1985)
School Worship (The National Society, 1989)
Geoffrey Marshall-Taylor (ed.), *The Children's Bible* (Octopus, 1980)
Oscar Wilde, *The Selfish Giant* (Puffin, 1982)

Contributors

Vida Barnett, after a career in teaching and teacher education, currently acts as a consultant to the Muslim Education Trust, IQRA. She is a freelance lecturer and writer, contributing to publications such as *RE Today*, *World Religions in Education* (Shap's Journal) and *Junior Education*. She is Advisory and Information Officer for the Shap Working Party and an Associate Secretary of the Christian Education Movement.

(Rabbi) **Douglas Charing** is the Founder and Director of the Jewish Education Bureau. He is also the part-time Director of Concord Multi-Faith Resources Centre in Leeds. Recent publications include *Glimpses of Jewish Leeds* (1989) and the CEM Judaism Posters. When not lecturing or writing he leads groups of teachers on study visits to Israel.

Owen Cole is a freelance lecturer and writer who also teaches at the West Sussex Institute of Higher Education where he was Head of Religious Studies until March 1989. Publications include *The Sikhs: Their Religious Beliefs and Practices* (Routledge, 1978); *Religion in the Multifaith School* (Stanley Thornes, 1983) and *Meeting Hinduism* (Longman, 1987).

Jill Davies is a former Advisory Teacher for Religious Education in the ILEA. Her responsibilities included Moral Education and Personal Relationships, but since 1982 her main responsibility and interest was to develop and support religious education for pupils with special educational needs. She has written on RE and Special Needs for *Resource* and other publications.

Peter Doble is currently Director of York Religious Education Centre, one of the major national centres and part of the College of Ripon and York St John. He was formerly head of Religious Studies at Culham College and has worked in India and the USA. His interests include study of South Indian religion, of the Christian traditions and stimulating concern for good religious education in schools and colleges.

Robert Green is a Lecturer in the Department of Arts Education at the University of Warwick teaching Initial Training and In-service courses in Music Education for the Primary age phase. As a violinist and conductor he is involved in practical music making of all kinds and with all ages. He writes materials for use in school and works with children to demonstrate and test them.

Rachel Gregory is currently County Adviser for Religious Education in

Bedfordshire; previously she was Headteacher of two small rural primary schools (in Leicestershire and Bedfordshire) followed by two years as CEM's National Primary RE Adivser. She writes on religious education and is General Editor of the *Bedfordshire RE Series* to which she contributed several titles including *Planning Primary RE* and booklets on stories from Biblical and other sources.

M. Abdel Haleem is Lecturer in Arabic at the School of Oriental and African Studies, University of London. He holds degrees in Arabic and Islamic Studies from the University of Cairo (BA) and Cambridge (PhD). His recent publications include 'The Qur'an' in G. R. Hawting (ed.), *Sacred Writing in Oriental and African Religions*, (University of London School of Oriental and African Studies, 1986) and contributions to recent issues of the *Islamic Quarterly*.

John Hallows was formerly Head of Theology at The Trinity School, Leamington Spa and is currently Deputy Headteacher at St Thomas More School, Chelsea.

Mary Hayward is Senior Lecturer and Deputy Director of York RE Centre in the College of Ripon and York St John. Working in a Centre with a national brief for RE, she is regularly involved in organising INSET courses for junior schools, and is a co-author of *Religious Education Topics for the Primary School* (Longman, 1989).

Jean Holm is a New Zealander who taught Religious Studies in four British Colleges of Education, most recently as Principal Lecturer at Homerton College, Cambridge. She has written *Teaching Religion in School* (OUP); *The Study of Religions* (Sheldon, 1977), and *Growing up in Judaism* (Longman) and is joint author of *Growing up in Christianity* (Longman, 1990) and joint editor with Peter Baelz of the *Issues in Religious Studies* series (Sheldon, 1977).

Robert Jackson is Reader in Arts Education at the University of Warwick. He has been Director of several externally funded research and curriculum projects on the religious nurture of children and on RE in Church Schools and has published widely in RE and Religious Studies. His books include *Approaching World Religions* (John Murray, 1982); *Religions Through Festivals: Hinduism* (Longman, 1989); *Approaches to Hinduism* with Dermot Killingley (John Murray, 1988) and, with Eleanor Nesbitt, *Listening to Hindus* (Unwin Hyman, 1990). He has contributed many programmes to BBC School Radio and is currently Chairman of the Shap Working Party on World Religions in Education.

Clive Lawton is Headmaster of King David High School, Liverpool. He is a member of the SEAC panel on Religious Education, a former Chairman of the Shap Working party and Consultant to the Liverpool SACRE. His recent publications include *I am a Jew* (Franklin Watts, 1984), *Passport to Israel* (Franklin Watts), and *Religion through Festivals: Judaism* (Longman, 1990).

Geoffrey Marshall-Taylor is Chief Producer, BBC Radio 5 and former Senior Religious Education Producer, BBC Schools Radio. He has taught in a North London Comprehensive School and is currently Associate Fellow in Arts Education at the University of Warwick. He is producer of several notable RE and assembly Radio series: *Together*, *Quest*, *Jesus* and *Tales of Narnia*. His publications include the best-selling *Come and Praise* assembly song book (BBC), *Let's Pray Together* (Collins, 1981) and *The Children's Bible* (Octopus).

Peggy Morgan is Senior Lecturer in Theology and Religious Studies at Westminster College, Oxford. She contributed to W. Owen Cole's *Six Religions in the Twentieth Century* (Stanley Thornes and Hulton, 1984) and is the author of *Buddhist Stories* (1987) and *Buddhist Iconography* (1987), both privately published, *Buddhism – an Illustrated Dictionary* (Batsford) and *Being a Buddhist* (Batsford, 1989). She is Reviews Editor for Shap's Journal, *World Religions on Education* and a regular contributor to Shap conferences and publications.

Eleanor Nesbitt is a Senior Research Fellow in Religious Studies and part-time Lecturer in the Department of Arts Education, University of Warwick. Her recent publications include 'Sikhism' in Zaehner (ed.), *The Hutchinson Encyclopaedia of Living Faiths*, fourth edition (Hutchinson, 1988), 'The Presentation of Sikhs in Recent Children's Literature in Britain' in O'Connel *et al.* (eds), *Sikh History and Religion in the Twentieth Century* (University of Toronto, 1988) and *Listening to Hindus* (Unwin Hyman, 1990), co-written with Robert Jackson.

Kenneth Oldfield is Director of the BFSS National Religious Education Centre at the West London Institute of Higher Education. He began his teaching career as a VSO volunteer in India where his interest in Jainism and Hinduism developed. His most recent publications in the CEM series *Illustrations in World Religions* are *Hindu Gods and Goddesses* (1982) and *Jainism: The Path of Purity and Peace*.

Jo Price, former County Advisory Teacher for RE for Warwickshire, is now Senior Teacher Adviser (Primary) in the same county. She has taught across the 5–16 age range over a number of years. She is particularly interested in developing RE on a cross curricular basis.

Merlin Price is a Primary Inspector in Warwickshire, having previously held two primary headships and a post as Advisory Teacher for Science. He was involved in the writing of Warwickshire's 1985 RE Agreed Syllabus and gained an MA from the University of Warwick for his research on the role of story in the religious education of young children. He is also the author of a number of novels for children.

John Rankin was formerly Head of Religious Studies at the West Sussex Institute of Higher Education in Chichester. He is founder of the Chichester Project and has written and contributed to many publications for RE in schools. His publications include: *Religious Education Topics for the Primary School* (1988) published by Longman for the Chichester Project and co-written with Alan Brown and Mary Hayward; *Religions* with Alan Brown and Angela Wood (Longman, 1988); and for the Chichester Project *The Eucharist* (Lutterworth, 1986) and *Christian Worship* (Lutterworth 1982).

David Self has been a teacher, a lecturer in drama at Bede College, Durham and has written and produced many religious education programmes for BBC School Radio. He is author of *The Macmillan Religious Education Course* and has compiled several anthologies for school assemblies.

Dennis Starkings is a Lecturer in the Department of Arts Education at the University of Warwick specialising in religious education at infant and junior levels. He has contributed to *Westminster Studies in Education*, to J. Sutcliffe (ed.), *A Dictionary of Religious Education* (SCM, 1984) and to R. Jackson (ed.), *Approaching World Religions* (John Murray, 1982). He has jointly edited *Resource* since 1978.

Jack Priestley is a Senior Lecturer in Education at the University of Exeter. Between teaching in both secondary and junior schools in Nottingham and Devon he spent three and a half years training junior school teachers in Zambia before entering teacher training in this country. He has published widely at all levels from junior school textbooks to academic journals in Britain, the United States, Canada, Germany and Scandinavia. He is currently a member of the Methodist Education Committee and represents the Free Churches as a co-opted member of Devon County Council Education Committee, where he has also been chairman of SACRE. He is married to author Fay Sampson.

Angela Wood is Adviser in Religious Education for Westminster. She has published several school materials especially on Jewish and Muslim subjects. As conference organiser for the Standing Conference for Interfaith Dialogue in Education, she is keen to promote storytelling and active learning, and has an interest in the relationship between multifaith RE and anti-racism. Against a long background as Head of RE at secondary level, in her advisory work she now appreciates the early years as the key to it all. She edited *Religions and Education* (BFSS, 1989), a volume celebrating 20 years of the Shap Working Party.

Keyword Index

agreed syllabus 3–4
art 135, 169–74
artefacts 78, 119
assembly 7, 220–1, 223
assessment 4, 23–4
attainment targets 21–4

Buddhism 31–6, 83–9
buildings 101, 117, 194–5, 203–4, 222–3

Christianity 37–50, 91–102
Christmas 162, 166, 214
collective worship 6–8

developmental approach 18, 96
discussion 84, 197, 201, 205, 206
drama 133, 162–8

Easter 93, 98–101
Education Reform Act 1988 3–13, 96
empathy skills 145
ethics 46, 59–60
ethnography 200–7
expressive element 11, 133, 170

fasting 53, 59
festivals 68–70, 85, 98–101, 118, 180, 190

Gurus 72–4

hajj 59, 113
Hinduism 51–6, 102–8

imaginative element 11, 174
INSET 12, 16, 220
integrated curriculum 186
interviewing skills 204–7

Islam 57–65, 109–15
issues 185–6

Jesus 37–41, 45–6, 49–50, 95, 151–4
Judaism 64–71, 116–23

life themes 221

methods 185–6
music 175–82

parish church 203–4
photography 195, 198
pluralism 5, 29, 30
prayer 224

questions 146, 157–61, 223
Qur'an 57–63, 109–15

relationships 38, 67–8, 172
religious experience of children 208–13
resources 75, 107, 121, 218

SACRE 3, 12, 81
salvation 39–40
secular 7, 11
sensitising element 9, 133, 170, 200–2
Sikhism 72–7, 124–9
special needs 185–6, 214–18
story 85–6, 87, 99–100, 124–9, 134–6, 137–41, 142–8, 149–54, 180

topic work 91, 95, 117, 187–91, 217

visits 111–12, 119–21, 192–9

withdrawal from RE 3, 5–7, 12
worship 48, 186, 219–25